THE

AMERICAN

CONSTITUTIONAL

TRADITION

THE

AMERICAN

CONSTITUTIONAL

TRADITION

DANIEL J. ELAZAR

University of Nebraska Press

Lincoln and London

Library of Congress Cataloging-in-Publication Data
Elazar, Daniel Judah.
The American constitutional tradition / Daniel J. Elazar.
p.   cm.
Includes index.
ISBN 0-8032-1813-3
1. United States—Constitutional history.   2. Federal
government—United States—History   I. Title.
JK31.E55 1988
320.973—dc19   87-33412 CIP
Acknowledgments for the use of previously published
material appear on page xiii.
Copyright © 1988, University of Nebraska Press
All rights reserved
Manufactured in the United States of America
The paper in this book meets the minimum requirements
of American National Standard for Information Sciences
—Permanence of Paper for Printed Library Materials,
ANSI Z39.48-1984.

To the memory of my friend,

colleague, and mentor,

Martin Diamond

CONTENTS

Preface, ix

Introduction: The Constitution and Federal Democracy, 1

Part One   Context

1. An Almost-Covenanted Polity, 13
2. Pluralism, Federalism, and Liberty, 39
3. Land and Liberty in American Civil Society, 54

Part Two   Covenants

4. The Declaration of Independence: The Founding Covenant of the American People, 89
5. The Principles and Traditions Underlying American State Constitutions, 107
6. Confederation and Federal Liberty, 124
7. Developing an American Theory of Federal Democracy, 140
8. The Constitution and the Blessings of Liberty, 162

Part Three   Continuity

9. Contrasting Models of Revolutionary Leadership, 181
10. The Constitution, the Union, and the Liberties of the People, 206
11. Coping with Constitutional Crises, 245

Appendix A: The Articles of Confederation, 255

Appendix B: The Northwest Ordinance of 1787, 262

Notes, 269

Index, 285

PREFACE

The bicentennial of the founding of the United States of America offers Americans a special opportunity to reflect on their country's civil society and its political institutions. Proper reflection on both requires consideration, first and foremost, of the American sense of vocation—its intellectual, social, and political sources—and how that sense was translated into reality and at what price. It needs to be concerned with the meaning of the economic forces that propelled the first Europeans to North America, brought Africans by force to join them, and created new economic realities that often stood in competition with the American vocation. It should consider the cultural realities of a pluralistic society that at its farthest reaches first confronted, then tried to absorb, Native Americans, and first excluded and later adoringly welcomed Asians.

Each of the chapters in this volume originated as an essay prepared for a bicentennial commemoration. Each is complete in itself, yet closely linked with the themes of the others. The Introduction, "The Constitution and Federal Democracy," presents my understanding of the place of the United States Constitution in giving the American people their identity and the implications of that reality for American civil society.

Chapter 1, "The Almost-Covenanted Polity," attempts to delineate why American civil society is federal through and through in the integral sense whereby federalism is not merely a device for organizing the structure of its political system. In doing so it explores the sources of the American polity, its vocation, and the pressures that have made Americans what Abraham Lincoln described as an almost chosen people—no more, but also no less. For the most part, the essay focuses on the colonial period, which culminated in the Declaration of Independence and the Constitution.

In Chapter 2, "Pluralism, Federalism, and Liberty," I turn to the pluralistic basis of federalism and liberty in American civil society, suggesting that pluralism, although indigenous to the American political experience, has taken different forms, beginning with the two faces of territorial democracy embodied in New England and the Middle Colonies and culminating in the radical individualism of contemporary California. In doing this, the essay explores the difference between federal and natural liberty, suggesting that a pluralism of primordial groups can survive and thrive only in a federal political culture.

Chapter 3, "Land and Liberty in American Civil Society," explores how Americans have always used land, especially freehold ownership, as a basis for fostering and maintaining individual liberty. The essay explores different systems of landownership and what they mean for different kinds of liberty. Going beyond the mere definition of liberty, it examines how the organization of the land in the westward expansion was designed to foster openness and accessibility in a free society and looks at the implications for today.

Chapter 4, "The Declaration of Independence: The Founding Covenant of the American People," examines the covenant that brought into being not only the United States of America but the American people. In this I follow Abraham Lincoln's understanding of the Declaration and its role in American life. The document itself is analyzed as a covenant following the classic covenantal form.

Both the Articles of Confederation and the Constitution of 1787 were designed to complete the American constitutional framework. Hence they are incomplete in themselves and rely on the constitutions of the American states as both their underpinning and their completion. Chapter 5, "The Principles and Traditions Underlying American State Constitutions," shows how during the revolutionary era those principles and traditions represented an American version of English revolutionary Whig ideas. That tradition contributed to the Federalist tradition of the United States Constitution of 1787 but was in great part set aside by it.

Subsequent state constitutions have represented syntheses of both traditions. These issues are explored in this essay.

Chapter 6, "Confederation and Federal Liberty," addresses how confederal forms of political organization continued to shape American political life even after the Articles of Confederation were rejected as the constitutional basis of the American regime and shows how they have reemerged on the world scene as a potential means of gaining the benefits of federalism under postmodern conditions. It also continues the examination of the contrast between federal and natural liberty introduced in Chapter 2.

Chapter 7, "Developing an American Theory of Federal Democracy," contrasts the thinking of George Mason and James Madison as part of the struggle to develop an American theory of federal democracy, to which both men were committed. Mason supported a confederal regime that emphasized the primacy of the states, and Madison urged a federation that would have a strong national government. As we all know, Madison won, and the Constitution of 1787 principally embodies his ideas, but they were modified by much that Mason and his confederates had to teach. Two hundred years later, when Americans seem to be busy contrasting early federalist ideas with decentralist notions, it is important to restore the original debate regarding federal democracy. This essay is a contribution to that end.

The American Revolution not only contributed new institutions for the establishment of democratic republicanism, it also introduced new canons of political behavior. Perhaps foremost among them was a new model of revolutionary leadership, exemplified by George Washington. Chapter 8, "Contrasting Models of Revolutionary Leadership," discusses the American experience and contrasts it with the leadership of other modern revolutions. Washington's sense of republican leadership became the model for other Americans in his time and subsequently enabled the United States to avoid the problems of either Jacobinism or Bonapartism that have plagued most modern revolutions. This essay tries to explain why.

Fourscore and five years after the declaration of American independence, Abraham Lincoln provided a summary and synthesis of the results of the American founding that should continue to serve subsequent generations of Americans. In the first whistle-stop tour in American political history, albeit after his election to the presidency, in February 1861 Lincoln journeyed from Springfield to Washington by a circuitous route that enabled him to speak to all sections and segments of the American public. In those speeches, culminating in his first inaugural address, he developed the basic theme of American federal democracy, namely the triad of "The Constitution, the Union, and the Liberties of the People." Chapter 9 explores Lincoln's synthesis, emphasizing his climactic discussion of the Declaration of Independence in front of Philadelphia's Independence Hall.

These essays are designed to illustrate how the American experience forms the basis for a coherent and comprehensive theory of democratic republicanism standing in sharp contrast to the Jacobin theories that constitute the primary competition for the allegiance of those who would be democrats in our times. There is a great need to articulate this comprehensive and coherent theory of democratic republicanism, because in the intervening years the American theory of federal democracy has been challenged, in many cases successfully, by Jacobin theories that represent a wholly different and, I argue, antidemocratic approach to the problems of liberty, equality, and self-government. The Jacobin challenge has been successful in great part because of the neglect of federal democracy as an alternate, indeed prior, theory. One of the most important tasks of the bicentennial commemoration should be to articulate a proper theory of federal democracy so that it may return, strengthened, to the arena in which the battle for men's minds is now taking place. This book is designed to be a modest contribution to that effort.

The Center for the Study of Federalism has tried to stimulate reflection on these questions through commemoration of the events of the bicentennial period, principally through conferences supported by Liberty Fund, the National Endowment for the Humanities, and the National Science Foundation and in part through special issues of *Publius: The Journal of Federalism*. In almost every case I was called on to provide the keynote for the deliberations of each gathering or for the collection. This gave me the opportunity to think through the American experience along the lines suggested above and to prepare a series of essays on various aspects of it that together present my understanding of that experience, particularly in its political dimensions.

Essays prepared for the series of Liberty Fund conferences in honor of the bicentennial of the United States of America and its Constitution include: "The

Principles and Traditions Underlying American State Constitutions" (1980), subsequently published in *Publius* 12, no. 1 (Winter 1982); "Confederation and Federal Liberty" (1981), subsequently published in *Publius* 12, no. 4 (Fall 1982); "Pluralism, Federalism, and Liberty" (1985); and "Land and Liberty in American Civil Society" (1985). "The Constitution, the Union, and the Liberties of the People" was first published in the *Publius* issue in memory of Martin Diamond (8, no. 3 [Summer 1978]). A different version of "The Almost-Covenanted Polity" was published in *This World* as "America and the Federalist Revolution," after presentation at a conference of the American Enterprise Institute as part of their bicentennial program under the directorship of Robert Goldwin. "Developing an American Theory of Federal Democracy" is based in part on a lecture I gave at George Mason University in 1985.

In presenting this book to the public, I would like to give special acknowledgment to my friend and colleague of the Center for the Study of Federalism, Ellis Katz, who has shouldered most of the responsibility for organizing the conferences for which these essays were prepared; to Liberty Fund, an exceptional American institution that does so much to achieve the purposes to which this book is dedicated and to its fine staff with whom we have worked: W. A. Hill, Charles King, Neil McLeod, and Kenneth Templeton; and to the Earhart Foundation and its staff, Richard Ware, Anthony Sullivan, and David Kennedy, who have supported my efforts to study and write about the American constitutional tradition. Thanks are due the National Endowment for the Humanities and the National Science Foundation for supporting aspects of the Center's bicentennial program. I am personally grateful to my research assistants, Gail Charette, Rasheeda Didi, and Joseph Marbach, for their help in my work and, as always, to my wife, Harriet, and long-enduring secretary, Mary Duffy, who make it all possible.

> Daniel J. Elazar
> Philadelphia, Pennsylvania
> in the 211th year of the
> independence of the United
> States of America

INTRODUCTION

THE CONSTITUTION

AND

FEDERAL DEMOCRACY

Had Alexis de Tocqueville written this book, he might have entitled it *How the American Constitution Is the Touchstone of American National Identity and Some Comments on the Character of the Polity It Establishes.* Those who observed the American scene during the 1960s and 1970s saw dramatic evidence of the degree to which the American polity is the source of American identity and the Constitution is the touchstone of American civil society. The American people have been able to weather many crises, including the sociopolitical crisis of the 1960s. Their confidence was shaken only when it seemed that their polity was in jeopardy and their Constitution somehow inadequate to deal with the problems confronting it. Vietnam and Watergate and the responses they evoked offer evidence that needs little elaboration.

One illustration comes prominently to my mind. At noon on August 9, 1974, when Richard Nixon resigned the presidency and Gerald Ford took the oath of office, I was in the offices of the American Revolution Bicentennial Administration. At that particular moment, some twenty to twenty-five people assembled in the foyer and watched television together. As Mr. Ford completed the oath of office there was an audible sigh of relief from those standing in the room, as if to express a general feeling that the Constitution had indeed provided Americans with a new president, the polity was intact, and we could build from there. I suspect that my experience was not in the least unusual—that others can recall similar responses revealing this American sense of the polity and the Constitution that is almost never put into words but is palpably there.

Precisely because the American people emerged by choice in the process of building a new society, they have required a conscious common touchstone to affirm the unity they seek. By and large, Americans have solved the problem of national identity by fostering a common way of life accepted, at least in principle, by those who claim membership in this new society. That common way of life is based upon a political touchstone. In this respect, the United States is a polity in the Aristotelian sense. It is not a society that will continue to function whatever the character of its governing institutions, as so many peoples of the world seem to do. Frenchmen and Italians can survive crises of regime and of constitution without threat to their "Frenchness" or "Italianness"; Americans cannot weather even relatively modest crises (by non-American standards) without challenging their very right to exist as a nation. The rest of the world looked upon Watergate as a very modest crisis, if not a tempest in a teapot, whereas Americans not only considered their Constitution in jeopardy but saw the fate of the whole polity hanging in the balance. I suggest that it is this quality of America as a new society—a society based on an accepted way of life rather than upon a sense of common ancestry—that lies at the basis of this response.

It follows that one of the significant system-affirming elements that came out of the 1960s was the demand by many radicals for a "renegotiation of the social contract" they saw as underlying the American polity. Most of those radicals, too poorly educated (in American schools) to know their own heritage, were utterly unaware that they were speaking in the rhetoric of the American Revolution—in the most traditional rhetoric of American society. The American polity itself is based upon a series of covenants and compacts. As I will show in chapter 1, the original political theory of the Americans explicitly recognized this, and even though later generations moved away from the theory to adopt an organic view of the state imported from Europe, the "true facts" remain what they are.

The United States Constitution itself is a compact that has acquired the status of a covenant—a morally grounded compact—in the minds of the American people, whether or not it was designed as such. The first Americans used the term covenant rather than compact in the colonial period precisely because of its religious and moral connotations. Compact became the preferred term in certain quarters only after the secularization of the Enlightenment took hold in the political realm, although those for whom the religious dimension continued to be vital continued to use both terms. Significantly, as Samuel Eliot Morison has pointed out, the first "compact" in American history, the so-called Mayflower Compact, was called a covenant rather than a compact, and a covenant was the only way America's new society could properly be brought together and given a sense of wholeness. We can understand the Declaration of Independence as a covenant in that sense (see chap. 4)—as Lincoln did (chap. 9).

The Constitution is couched in affirmative language, yet that language provides a framework of limitation, thus creating a compact for organizing power that affirms unity while providing the negatives necessary to maintain the liberty Americans strive for.

The American Constitution is a federal document in two senses. In the modern sense, it unites states into a federal polity. But it is also a federal document in the original meaning of the term—from the Latin *foedus*, which means "covenant," derived in turn from the Hebrew *b'rit* via the Vulgate translation of the Bible—a covenanting together of several parties desiring to preserve their own respective integrities even as they create a new union and a new unity. The United States Constitution was designed to perfect the new American union and to preserve its constituent elements, both people and states. Thus, while it gave birth to modern federalism, the Constitution also represents a reconstruction of federalism in its most ancient form (see chap. 7). Even older than that of the Greek leagues, which were based upon very limited ties among separate polities—the kind of confederation the Constitution was designed to replace—this is the federalism of the Bible, creating a new compound polity under a common law with common institutions, the way the twelve tribes of Israel were united.

Was the founding generation aware of those biblical roots? There is considerable evidence that it was. If the United States was the first modern nation, in many respects biblical Israel was the first new nation of all time. Indeed, the Bible sets forth the paradigm of how a new nation is created. Abraham is told to leave his father's house to go to a new land where he has no old idolatrous associations and can build anew. He must participate in a founding and act as a founding father. But one founding is not enough to build the new society; there must be a refounding after the exodus from Egypt in which a whole people moves from the familiar to the unfamiliar to undergo the founding experience.

The American founding fathers were quite aware of this paradigm and how closely it related to the American experience, including much of what they did. My assessment is that they well understood the relationship between the two experiences. Yet there is one major difference between them: the American polity is based upon a political transformation of a religious experience whereas the original Israelite founding was based upon a religious transformation of a political experience. In a sense the exodus and the settlement of the land constituted a political experience that was transformed religiously into something that, for the Jews and Western civilization as a whole, proved enduring indeed.

American constitutional history, I suggest, can be read as a playing out of these two meanings of the concept of federalism. The playing out involves a federalistic politics that has had to come to grips with a continuing frontier, both emphasizing ways to achieve liberty and equality. Chapter 2, "Pluralism, Federalism, and Liberty," suggests how this was so. In this respect, as in so many others, Thomas Jefferson embodied the thrust of American constitutional history. When he announced at the beginning of his administration that "we are all federalists, we are all republicans," he indicated that the Jeffersonian Republicans had preempted the federalist dimension of the Federalist party and turned it to their own ends. He then proceeded to purchase Louisiana, an exercise of presidential powers of Federalist proportions but with the clear intention of ensuring the American people a Republican goal—enough land (or frontier) for the indefinite expansion of Jefferson's "ward republics" that were to preserve American liberty. That is the theme of chapter 3, "Land and Liberty in American Civil Society."

The United States is like every other civil society—filled with tensions, contradictions, and paradoxes. While other civil societies have attempted to resolve, or at least balance, these by building from a firm and often inflexible tradition to encompass a golden past and to preserve the society's mythic memories of that past, the United States, as the first modern nation, looks to a continuing frontier to move the society toward a golden future. Like the model of the universe of eighteenth-century physics out of which the American political founding emerged, the United States depends upon creating some degree of perpetual motion to balance its own tensions, contradictions, and paradoxes. This effort to found a civil society in perpetual motion is manifested in both the governmental and social institutions and processes of the United States. The effort to build checks and balances into every aspect of the American polity was designed to create a condition not of homeostasis but of perpetual motion—a civil society that is active, not static, whose institutions would counterbalance each other by interacting.

The frontier has been the American means for achieving this perpetual motion in the socioeconomic realm, beyond the immediately political and constitutional. Frederick Jackson Turner, who in a sense told us this secret of American life, also raised a crucial question with regard to it: Can the frontier be maintained? Can the momentum—and indeed the perpetual motion—be maintained? For Turner the issue was at best in doubt, for he saw the frontier as no more than the land frontier that persisted for the first two and a half centuries of American existence and that came to an end, to all intents and purposes, in his time. I suggest that Turner's view was too limited, that the land frontier itself (more properly the rural-land frontier) set off a kind of chain reaction that, though not producing subsequent frontiers that would have suited the taste of Daniel Boone or those who romanticize the Old West, nevertheless did generate frontiers that have met the political, economic, social, and psychological tests Turner found in the land frontier and, by creating a continuing frontier experience, have served to maintain the country's momentum.

Even while the rural-land frontier was in the process of being conquered—I use the old-fashioned word, out of style in the United States today, that was used at the time—it generated a new urban-industrial frontier where cities developed not merely as commercial service centers for rural areas but as wealth generators in their own right. They were based upon new uses of land for high-density settlement, new forms of economic activity, particularly industrial, and new forms of social and geographic mobility, continuing the momentum of the land frontier. Perhaps a different set of people were the principal beneficiaries of this new frontier, but the societal effect was the same.

When the urban-industrial frontier that reached its heyday at the end of the nineteenth century completed its course, a metropolitan-technological frontier emerged. Based upon a new form of settlement—the low-density multicentered metropolitan region—a radically transformed technology, and newer forms of economic, social, and geographic mobility, the new frontier offered the same possibilities as its predecessors. That some 80 percent of all contemporary job classifications in the United States did not exist two generations ago says a great deal about widespread opportunities for individual mobility. The migration of tens of millions of Americans within the United States that accompanied these other changes further reinforced them.

The metropolitan-technological frontier reached its peak in the post–World War II generation. At present the United States is entering a fourth frontier stage: a rurban-cybernetic frontier based upon the reorganization of settlement into city belts where urban and rural are intertwined by relying on cybernetic technology. It seems to me that much of the hope of America depends upon whether this fourth frontier stage fulfills its promise, because America has invested its hopes—staked its all—on maintaining itself through perpetual motion.

For all of that, these dimensions of American civil society have been less than fully recognized by American scholars and even by the American people in recent years. Two centuries ago John Adams used the word "form" to describe both the frame and the content of institutions—that which informs them. I suggest that federalism is the form of American government in this sense. Various commentators have noted the amazing persistence of federalism in the United States despite the drastic changes that have taken place in the past two hundred years and most particularly in the twentieth century. They are quite correct in suggesting that the one dimension of American civil society that remains essentially intact despite the great changes that have taken place is its federalistic form.

The founding of the United States was itself a federal act (general plus constituent polities working together). The resolution for independence was adopted by the states acting collectively through the Continental Congress but voting state by state. The Declaration itself is phrased in the ambiguous way that federal acts are sometimes stated, so as to raise the question whether independence is being declared by one entity or by thirteen collectively. This ambiguity is often a necessary part of the federalist political orientation because federalism both unites and separates. But even the process leading up to the Declaration of Independence and following out from it toward the adoption of the first constitution of the United States, the Articles of Confederation, was fully federal (see chap. 6, "Confederation and Federal Liberty"). A look at the historical record reveals a dramatic interplay between the states and the Continental Congress, between certain localities and their states, and even between certain localities and the Continental Congress, building up a certain sentiment and a documented body of commitments for independence.

In the half-generation between the mid-1770s and the early 1790s, the modern world was given the two competing conceptions of democracy that have struggled on the world stage ever since, with each other as well as against the old order. Just as federal democracy represents the key American contribution to the modern revolutionary era, the French Revolution produced Jacobinism, a radically different approach, as its key contribution. Together they encompass the principal revolutionary responses of the modern era.

Federal democracy is based on the premise that civil society is compounded of many different groups and hence must be organized around multiple centers of power, each able to preserve its own integrity even as it functions within a common political matrix. For the sake of liberty all governmental powers must be limited and must check and balance each other. Federal democracy in this sense is to be found in the American state constitutions as much as in the federal document (chap. 5).

Jacobinism is based on the premise that civil society is guided by the general will, to be expressed through a single center where maximum governmental power can be concentrated in the name of the whole. In our own time we can see federal democracy working itself out through mainstreams and byways in the United States and various other polities influenced by the American way, and we can see one version of Jacobinism working itself out in democratic France and another, more sinister version, in the totalitarian Soviet Union and in other polities influenced by each.

For over a century, the idea of Jacobinism flourished while the idea of federal democracy was neglected. The emergence of two doctrinal forces in the nineteenth century, Marxism in Europe and what may be termed Wilsonianism in the United States (which transformed the accepted understanding of the British parliamentary system to apply the notion that every polity requires a single governmental center of power, to the American scene), led to a climate in which the basic premises of federal democracy came under great challenge, first in the academic community, then in the community of reformers, and finally in the body politic as a whole. On the intellectual and doctrinal—or perhaps more correctly on the ideological level—a new social science was constructed upon a Marxian framework that emphasized the Jacobin view of the polity as the measure of all things. Even the anti-Marxists became Marxians in that sense, responding to the issues as the Marxians defined them. Once the problems are defined in that way, a federalist analysis seems diversionary and misleading if not downright wrong. For Marxians (orthodox, neo-, crypto-, or unconscious), the real concerns must be classes and cities, not federal power sharing and frontiers. Hence even among those who advocate what they believe are federalist policies, there is a strong tendency to consider them on terms other than those in which the American founding fathers sought to frame them.

Here the differences in principle and orientation must be recognized for what they are. When, in the late nineteenth-century United States, there developed a view of proper government based upon the Westminster model, best articulated by Woodrow Wilson, it stressed that any proper system of government should not be based upon organized division of powers but should have some center of power. The distinction between "powers" and "power" is crucial. Wilson started by focusing on Congress as the single center of power; he ended up by focusing on the presidency. The early twentieth-century reformers went a step further to focus on the administration—the bureaucracy in the broadest sense. We have seen the consequences of these shifts all too well in recent years.

All three approaches contradict the federal principle of organizing powers as fully as the Marxian analysis of the social scientists and intellectuals contradicts the federalist view of the condition of humanity. In the twentieth century the two together have become powerful forces that have led Americans, and people outside of the United States, to ignore the central teaching of the American founding—federal democracy. I hope that the bicentennial of that founding will provide the impetus for a rediscovery of that teaching.

Yet that goal is not so easily accomplished. Perhaps because American society is so modern and so self-made, Americans continue to believe that all problems are solvable and that political means, in the larger sense of cooperative human action as well as in the immediate sense, can be mobilized to solve them. And yet American society now is up against problems that are beginning to teach its people something about the limits of politics. One of those problems is the atomization of society. The extension of individualism beyond the limited kind sought by the prophets of individual self-fulfillment of the seventeenth and eighteenth centuries (what John Winthrop described as "federal liberty"), has led to the point where no ties, not even family ties, are considered necessarily permanent or deserving of support through the normal legal and social sanctions that historically have encouraged permanence.

On the other hand, we are witnessing the extension of another strain in American society—corporatism. This is not corporatism in the European sense, but the tendency to rely upon corporate entities, public or private, to undertake the activities of society. American corporatism can be traced back to the first great English companies established to create settlements on American shores in the sixteenth and seventeenth centuries. It has continued to exist in one form or another ever since, with its importance waning, then waxing again. Consequently there has been an interplay between individualism and corporatism that Americans, including students of American society, have neglected to examine very fully. Recently corporatism has also gone beyond the limits of the old interplay. For the first ten generations of American existence, individualism and corporatism struggled with one another through important mediating institutions. Today, with those institutions weakened, the individual and the corporate world seem to say to each other, "You do your thing and we'll do ours," so that together they drain the healthy lifeblood of the society in pursuit of gain.

The twentieth-century response to this unholy alliance has been, by and large, to seek collectivist solutions, to use the government to restrain corporatism and replace individualism. Americans today are not all certain this has been a felicitous choice. They may indeed be ready to again explore earlier communitarian and federalist forms that were once used to mediate between individualism and corporatism in American society.

What is clear is that a serious problem exists. It is reflected in the consumerism of American society. Americans are confronted with the problems of a society in which consumerism has come to rival citizenship as the basis for political self-definition. The politicosocial order emphasizes the delivery of goods and services in place of civic participation.

The reaction to this consumerism run rampant is now beginning to appear. A few years ago the Center for the Study of Federalism held a conference on "Serving the Public in a Metropolitan Society." To our pleasant surprise there was a groundswell from all quarters, left, right, and center, to issue a major challenge to the consumerist premises that had come to be generally accepted with regard to serving the public, precisely because they seemed to be challenging the very possibility of citizenship. Even though Americans do not like to talk about their obligations as distinct from their rights, all the participants recognized that democratic citizenship does involve obligations that have not been properly discussed, and that the problem has become intense. In recent years this theme has echoed in a growing number of quarters, along with a new concern for the civic arts as vital to the health of a democratic society. This new consciousness offers the promise of reconsidering post–World War II consumerist goals.

The basic tensions, contradictions, and paradoxes in any civil society are never fully resolved as long as the society lives. When the tensions are gone, the society is dead. Moreover, people being what they are, a full understanding of the society can come only at that moment of truth that is also the moment of death. Fortunately, Americans continue to wrestle with these forces and, by doing so, demonstrate that their society is vitally alive. Understanding American federal democracy is necessary to keep it vital.

PART ONE

CONTEXT

1

AN ALMOST-COVENANTED POLITY

America and the Federalist Revolution

Two hundred years ago, the newly independent United States of America invented modern federalism. Today, as we commemorate the bicentennial of the American founding, federalism is a world revolutionary movement, no less though it is the hidden revolution of our times than if it were advancing to ideological trumpets.[1] The development of modern federalism parallels the development of the United States. At the time of the first colonial settlements in British North America, the Dutch and the Swiss were pioneering the development of federal polities whose links were postfeudal in character yet not quite modern. It remained for the United States to invent modern federalism in its full form.

With the establishment of the American federal union, federalism emerged as a viable option in the development of modern nation-states. Today some 40 percent of the world's population lives within the nineteen polities that have adopted constitutions at least purporting to be federal in character, while another 32 percent lives within the eighteen political systems that utilize federal principles to some degree within a formally unitary framework. If we were to add into our calculations supranational federal arrangements such as the European Community, the number of polities involved would be even larger and the share of the world's population directly touched by the federalist revolution substantially increased. While the variety of forms the federalist revolution has taken is great, the American federal system remains the single most influential standard against which others are measured, for better or worse. Thus an understanding of American federalism becomes crucial not only for understanding the American polity but for comprehending a major phenomenon let loose upon the world as a result of the American revolutionary effort.

Since federalism is the *form* of American government (in the eighteenth-century meaning of the term—that is to say, the principle that informs the American polity in its every aspect), it should not be surprising that the foundation of the United States was a federal act par excellence, involving a consistent and protracted interplay between the colonies-cum-states and the Continental-cum-United States Congress they created as a single national body to speak in their collective name.[2]

In the year when the representatives of the people of the colonies collectively declared the independence of the United States, other representatives of the same people were reconstituting the colonies themselves as states. Four colonies—New Hampshire, South Carolina, Virginia, and New Jersey—adopted state constitutions in 1776 before the adoption of the Declaration of Independence, and before the year was out four more—Pennsylvania, Maryland, Delaware, and North Carolina—did likewise. Within sixteen months, all the former colonies except Massachusetts had adopted constitutions (Massachusetts wrote one, but it took several years before it was formally ratified by the voters). In the interim, the Continental Congress drafted the Articles of Confederation as a constitution for the United States (though they too were not fully ratified until 1781). At one time this fact was used to argue that the creation of the states preceded that of the Union. Today it is generally agreed that they came into existence simultaneously—in the original federal act of the United States as such. In sum, all the ambiguities of diversity in unity endemic to federalism are—fittingly—"present at the creation." Even local governments (in this case the towns and counties) got into the act as participants in the constitutional drafting and ratifying processes, then as now, not because they were asked but because they felt that they had as much right to do so as any government.

To understand the more than two hundred years of the American federalist experience, we must examine American federalism in the broadest sense of the term—not as intergovernmental relations, as federalism has come to be interpreted from the managerial perspectives of the twentieth century; not as a matter of the constitutional distribution of powers between the general and state governments, as the constitutional lawyers are wont to see it; not even as the grand political struggle between the Union and the states that covered the canvas of nineteenth-century historians; but as something close to what the French term "integral federalism," as the animating and informing principle of the American political system flowing from a covenantal approach to human relationships.

Let us begin at the beginning with the founding of the first British North American colonies. We must do so because American federalism begins at the beginning. Indeed, it is the development of the social, economic, and constitutional as well as the political bases of American federalism in the colonial period that created the federalist political culture upon which a formally federal system was subsequently erected. As in every other aspect of American life, the colonial background was crucial, for it was within the five generations of American colonial history that the basis was laid for a covenantal federalism. Indeed, it was so well laid that Americans have taken it utterly for granted and virtually ignored it ever since.

The Four Roots of American Federalism

As the form of the American polity, federalism has its roots not only in the political dimension of American society but in the economic, social, and religious dimensions as well.[3] This point is often overlooked and has been especially neglected in our own time. The political roots of American federalism spring to mind most easily, the Articles of Confederation and the Constitution being the foremost examples. In fact, those roots go back at least to the Mayflower Compact, a federal document in the original meaning of the term as a covenant among parties seeking to unite for common purposes while preserving their respective integrities. For all intents and purposes, the Mayflower Compact marked the first federal act on the part of people who were to become Americans. Between the Mayflower Compact and the Constitution of 1787 were uncounted compacts, covenants, and constitutions creating churches and towns and colonies, and at least one intercolonial confederation as well. Since we will have considerable occasion to examine the political behavioral roots of federalism in the following pages, suffice it to say at this point that these constitutional documents reflected as well as stimulated those behavioral patterns.

The economic roots of American federalism can be traced to the early trading companies that sponsored British and Dutch settlement of North America and to the system of governance the settlers encountered on the voyage over. The trading companies were royal monopolies organized so that both ownership and control were spread among shareholders. In some cases, the shareholders remained in Europe and tried to hold the actual settlers within their grasp through their control of the company. Invariably this failed for political reasons. In a few cases some significant portion of the settlers were themselves shareholders and thus combined political and economic control. In both cases the pattern of shareholding led to a corporate structure that was at least quasi-federal. The governance of ships had a contractual character that involved federal principles (in the original sense) whereby every member of a ship's crew was in some respects a partner in the voyage. By signing the ship's articles, a crew member was entitled to an appropriate share of the profits while at the same time submitting himself to the governance of the captain and ship's officers. Thus every voyage was based on a prior compact among all participants determining the economic and political arrangements that would prevail for that voyage. This system resurfaced in slightly different form in the organization of the wagon trains that crossed the plains, whose members compacted to provide for their internal governance during the long trek to the Pacific.

The religious expression of federalism was brought to the United States through the federal theology of the Puritans, who viewed the world as organized through the covenants God had made with mankind, binding God and man into a lasting union and partnership to work for the redemption of the world, but in such a way that both sides were free as partners must be to preserve their respective integrities. This daring notion lies at the basis of all later perceptions of human freedom, since only free people can enter into covenants. Thus, implicit in the Puritan view is the understanding that God relinquished some of His omnipotence so humans could be free to compact with Him.[4]

According to the federal theology, all social and political relationships are derived from that original convenant. Thus communities of believers had to organize themselves by covenant into congregations, just as communities of citizens were required to organize themselves by covenant into towns. The entire structure of religious and political organization in New England was a reflection of this application of a theological principle to social and political life, and its echoes can be found in the economic life of the New England colonies as well.

Outside New England, perhaps half of the religious congregations and a fair share of the local governments were organized on the basis of covenants. It has been demonstrated that early Virginia was also influenced to a great extent by Puritan ideas. Even after the eighteenth-century secularization of the covenant idea, the behavioral pattern persisted, to resurface on every frontier, whether in the miners' camps of southwestern Missouri, central Colorado, and the mother lode country of California or in the agricultural settlements of the upper Midwest.

It should not be surprising that the social dimension of federalism became so pronounced, given the convergence of these political, economic, and religious factors. Americans early became socialized into a kind of federalistic individualism—not the anarchic individualism of Latin countries, but an individualism that recognized the subtle bonds of partnership linking individuals even as they preserve their individual integrities. William James was later to write about the federal character of these subtle bonds in his prescription for a pluralistic universe.5 Indeed, American pluralism is based upon the tacit recognition of those bonds. Even though in the twentieth century the term pluralism has replaced all others in describing them, their federal character remains of utmost importance. At its best, American society becomes a web of individual and communal partnerships in which people join with one another to accomplish common purposes or to create a common environment without falling into collectivism or allowing individualism to degenerate into anarchy. Their links usually manifest themselves in the web of associations that we associate with modern society but that are particularly characteristic of covenanted societies like the United States.

In a covenanted society the state itself is hardly more than an association writ large and endowed with exceptional powers, but it is still an association with limited means and ends. Were Americans to adopt a common salutation for some farfetched reason, like "comrade" in the Soviet Union or "citizen" in the days of the French Revolution, in all likelihood the American salutation would be "pardner," the greeting of the archetypical American folk figure, the cowboy who embodies this combination of individualism and involvement in organized society.

The Individual and Society: Contrasting Orientations

Implicit in the foregoing is a specific conception of the proper relationship between the individual and society. Perhaps more than any other polity in human history, the United States has consciously and explicitly focused upon that relationship as the cardinal question of politics. American history can be understood as a struggle between four major orientations toward the relationship between the individual and civil society (that by now slightly archaic early modern term that conveys so well the way all comprehensive societies necessarily have a political form and the way all good societies keep that political form from becoming all-embracingly totalitarian). All four orientations can be traced back to the first foundings of American settlement and have continued to manifest themselves in the American experience ever since. One of these is individualism. It is perhaps the best known and most celebrated, so much so that it is often thought to be the *only* legitimate American orientation. Another is collectivism, viewed by most as the opposite of individualism and as a kind of bogeyman to be rejected by all right-thinking Americans. A third is corporatism, rarely identified in its own right yet a powerful influence on the course of American history. The fourth is federalism, a term as familiar to Americans as individualism, in its own way almost as hallowed and certainly as misunderstood.

Americans and foreign observers alike have tended to emphasize American individualism. The American has been portrayed as the Lockean man, the solitary individual confronting a society he has made through his contract with other solitary individuals, assessing both his rights and his duties within the society on the basis of individual self-interest, rightly understood. The society in turn confronts the individual with all its massiveness, uncushioned by mediating groups of other than transient character. At its best, America as an individualistic society emphasizes the importance of individual rights, the limitations the existence of those rights places upon government, and the responsibility of government to preserve and protect those rights. On the other hand, individualism has also provided a cover for social irresponsibility, especially (but not exclusively) by the rich and the powerful, and the fuel for an overwhelming alienation of the detached individual.

It was in answer to the latter strains within American individualism that collectivism emerged as a major force on the American scene. Collectivist strains can be found from the very beginnings of American society. The first efforts at colonization by the English, both at Jamestown and at Plymouth, were based on collective effort and ownership. In both cases, within a year or two the experiment was abandoned as a failure in favor of encouraging individual enterprise, which brought far better results. The collectivist strain periodically resurfaced in other colonization efforts, particularly in the utopian colonies of the nineteenth century. These experiments represented the first attempts to utilize collectivism as an antidote to what were considered the evils of individualism, and they were initiated for the best of reasons. As long as the collectivist impulse was confined to a few relatively small experiments and all the colonies either disappeared or transformed themselves into noncollectivist communities, it had little influence on the body politic as such. Beginning with the New Deal, however, a collectivist approach began to be imposed on a national scale through massive government intervention.

The intellectual origins of this collectivist approach can be found in the post–Civil War years, in the last generation of the nineteenth century, when intellectual reformers seeking to eliminate the evils of industrial society while retaining the benefits of industrialization began to propose collectivist solutions to current social problems. Perhaps the foremost example of this new collectivist utopia was provided by Edward Bellamy in his novel *Looking Backward*.[6] In it he describes a society organized on military principles, in which every person is mobilized for the active adult portion of his or her life within one grand pyramid to undertake the tasks of society. At the time Bellamy's utopia was widely admired, and clubs were established all over the country to advance his scheme. Today, in retrospect, with the experience of such utopias in other parts of the world before us, we are appropriately horrified by the collectivist regimentation involved and appalled at Bellamy's naiveté regarding human nature and the exercise of power.

Less radical expressions of this collectivist impulse were expressed by people like Herbert Croly, often identified with the Progressive movement.[7] Croly's ideas had more impact in that he did not seek an utter transformation of American society but rather sought to ameliorate existing conditions through greater national government effort on a collectivist basis. The Crolyan image provided the basis for the kind of collectivism that emerged during the New Deal.

This is not to say that the New Deal was itself collectivist. It was far too unsystematic for that, and it is unlikely that Franklin D. Roosevelt wished to foster a collectivist America, but among those around him were people who saw in collectivism—democratic collectivism to be sure—the only solution to the problems facing the country. Capitalizing on the moralistic strain in American society that periodically encourages Americans to try to impose single standards of behavior, even in delicate areas, upon the American public, they and their heirs have succeeded in the intervening decades in creating a substantial collectivist thrust within the body politic. Needless to say, it is not known by that name. Sinclair Lewis once wrote that fascism could come to the United States only in the name of liberty. So too with collectivism.

Collectivism American style has often been encouraged by a third strain in American life, that of corporatism. In this context corporatism may be defined as the organization of civil society through corporate structures that can efficiently focus considerable power and energy on the achievement of specific goals and that tend to combine with one another to control common fields of endeavor, primarily economic but potentially political as well. Such corporate bodies, while nominally broad based, in fact are excellent devices for concentrating control in the hands of managers who formally are trustees for the broad group of owners (shareholders) but in fact have great freedom of maneuver. The shareholders, in return for relinquishing control to managers through the corporate framework, are in a position to profit without sharing responsibility, since the corporation becomes a reified person standing apart from those who have combined to form, own, and manage it.

It is easy to see how corporatism of this kind can be closely linked with a kind of collectivism. In fact that linkage also began with the very first English settlements on American shores. The first settlers were sent out by the great trading companies of England and Holland, the predecessors of the modern corporation, which sought to use collectivist mechanisms to build their colonies until those mechanisms proved themselves unprofitable. This phase of corporatism did not last much beyond the first generation of settlement in each of the colonies. But the mere fact that the original colonies tended to be settled through such corporate structures has a significance that has often been overlooked in American history. It was only after corporate endeavors had laid the groundwork that other settlement agencies would pick up the momentum.

Much the same pattern recurred at each successive take-off point in the advance of the land frontier. Thus settlement of the trans-Appalachian West owed much to the initial work of fur and land corporations, and subsequent settlement of the trans-Mississippi West was in no small measure initiated by larger fur corporations and the great railroad corporations. Needless to say, the urban-industrial and the metropolitan-technological frontiers are closely related to corporatism. Even the initial wave of entrepreneurs on the urban-industrial frontier rapidly came to institutionalize their efforts in corporate structures. Indeed, the struggle in the Jacksonian era over the freedom to incorporate was crucial to the opening and development of the urban-industrial frontier. By the opening of the metropolitan-technological frontier, pioneering was again a corporate activity, even more than in the earliest days of land settlement.

In the era of the land frontier, corporatism had strong competitors, so its role remained significant but not dominant, intervening at key junctures in American development but then having to retreat before other factors. Even the nascent corporations were subject to other strong influences, so that corporatism as such had less impact. It was only on the urban-industrial frontier that corporatism acquired a major role, though still by no means a dominant one. Corporations took on significant economic roles and involved themselves in politics as a result, primarily to protect and advance their own interests. However, even the most ruthless among them did not seek to provide a model for organizing the polity. Everyone assumed that corporate and political organizations existed for different purposes and hence drew from different models. Here too it was the intellectual reformers in the last generation of the nineteenth century who borrowed corporate models as the basis for many of their reform proposals. In the Progressive Era they were joined by spokesmen for corporate interests, who saw in the smooth workings of the great business corporations models to be adopted by governments, particularly municipal governments, to improve their efficiency.

Still, it was only with the coming of the metropolitan-technological frontier in the generation following World War II that the corporate model became identified with progress in the political realm. In that generation there was a movement toward linking corporatism and collectivism. This in itself marked a revolutionary shift. Collectivism was originally fostered in government to fight corporate power, but in the end the natural alliance between the two has tended to bring them together, at the expense of individualism and federalism.

The American people, who pride themselves on their individualism, are for the most part unaware of the role corporatism has played in their history, even though they have come to share many of its basic assumptions, often unknowingly. For example, since Americans have inevitably defined efficiency in commercial terms (what is efficient for the promotion of commerce is accepted as efficient for all purposes), they increasingly have come to accept corporate definitions of efficiency as corporations have become the dominant forces in commerce. Thus political life has also been pushed in the direction of corporatist ideas, with little questioning whether the basic assumptions of corporatism are applicable or appropriate in a democratic political arena.

Federalism is a fourth orientation in American life, one that has so dominated the mainstream of the American experiment that it has been utterly taken for granted. Since the days of the Puritan and Revolutionary founders, when John Winthrop could still talk of federal liberty and Thomas Jefferson of ward republics, federalism in this sense has sunk deep into the American psyche. It is only in civil societies in which there are people searching for the federalist way—France, for example—that federalism is identified as a sociopolitical orientation in its own right. Intellectuals in those countries write about "integral federalism."[8] But federalism has always been integral to the American experience; hence there has been no incentive to discuss integral federalism as a concept.

Federalism as an orientation emphasizes each individual's place in a network of cooperative communities where individualism is defined not through one's detachment but through partnership with others, a network in which the individual does not confront society alone but works through such mediating institutions as the family, the religious community, or an ethnic group. It is this federalist way that has limited the anarchic tendencies inherent in individualism, to generate the kind of disciplined independence that has been characteristic of American society. It is this federalist way that has enabled Americans to undertake collective action without embracing collectivism. It is this federalist way that has provided both the political and the social dimensions necessary to harness the power generated by corporatism and direct it toward the goals of justice that animate American civil society.

The Origins of American Federalism

As the literature of the constitutional ratification campaign, both Federalist and Anti-Federalist, indicates, federalism was designed by the founding fathers to be more than a structural compromise making it possible to unify the several states under a single national government. It was also meant to achieve more than a geographic division of power for expediency's sake. Federalism, to its American creators, represented a new political alternative for solving the problems of governing civil societies, an alternative that from the first embraced the whole panoply of political theories, institutions, and patterns of behavior that form a political system.

The federalism of the founders was designed to provide substantially new means of developing a viable system of government and politics, a reasonable approach to the problems of popular government, and a decent way of securing civil justice and morality. Moreover, its inventors conceived of federalism as a uniquely valuable means of solving the perennial problems of any civil society seeking to transform itself into a good commonwealth, particularly one built on the rock of popular government—the problems of balancing human liberty, political authority, and governmental energy so as to create a political system at once strong, lasting, democratic, and just. They believed their invention was based on valid fundamental principles and could employ proper, if new, political techniques to carry them out. They were convinced of this—and were soon joined in their conviction by the American people as a whole—because their invention directly resolved important substantive questions that they anticipated would confront the United States. The essence of their solution was to apply the federal principle not only to relations between governments but to the overall political relationships of groups ("factions" in Madison's terminology) and individuals to government.

The founders' own sources try to justify their stand by telling us why they felt as they did. Unfortunately, current myths prevent many people from considering those sources on their own terms. For one thing, many believe American federalism is the product of circumstances alone, that nature itself (or at least prior experience) dictated that the American republic be built on the rock of diffused governmental powers so that any discussion of a "federal principle" is an ex post facto attempt to discover an original political invention when common political considerations actually sufficed. Pointing to the vast expanse of land under the American flag even in 1787, the great diversity of peoples gathered under its protection, the general commitment to popular government prevalent in the land, and the preexistence of the thirteen colonies, many people conclude that a formal distribution of power among "central" and "local" governments was inevitable if there was to be any union at all and that the founders of the republic simply worked out the mechanisms needed to make the status quo politically viable.

This idea has become widespread in the twentieth century because it is particularly useful to those who accept two companion views of American federalism current today. One is the notion that the framers of the Constitution were hostile to popular government and used federalism to limit "democracy" by distributing powers undemocratically. This school sees subsequent American history as the struggle to establish popular government against the will of the founders' Constitution. Accordingly, they believe that the Constitution's system for distributing power grew obsolete as the nation became more "democratic." The other view accepts the premise that the founders were antidemocratic but "excuses" them on the grounds that problems of communication over such a vast and diverse area required the federal distribution of powers. Their claim is that as problems of communication are lessened, this distribution of powers becomes unnecessary.

At first glance, history appears to support the current myths. The implantation of settlements on the American shores under different regimes and charters had led to the emergence of at least thirteen firmly rooted colonies-cum-states by 1776. The new nation did inherit the basis for some type of federal plan and, it might even be said, had no choice in the matter. Recent research has heightened the plausibility of this view by showing how far the American colonies enjoyed a de facto federal relationship with the English king and Parliament before independence.[9]

The existence of states, however, was no guarantee that they could be united under one government. Moreover, there was no guarantee that unification could take any form other than loose confederation so long as the states remained intact as sovereign civil societies, or any form other than consolidation if they did not. In this respect the factors of size and diversity were in no way determinative. Distribution of power, as opposed to concentration, is a function not of size and diversity per se but of republican political inclinations.

Students of comparative government—from the days of Aristotle to our own and including the generation of the founders of the republic—have been aware of the possibilities for centralized government in even the largest and most diverse empires. In Aristotle's day the Persian empire extended for over three thousand miles, "from India to Ethiopia," and included more than a hundred nationality and ethnic groups, each in its own land. Yet throughout its two hundred years of existence, it was governed by a despotism that, while maintaining a benevolent attitude toward the maintenance of local customs and laws, carefully concentrated as much political power as possible in the hands of the emperor.

Locke, Montesquieu, and the founding fathers were acquainted with the similarly organized Ottoman empire. They, like our own generation, also encountered one of the greatest centralized despotisms of all time in the form of the Russian empire. When Cortez was viceroy in Mexico, the Russian empire under Ivan the Terrible already covered an area larger than the original United States (888,811 square miles in 1789). The Russians began their march eastward in the sixteenth century, and at the time the Puritans were settling New England they reached the Pacific. By the year of the Glorious Revolution and the establishment of parliamentary supremacy in England, the Russians had consolidated their centralized rule over some seven million square miles and dozens of nations, people, and tribes. An eighteenth-century Russian, if asked about the political consequences of a large domain, would have been likely to say that an expanse of territory is useful in protecting absolutism, since the difficulties of internal communication it creates help prevent popular uprisings on a nationwide scale.

A Frenchman of the same century, if asked the best method of creating a nation out of a number of smaller "sovereignties," would undoubtedly have recalled the history of France and advocated the complete political and administrative subordination of the entities to be absorbed under a central government and the elimination of all vestiges of their local autonomy so as to minimize the possibilities of civil war. Even an eighteenth-century Englishman, aware of the centuries-old problem of absorbing Scotland within Great Britain, would have been likely to approach the problem of national unification in a somewhat similar manner, except that he might have added a touch of decentralization as a palliative to libertarian sentiments. Thinking Americans were aware of all these examples in 1787. It is no accident that *The Federalist* had to concentrate heavily on refuting the argument that a stronger national government would inevitably open the door to centralized despotism.

Closer examination of the situation between 1775 and 1801 provides convincing evidence that, regardless of the factors encouraging some form of division of power between a general government and the state governments, the development of a federal system stronger than that embodied in the Articles of Confederation was by no means foreordained. Such an examination reveals how far the founders of the United States were committed to the idea of popular government and were searching for the best form of organization—the best constitution—for the republic, one that would secure the liberties of the people while avoiding the weaknesses of past experiments in popular government.

Even here the founders had little precedent to guide them. Not only were there no extant examples of the successful government of a large territory except through a strong centralized government, but there were few small territories governed in a republican manner and none that offered the example of federalism as Americans later came to know it. The two nations then existing that had come closest to resolving the problems of national unity without government centralization were the United Provinces of the Netherlands and the Swiss Confederation. Not only were both very small republics indeed (each covered about 15,000 square miles at that time), but the failure of the former to solve its constitutional problems and its consequent lapse into government by an incompetent executive and an antirepublican oligarchy was well known, while the latter was hardly more than a protective association of independent states with little national consciousness. Neither could be an attractive example to the American nation builders, who were committed to both republicanism and the common peoplehood of all Americans.

In one sense, then, the founding fathers had only two contemporary models to choose from, both of which showed great weakness and promised little for the perpetuation of popular government. They could have attempted to bring the several states together in a single unified but decentralized state on the order of the government of Great Britain, or they could have been satisfied with a loose confederation of sovereign states, united only for defense and foreign relations, that could barely govern adequately even in the areas of its responsibility but would offer minimal opportunities for national despotism.

There were those who advocated the former course, particularly among the younger officers of the Continental Army. At various times they urged Washington to establish a constitutional dictatorship (which might have led to a political system akin to the kind of Jacobin dictatorship established by Napoleon in France in the 1790s) or to assume the crown as a constitutional monarch (which presumably would have led to the kind of aristocratic oligarchy that existed in eighteenth-century England). Although Washington effectively subdued most of these officers on several occasions during the war itself (the most famous was his appearance at Newburgh), one of their number, former lieutenant colonel Alexander Hamilton, continued to advocate the latter position as much as he dared right though the Constitutional Convention.

The second course was the one followed during the war as a natural outgrowth of the Continental Congresses assembled from 1765 through 1775. If the founders had been content with a "foreordained" system, one "dictated" by the actual status of the United States in 1776, they would have accepted this alternative and retained the Articles of Confederation, which were adopted to ratify just that kind of confederacy. That system has been most frequently compared to the various Hellenic leagues that united several city-states only insofar as they shared a common purpose—invariably defense. Such leagues embraced small despotisms as well as small democracies. They had no role to play in determining the internal regimes of member states and were in no sense protectors of human liberties or popular government.

Among those who advocated this course of action were some of the most notable patriots of the early revolutionary struggle. Above all, they feared despotism in large governments and distrusted any notion that a national government with energy could be kept republican. Whatever their views on the potential tyranny of the majority, they were more willing to trust smaller governments with supervision of the people's liberties on the grounds that they were more accessible to the people. Patrick Henry was the most outspoken of this group. He held his ground to the bitter end, uncompromising in his belief.

Popular Government and the Federal Solution

As we all know, the founders chose neither alternative, instead inventing one of their own, animated by a desire to perfect the union of what they believed to be an already existing nation and to give it the power to act as a government while keeping it republican and democratic. In developing their solution, they transcended the limits of earlier political thought in order to devise a way to protect the people's liberties from every threat.

Their alternative reflected a great step forward in thinking about popular government because they refused to accept the simplistic notion that the possibilities for despotism increased in direct proportion to the size of the country to be governed. They were fully convinced by history and personal experience that small governments, in their case the states, could be as despotic as large ones.

Moreover, the founders were convinced by history and experience that democratic governments could be as tyrannical as autocratic ones if they were based on simple majoritarianism. Pure democracies, in particular, were subject to the sway of passion and hence to the promotion of injustice, and even republics were susceptible if faction was allowed to reign unchecked. As friends of human liberty and popular government, they felt it necessary to create a political system that would protect the people from despotic governments whether large or small, democratic or not.

Their solution, federalism, was designed to deal with all these contingencies by balancing them against one another to create a number of permanent points of tension that would limit the spread of either popular passion or government excess, that would break up or weaken the power of factions, and that would require broad-based majorities for significant political actions. To the founders, locating all sovereignty in the people as a whole while dividing the exercise of sovereign powers among several governments—one general, the others constituent—was a means of checking the despotic tendencies, majoritarian or other, in both the larger and the smaller ones while preserving the principle of popular government. The interdependence of the national and state governments was meant to ensure their ability to check one another while enabling them to cooperate and govern energetically. In the words of *The Federalist*, they advocated republican remedies for republican diseases.

In organizational terms, the perennial tug-of-war between centralization and decentralization was to be avoided by the introduction of the principle of noncentralization. The difference is a crucial one. Decentralization, even as it implies local control, assumes the existence of a central authority with the power to concentrate, devolve, or reconcentrate power more or less at will. Noncentralization assumes that there is no central authority as such but that power is granted to several authorities, general and regional, directly by the people. Even though the general authority may enjoy an ultimate preeminence that is real indeed, those authorities cannot legitimately take basic powers away from each other.

True federal systems must be noncentralized. Even when, in practical situations, there seems to be only the thin line of the spirit between noncentralization and decentralization, that line determines the extent and character of the diffusion of power in a particular regime.

The American people and their leaders were to extend this aspect of federalism, known in common parlance as the "checks and balances" system, into most areas of their political life. Both the state governments and the national government have powers that cannot be taken from them even when both share in their exercise. The principle was further applied to relations of the various branches of government—executive, legislative, and judicial—within each plane even before the invention of federalism. It was subsequently applied to the structure and organization of the party system, which consists of two national coalitions of substantially independent state and local party organizations further checked by the independence of action reserved to the "congressional parties" within each of the coalitions. It was applied to the other processes of politics and even to the nation's economic system in ways too numerous to discuss here.

The federal principle sets the tone for American civil society, making it a society of balanced interests with egalitarian overtones, just as the monarchist principle makes British civil society class and elite oriented despite democratic pressures, and the collectivist principle sets the tone for Russian civil society, making it anti-individualistic even when egalitarian. In political terms, this is because the federal principle establishes the basic power relationships and sets the basic terms for the processes of distributing power within American civil society. The founders understood the role of such governing principles in building the framework for a political system. They knew that though the roots of the governing principle of every civil society are embedded in its culture, constitution makers do have a significant opportunity to sharpen the principle's application and direct its growth.

In sum, federalism as the founders conceived it was an effort to protect the rights of men by consciously creating institutions and procedures that would give government adequate powers while forcing the governors to obtain a high level of consent from all segments of the public they served before acting in other than routine ways. Requiring extraordinary majorities for great actions, the Constitution was based on the idea that there is a qualitative difference between a simple majority formed for a specific issue and the larger consensus that allows governments to continue to function from generation to generation.

The Covenant Idea and the Federal Principle

The creation of the American federal system was both a new political invention and a reasonable extension of an old political principle—a considerable change in the American status quo and a step fully consonant with the particular political genius of the American people. Partly because of their experiences with the model before them and partly because of the theoretical principles they had derived from the philosophic traditions surrounding them, the American people rejected the notions of the general will and the organic state common among their European contemporaries. Instead, they built their constitutions and institutions on the *covenant* principle, a very different conception of the political order and the one most conducive to the theory and practice of federalism.

This idea of covenant, of a lasting yet limited generally grounded agreement between free people, entered into freely by the parties concerned to achieve common ends or to protect common rights, has its roots in the Hebrew Bible. There the covenant principle stands at the very center of the relationship between man and God and also forms the basis for the establishment of the holy commonwealth. The covenant idea passed into early Christianity only after losing its political implications. Its political sense was restored during the Protestant Reformation, particularly by the Protestant groups influenced by Calvin and the Hebrew Bible, the same groups that dominated the political revolutionary movements in Britain and America in the seventeenth and eighteenth centuries. Much of the American reliance upon the covenant principle stems from the attempts of religiously inspired settlers on these shores to reproduce that kind of covenant in the New World and to build their commonwealths upon it. The Yankees of New England, the Scotch-Irish of the mountains and piedmont from Pennsylvania to Georgia, the Dutch of New York, the Presbyterians, and to a lesser extent, the Quakers and German sectarians of Pennsylvania and the Middle States were all nurtured in churches constructed on the covenant principle and subscribing to the federal theology as the means for properly delineating the relationship between man and God (and by extension between man and man) as revealed by the Bible itself.

By the middle of the eighteenth century, however, the covenant idea had been plucked from its religious roots and secularized by men like Hobbes, Locke, and Rousseau. They transformed it into the concept of the *social compact*, the freely assumed bond between man and man that lifted them out of an unbearable state of nature and into civilization. In the Lockean view widely admired by Americans, it was this social compact that made popular government possible. The availability of the covenant idea in two forms meant that those Americans who did not acknowledge the political character of the covenant between man and God inevitably recognized the political character of the social compact between man and man and built their constitutions upon that.

The evidence is overwhelming that the covenant principle translated into the larger political realm as part of the development of modern popular government produced the idea of federalism. The history and meaning of the term itself reveal this. The word *federal* is derived from the Latin foedus, "covenant." It was first used in 1645 in the midst of the English civil war to describe covenantal relationships of both a political and a theological nature. Apparently, as its theological usage indicates, the term implied a closer or more permanent relationship than its slightly older companion *confederal*, a Middle English derivative of the same Latin root. At first the two words were so closely related that they were used synonymously until the American Civil War added an additional dimension to the theory of federalism by sharpening the distinction between them. Federal was not used in its present sense until 1777, during the American Revolution. Its modern usage, then, is an American invention. The creation of the term federalism to indicate the existence of a "federal principle or system of political organization" (quoting the *Oxford Universal Dictionary*) did not come until 1793, after the principle was already embodied in a great work of political theory and the constitution of a potentially great nation.

Covenant (or federal) theory was widely appreciated and deeply rooted in the American tradition in 1787 because it was not the property of philosophers, theologians, or intellectuals alone. In its various adaptations, it was used for a variety of very public enterprises from the establishment of colonial self-government to the creation of the great trading corporations of the seventeenth century. Americans regularly made covenants or compacts to establish new civil societies. Witness the Mayflower Compact (1620):

> In the name of God, Amen. We whose names are under written . . . Having undertaken for the Glory of God, and Advancement of the Christian Faith, and the Honour of our King and Country, a Voyage to plant the first colony in the northern Parts of Virginia; Do by these Presents, solemnly and mutually in the Presence of God and one another, covenant and combine ourselves together into a civil Body Politick, for our better Ordering and Preservation, and Furtherance of the Ends aforesaid.

The Virginia Bill of Rights (1776):

> [A]ll men are by nature equally free and independent, and have certain inherent rights, of which, when they enter into a state of society, they cannot by any compact deprive or *divest* their posterity, namely, the enjoyment of life and liberty, with the means of property, and pursuing and obtaining happiness and safety.

The Vermont Declaration of Independence (1777):

> We, the inhabitants [of the New Hampshire grants], are at present without law or government, and may be truly said to be in a state of nature;

consequently a right remains to the people of said Grants to form a government best suited to secure their property, well being and happiness.

The Constitution of Massachusetts (written by none other than John Adams in 1779):

> The body politic is formed by a voluntary association of individuals. It is a social compact by which the whole people covenants with each citizen and each citizen with the whole people, that all shall be governed by certain laws for the common good. It is the duty of the people, therefore, in framing a Constitution of Government, to provide for an equitable mode of making laws, as well as for an impartial interpretation and a faithful execution of them, that every man may, at all times, find his security in them.

Covenant making remained a part of the settlement process throughout the days of the land frontier. Men gathered together in every one of the thirty-seven states admitted to the Union after the original thirteen to freely frame constitutions for their government in the manner of the first compacts establishing local self-government in the New World. Cities and towns were created by compact whenever bodies of men and their families joined together to establish communities devoted to common ends.

With the rise of organizations, the covenant principle was given new purpose. Scientific and reform societies, labor unions, and professional associations as well as business corporations covenanted with one another to form larger organizations while preserving their own integrity. They initiated a new kind of federalization that continues to this day.

As a consequence of these manifold uses of the covenant idea, the American "instinct" for federalism was extended into most areas of human relations, shaping Americans' ideas of individualism, human rights and obligations, divine expectations, business organization, civic association, and church structure as well as their notions of politics. While there were differences in interpretation of the covenant principle among theologians, political leaders directly motivated by religious principles, and those within a secular political outlook; among New Englanders, residents of the Middle States, and Southerners; and from generation to generation, there was also a broad area of general agreement that unified all who subscribed to the principle and set them and their doctrine apart within the larger realm of political theory. All agreed on the importance of popular or republican government, the necessity to diffuse power, and the importance of individual rights and dignity as the foundation of any genuinely good political system. At the same time, all agreed that the existence of inalienable rights was no excuse for anarchy, just as the existence of ineradicable human passions was no excuse for tyranny. For them the covenant provided a means for free men to form political communities without sacrificing their essential freedom and without making energetic government impossible.

The implications of the federal principle are brought home forcefully when it is contrasted with the other conceptions of popular government developed in the modern era. Other revolutionaries in the "age of revolutions" that has existed since the late eighteenth century—most prominent among them the Jacobins—also sought solutions to some of the same problems of despotism that perturbed the Americans. But in their efforts to hurry the millennium, they rejected what they believed to be the highly pessimistic assumptions of the American constitution makers that unlimited political power could corrupt even "the people" and considered only the problem of autocratic despotism. They looked upon federalism and its principles of checks and balances as subversive of the "general will," their way of expressing a commitment to the organic unity of society, which, like their premodern predecessors, they saw as superior to the interests of mere individuals. They argued that since their "new society" was to be based on "the general will" as a more democratic principle, any element subversive of its organic unity would be, ipso facto, antidemocratic.

By retaining notions of the organic society, the Jacobins and their revolutionary heirs were forced to rely upon transient majorities to establish consensus or to concentrate power in the hands of an elite that claimed to do the same thing. The first course invariably led to anarchy and the second to the kind of totalitarian democracy that has become the essence of modern dictatorship. Although the "general will" was undoubtedly a more democratic concept than the "will of the monarch," it has proved no less despotic and usually even more subversive of liberty.

The history of the extension of democratic government since the eighteenth century has been a history of the rivalry between these two conceptions of democracy. Because of the challenge of Jacobinism, the meaning of the American idea of federal democracy takes on increased importance.

The American Federal Consensus

The framers of the Constitution capitalized on the American instinct for federalism that had already revealed itself in the nationwide organization for the revolutionary struggle and in the first constitution of the United States. In one sense they simply tried to improve the American political system within the framework of the covenant idea by creating—as they put it—a "more perfect union."

The results of their work were not accepted uncritically at the time, nor did they remain unmodified after the ratification of the Constitution. Their emphasis on the "national" as distinct from "federal" aspects of the new Union (the terms are those of *The Federalist*) did not sit well with most of the American people, who felt keenly that emphasis on the federal aspects was necessary to keep government limited, taxes low, and liberties secure.

The Anti-Federalists lost their fight to prevent ratification of the Constitution, but by immediately accepting the verdict and entering into the spirit of the new consensus, they soon won over a majority of the American people. After the Jeffersonian victory in 1800, the dominant theoretical emphasis around the nation was on the primacy of the states as custodians of the nation's political power, an emphasis that was dented from time to time—substantially between 1861 and 1876—but not altered until the twentieth century. This emphasis provided a very hospitable environment for the development of the "states' rights" heresy that colored the actions of Southerners during the Civil War generation.

In reality, the debate over the meaning of the American covenant and its federal principles began anew under the Constitution, has continued ever since, and will no doubt go on as long as the American people remain concerned with constitutional government as an essential element of the American mystique. Its very existence enhances the health of the body politic. Yet from first to last it has remained a debate over interpretation of the meaning of the federal principle, not over the validity of the principle as such.

Though the debate has involved vital questions of the first magnitude, it has been carried on within the context of a political consensus that is all the more remarkable for having changed so little in some two hundred years. Though rarely, if ever, given verbal expression as a whole, this consensus is attested to by scores of commentators on the American scene, from Crevecoeur to Max Lerner and from de Tocqueville to D. W. Brogan.[10] More impressive testimony is found in the behavior of the American people when that consensus has been threatened. Abandoning their more transient allegiances, they have invariably responded to the call, changing their "normal" patterns of behavior—often to the amazement of observers lacking historical perspective—for others more appropriate to the situation. It is this inherent understanding of the basics of the American political system that sustains popular government despite the mistakes of transient majorities. The consensus itself is imbued with the spirit of federalism through and through, though it extends much beyond a concern with the strict institutional aspects of the federal system to embrace the ideas of partnership and balance that, put together, give birth to the federal principle.

Like the other orientations, the federalist approach is not a single way of doing things, but rather a direction, a path. Thus federalism provided a basis both for the secession of the southern states and for their reintegration into the Union on an equal footing with their northern sisters once the Union forces won the Civil War. Federalism has been interpreted both as limiting government action and as providing the basis for government intervention to force private individuals to behave in a morally correct way. It is unfashionable for contemporary Americans to endorse John Winthrop's conception of federal liberty, which he defined as the freedom to do what is right.[11] But the recent history of government enforcement of civil rights on the basis of United States Supreme Court decisions is precisely an example of federal liberty—of the abridgement of the rights of individuals to do wrongs to other individuals.

For three and a half centuries, two of them under the same constitution, Americans have managed to follow the federalist way without being conscious that they were doing so except in the narrowest institutional sense. Now, however, the federalist way has come under assault from the twin pressures of corporatism and collectivism. We shall have occasion in the course of this volume to see how these pressures developed, in no small measure in response to an individualistic heresy, no less problematic than the collectivist and corporatist heresies now confronting Americans. An understanding of organization based upon corporatist models of efficiency coupled with a set of expectations from government based upon collectivist models, which have come at the same time as a reorientation of individualism in the direction of license, have combined to weaken the federalist mainstream of the American experiment. Hence it becomes vital for those who understand that mainstream to articulate the concept and to bring it to the attention of those who have taken it for granted and are now puzzled by the transformations taking place in American society.

The year 1976 marked the end of the eleventh generation of American history and the sixth generation of American independence. It also marked the end of the first generation of the postmodern epoch. The United States, aptly called by Seymour Martin Lipset the first new nation, was born at the beginning of the modern epoch, achieved its independence as that era reached its apogee five generations later, and matured over the next five generations until the modern epoch came to an end.[12] Today, only Americans over the age of fifty were raised when it was still possible to talk about the United States as being on the threshold of maturity—when as much time separated the founding of the American colonies from the Revolution as separated the Revolution from them. Since then America has experienced a generation of full maturity—of great world responsibility, of tragic foreign involvement, of constitutional crisis at home derived from the attempt to substitute imperial for republican styles of behavior in the highest offices of the land. We have crossed a divide at least as formidable as that crossed when the era of the land frontier came to an end.

The Bible reminds us that with every tenth generation a new epoch begins. During the first epoch of American history, the American people forged a unique synthesis of constitutionalism, republicanism, and democracy. As we reflect from the vantage point of the twelfth generation, we are well advised to consider the character and meaning of the first epoch. Federalism is the glue that has held constitutionalism, republicanism, and democracy together during eleven generations of American history. Like all glue, it has in turn the properties of flexibility and hardness and, once set, tends to be invisible or at least unnoticed in the midst of the materials it has joined together. But without the glue, the materials fall apart. Contemporary Americans have shown that they have no less concern for constitutionalism, republicanism, and democracy than their forefathers, but if the second epoch of American history is to reflect the fulfillment of the American promise, we must not neglect the glue.

2

PLURALISM, FEDERALISM, AND LIBERTY

The United States of America is often considered the pluralistic commonwealth par excellence, in the sense that plural ways of social, religious, and to some degree political and economic expression are accepted as part of the natural order of things.[1] American pluralism as we know it today, in its most widespread if not normative form, is in many respects modeled after the commonwealth William Penn founded three hundred years ago. Pennsylvania was the first deliberate effort to build a commonwealth on pluralistic social foundations, an extension of the Quaker doctrine that every individual is guided by his or her inner light.

The largest of the middle colonies/states until it was surpassed by New York after the beginning of the nineteenth century, its influence extended far beyond its borders. During the eighteenth century, Philadelphia was the largest city in North America and second only to London in the British Empire—the intellectual and commercial center of the colonies. Pennsylvania led the way west for northerners; its impact is visible to this day in the layout, street names, and architectural design of cities and towns across the United States from coast to coast, copied and transplanted by settlers moving westward.

However monolithic government was in colonial Pennsylvania, the commonwealth soon fulfilled Penn's commitment to social pluralism by welcoming a wide variety of religious and ethnic groups on the basis of complete and mutual toleration. It is hardly surprising that the Revolution in Pennsylvania made it the most democratic of the states. Indeed, the Commonwealth of Pennsylvania is notable for having maintained its posture of mutual toleration with relatively few lapses throughout its history, and those lapses involve struggles over control of economic or political power rather than over the issue of pluralism per se.[2]

Six American Models of Pluralism

Pennsylvania deserves special recognition as the first deliberately pluralistic commonwealth, but it was not the only pluralistic colony in British North America, nor has it provided the only model of pluralism to take root in the United States, however close to normative it may have become. In fact, Pennsylvania's is one of six models of pluralism that have developed in the United States, each beginning in a different state and spreading throughout particular regions or sections of the country.

At the time of Pennsylvania's founding, if not before, New York was developing its own model of the pluralistic commonwealth. New Yorkers might even claim their model preceded that of Pennsylvania, but New York became pluralistic by default, not by design. Indeed, as the colony of New Amsterdam, the form in which it was founded, it was far from pluralistic in intent. It was only the desire of the settlers and the mother country to make money by strengthening commerce that opened the back door to the development of a pluralistic society in what was to become the Empire State.[3]

The critical case was the first Jewish settlement in New York, which became the first Jewish community in North America. In 1654 twenty-three Jewish refugees from Recife, Brazil, arrived in New Amsterdam. They had originally settled in Recife as Dutch subjects as part of the Dutch colonization effort in northeastern Brazil. After the region was reconquered by the Portuguese they left the colony because Jews were banned from any Portuguese territory. They came to New Amsterdam because of their Dutch connection, but Governor Peter Stuyvesant also did not want to accept Jews—clearly a rejection of pluralism, which he, like most others of his time, viewed as dangerous to the body politic. They appealed to the Dutch West Indies Company. A number of its shareholders were Jews, and pressure from them, effective because of the profit-making instincts of the company, led to a reversal of Stuyvesant's expulsion order and to permission for the Jews to stay, albeit as second-class residents at first. It took a century of struggle before all restrictions on Jews were removed.[4]

No one should dismiss the importance of the pursuit of wealth as an instrument of social progress. That commerce led to the development of pluralism by default in New York State not only does not diminish the importance of New York as a model, it even suggests that New York should take its place alongside Pennsylvania as one of the normative models of pluralism in America.

Pluralism in New York evolved as the pluralism of the marketplace. Whoever was prepared to abide by the rules of the game could participate and be rewarded according to his success. The Jews of New York capitalized on that opportunity from those early beginnings until the present, as have so many other groups since then. Pennsylvania has never become quite so pure a marketplace, giving every group an equal claim to participation. Where left to its own devices, it still maintains certain tests of legitimacy that have moral rather than commercial foundations. That, indeed, was part of the Penn model.

In both states pluralism is primarily social, most particularly a pluralism of primordial groups (ethnic, racial, religious), and it is largely unsegregated, except by action of the marketplace. A very different kind of pluralism developed in New England, particularly in Massachusetts which by no means set out to become a pluralistic commonwealth. In a certain way, its founding was a revolt against the necessity of having to live in what had become by default a religiously pluralistic polity—pre–civil war England.

The founders of Massachusetts sought to build a commonwealth based upon religious purity, meaning a purity of religious ideology and the forms of its common expression. We all know that those founders expelled or executed Quakers, Baptists, and any other dissenters who happened to be in their midst, even native sons and daughters. Yet the settlers of Massachusetts could not help but be aware that their idea of truth was not shared universally, hence they had to offer some means of accommodating diverse visions, especially when those visions sought concrete expression in civil society. Their formula was pluralism via physical separation. In other words, they had no objection to non-Puritans going out into separate parts of the wilderness and founding their own commonwealths, just as long as they did not try to settle in Massachusetts. There could even be limited cooperation between commonwealths motivated by different visions, as in the case of the New England Confederation, directed toward maintaining common security against the Indians and common rights against England. Since each proper commonwealth would be animated by its own vision and seek to give form to that vision (e.g., by establishing a state religion), pluralism would have to be expressed through separate commonwealths for each vision.[5]

We might say that the New York and Pennsylvania models on one hand and the Massachusetts model on the other represent the two faces of territorial democracy. The United States from the first was based on strictly territorial communities, in contrast to Europe, where modernism emerged from a society divided into corporations and estates that, while occupying and sharing the same territory, were each governed by their own institutions and leaders. This kind of corporate pluralism was already declining in Europe when the first settlers came to British North America, giving way there to the territorial organization of civil society.

The Americans did not have to go through that struggle. They adopted territoriality as the only legitimate basis of political organization from the first, but they expressed that commitment in two ways. The first, characteristic of New York and Pennsylvania, was based on the neutrality of territory. Whichever groups came to settle in a particular territory would gain the rights of citizenship and share political power according to their size and strength. If one group replaced another, then so be it.

The second face of territorial democracy was that represented by Massachusetts and most of New England, whereby different groups were expected to settle in different territorial entities and build polities that would protect their separate group interests. Territory became a basis for maintaining separation through mutual respect and cooperation rather than an arena for determining the relative power of different groups. Although the first face became more widespread in the United States and indeed has been made normative by recent decisions of the United States Supreme Court if not by the federal and state constitutions, the second face has continued to exist and has an ancient and honorable place in American society.

When the United Sates was essentially an agricultural society, rural settlement was quite homogeneous, with different groups settling together in different townships or even counties. Urbanization substantially changed that pattern, leading to the present situation. Where the second form of territorial democracy continues to exist, it tends to be like the pluralism espoused by Puritan Massachusetts, a pluralism based on religious or, in a few cases, ideological communities where the sharing of a common vision that requires local homogeneity for its preservation or fulfillment legitimizes some degree of territorial exclusiveness.

Yet a fourth model of "pluralism" emerged out of colonial North America—a pluralism of caste, separating whites and blacks and rooted initially in human slavery. Although slavery was widespread throughout the colonies during the seventeenth century and much of the eighteenth, this kind of pluralism received its first full expression in the Commonwealth of Virginia in the late seventeenth century when the white population of that commonwealth transformed indentured servitude for blacks (as distinct from whites) into permanent bondage.[6] This pattern was to spread throughout the South even as slavery ceased to exist in the North during and after the Revolutionary War and indentured servitude for whites disappeared throughout the country.

As a result of the Civil War and the emancipation of the slaves, a hierarchical pluralism of caste was reinstituted by southern whites and remained the dominant pattern until the civil rights revolution of the 1960s. During that time, each racial caste developed a complete society of its own. While many of the most overt aspects of this caste division have since disappeared, it remains a factor in southern society and beyond to this day.

Pluralism of caste was never considered fully legitimate in the United States and, as we shall have occasion to discuss below, represents the dark side of pluralism. It, more than any other form, is associated with particular states in a particular section in the American public mind, but in fact the other forms of pluralism are so associated as well.

A fifth model of pluralism is the pluralism of associations, whose mother state was Ohio and which is associated in American popular culture with the Midwest. Ohio's prominence as the exemplary state of the pluralism of associations is reflected in American folklore in the image of small cities dominated by networks of associations, whether the various fraternal bodies—Elks, Kiwanis, Moose, Masons, Rotary—or civic associations such as the Chamber of Commerce, or even the two major political parties—political associations that became foci for multigenerational commitments. Ohio, then, as the first state of what is generally known as the Midwest, originally the Old Northwest and perhaps most appropriately the Near West, was the mother state of this pluralism of associations.

Unlike Pennsylvania and New York, what counted most in Ohio and the Midwest was not one's primordial group but the associations one joined. Links with particular associations were not matters of the moment; one joined for life and in many cases expected one's children to follow into the same network. But they were associations nonetheless, reflecting personal choice in joining, not inheritance. Intergenerational patterns of associationism in particular communities or areas might lead to the emergence of what Ellsworth Huntington has termed a kith, a multigenerational group united by a common culture. But even where ties are intergenerational, it is the association that determines the kith in the Midwest, whereas in the Northeast the kith determines the patterns of association.

This pattern of associations became the norm throughout the Midwest, serving as a basis for uniting Protestants of different primordial group backgrounds in the Republican party and for the Americanization of Catholic and Jewish settlers in the section. Indeed, it became the model for late nineteenth-century Protestant America, a nation of "joiners." It even functioned within the two castes that constituted the basis for southern pluralism. Where Yankee-style pluralism prevailed, it took on a moral character. It provided an even more Americanized basis for the group pluralism of Pennsylvania or New York, whether in the form of churches and synagogues or fraternal societies as associations of people from the same ethnic group, or as family clubs (the transformation of the clan into an association). If no longer as firm as in small-town America, in the twentieth century this kind of pluralism permeated all segments of American society and remains a powerful force, influencing all the other models.[7]

In our times a sixth model of pluralism has emerged, clearly identified with the state of California. It is a radical pluralism of individuals, according to which everyone is so singularly separate that he or she need not maintain permanent ties with any other individual or group, abandoning not only primordial ties such as ethnicity and associational ties such as church and political party, but even family ties, including marriage ties, at one's convenience. This radical pluralism of individuals has spread rapidly throughout the United States since the late 1960s, adding another dimension to American pluralism, being absorbed in each state and section according to the previously dominant patterns of pluralism and with correspondingly different effects.[8]

Varying Conceptions of Liberty

All six of these models of pluralism have mixed social and political characteristics, implications, and impact. For example, each reflects its own conception of liberty. The first two emphasize the liberty to maintain group identities within a shared polity, with its corollary of the market model based upon shared rules of the game. The difference between them is in that one emphasizes the moral foundations of civil society and the other emphasizes civil society as a marketplace pure and simple. The third emphasizes the liberty to build communities, each with its own way of life and the necessity to make distinctions as to who can build what where.

The fourth model emphasizes the liberty of one group at the expense of another and hence has been judged severely wanting in terms of American ideals. It is the one form of pluralism that has been formally rejected as illegitimate in the American contest and has been subject to direct assault by American political institutions in the name of the Constitution.

The fifth model, like the first, emphasizes the liberty of the marketplace based upon common subscription to the rules of the game, but it goes beyond in emphasizing the liberty of the individual to choose primary associations as well as secondary ones. This liberty is limited only by the shared recognition that it is necessary to have binding, long-term primary associations, however free one is to choose them. The sixth model rejects even that, seeking radical liberty for everyone, even to the point of questioning the extent to which individuals are bound by shared rules of the game.

It is in this connection that we confront both the virtues and the problems of pluralism. Pluralism is a necessary concomitant of democracy American style. It may not be a necessary concomitant of every democracy. Indeed, strong arguments have been made by various political philosophers and others that true democracy can function only under conditions of social homogeneity. The United States, as a nation of immigrants, has chosen to take another path, fraught with its own problems as well as blessed with its own virtues.

What kinds of pluralism are legitimate and what kinds are not? I have already suggested that Americans have rejected the pluralism of caste as being inevitably discriminatory. There is no such thing as "separate but equal." In fundamentally antihierarchical American society, a pluralism that by definition is hierarchical has no place. But even that position is a relatively recent development, since the pluralism of caste was accepted as reasonable throughout the nineteenth century and tolerated by default until the post–World War II generation. Today a declining pluralism of caste is being transformed into a pluralism of primordial groups in either the original New York or the original Pennsylvania style.

While the American people, more or less as a whole, were rejecting the pluralism of caste, the United States Supreme Court was rejecting the pluralism of communities developed in colonial Massachusetts—the nonneutral face of territorial democracy. The reapportionment cases are perhaps the most striking examples of this, though by no means the only ones. By coming down hard in favor of the neutrality of territory, the Court has made it extraordinarily difficult for communities to separate themselves through control of particular pieces of territory, even on the basis of mutuality.

It is not at all clear that the American people are in sympathy with this thrust of the United States Supreme Court. The issue has never really been joined, because it has never been raised as a matter for serious debate. Rather, the Court's position has been taken as a given, in great part because it coincides with the radical pluralism of individuals that has been sweeping the country and that makes unfashionable the notion that communities have the right to restrict individuals within their boundaries on behalf of common goals or standards, particularly among those circles that determine the American agenda in such matters.

For a while in the aftermath of World War II, with its great impact on the breaking down of barriers in American society, it seemed that the kind of pluralism grounded in primordial groups in which Pennsylvania pioneered was doomed to disappear. As the barriers restricting different racial, ethnic, and religious groups from full participation and opportunity in American society fell, there seemed no likelihood that such groups would maintain themselves. Then in the late 1960s there came the "ethnic revival" or "new ethnicity"—what seemed, at least for a brief moment, to be a reethnicization of America.[9]

Although much of what seemed to be happening turned out to be a passing phase, and though its impact was much exaggerated by commentators at the time, it did generate, at least for the moment, a new legitimacy for primordial group identification in the United States, though clearly in tandem with associationalism and even radical individualism. According to the new theory, though one could choose to make primordial ties the most meaningful without being treated as a "hyphenated American" (a term from the late nineteenth-century melting-pot theories and expectations that dominated the American establishment), one is not bound to one's primordial group a priori.

As it turned out, the "ethnic revival" was, for most of the "ethnics," a last gasp of ethnic self-perception before their complete assimilation into the new America. In this respect it can be compared to the ethnic revival that took place in the 1880s and 1890s among groups from the British Isles and northwestern Europe—Dutch, German, Scottish, and Welsh—who by asserting their own ethnic identity and collective contribution to American civilization legitimized their entry on equal terms into what had become an English-dominated civilization. Similarly in the 1960s and 1970s, southern and eastern Europeans sought what can be defined as better terms for total submergence into a common American culture by emphasizing their roots and heritage and their contribution to American life. However, though the new ethnicity turned out to be a passing phase, the legitimacy of primordial group pluralism was renewed and even given new life for those who chose that way of self-expression.

The pluralism that the changes of the past decade particularly advanced was the radical pluralism of individuals. The causes for this transformation are to be found in a convergence of factors: United States Supreme Court decisions breaking down barriers to radical individualism (the abortion decisions are good examples of that); media emphasis on hedonism as a "good;" widespread affluence, making hedonism and radical individualism possible—that is to say, people could afford it; disillusion with old ways on the part of the young; and so forth.

To the extent that this kind of radical individualism was a phenomenon of the American West, its spread throughout the country can be seen as a kind of "westernization" of America that ran parallel to its ethnicization. If these seem to be contradictory trends, so be it. I have already suggested that there was a mutual influence, with primordial attachments becoming a matter of individual choice. It also is possible that the penchant for radical individualism may be more widespread among people from certain primordial groups. Needless to say, the effectuation of the synthesis draws heavily upon the pluralism of associations that had spread countrywide even earlier. Associationalism is also transformed by radical individualism. In politics, the new synthesis emphasizes "California style" participatory politics, heavy media involvement, and "citizens for . . ." groups with shifting activists as well as single-issue groups dominated by uncompromising cadres who approach their cause with near-messianic fervor.[10]

Federalism and Liberty: Maintaining and Containing Pluralism

Whatever its character and dimensions, it is clear that pluralism is alive and well in the United States. Its maintenance is not a problem. Rather, there may be a problem of containing pluralism or at least certain forms of it for the health of the body politic. John Adams told of an encounter with a jockey in Boston at the outbreak of the Revolution. The rider told Adams how grateful he was that the Patriots had liberated them all so that every man could do as he pleased. Adams was shocked at this misinterpretation of the meaning of political liberty, rejecting the jockey's equation of liberty with anarchy. He sought what his Puritan ancestors and several of his contemporaries referred to as federal liberty—liberty limited by covenant. That kind of liberty is both morally grounded and mutually agreed upon; hence it is the liberty to do what is morally right and to play according to the rules of the game to which the participants have consented.[11]

Anarchy has never been an American vice, but federal liberty has had to contend with natural liberty throughout American history. While half of the American character seems to be attuned to federal liberty and proud of its biblical-Puritan foundations, the other half has celebrated natural liberty—that of natural man, not bound by convention, but able to pursue true freedom in nature.[12] Much of the myth of the American West is associated with natural liberty and natural men, implicitly rejecting federal liberty; yet the reality of westering, whether in wagon trains or mining camps—not to speak of temperance colonies or settlements of sober farm folk—rested upon the introduction of federal liberty into the wilderness.

This struggle between federal and natural liberty can be traced back to the earliest days of the American experience, in the confrontations between the Puritan ideal and the Rousseauian ideal of the noble savage. It was expressed in an earlier generation of this century as "doin' what comes naturally" and today is known as "letting it all hang out," a kind of pluralism run wild. Natural men in the western wilderness were limited by raw nature, which they confronted daily and thoroughly respected. Hence they were no more unlimited in their freedom than those bound by covenant. When people within civilization seek to behave as natural men, however, it is another matter entirely. In fact, even they are finally restrained by nature, as reflected in the number of young celebrities and others who die from drug- or alcohol-related causes, often after damaging the lives of many of their peers.

Here we come to the intersection of politics and pluralism. Democratic politics must both maintain and contain pluralism if democracy is to survive. There are many elements in politics that are necessary or useful in fostering a polity conducive to accomplishing both tasks, including proper political structure and processes, embedded in a proper constitutional framework and rooted in turn in a proper political culture, encouraged by appropriate social and economic conditions.

Americans have found federalism, though they have not always recognized it as such, to be an extraordinarily important element in both maintaining and containing American pluralism. In a classic but perhaps too-little-known exchange, Martin Diamond made this point to Morton Grodzins.[13] Both were at the height of their work on the origin and operation of the American federal system. Grodzins, in the spirit of contemporary political science, argued that it was the American party system that preserved the pluralistic dimensions of the American polity. Decentralized parties, in his words, allowed the continuation of decentralized government despite twentieth-century pressures toward centralization. Diamond responded that the decentralized parties existed in no small measure because of the constitutional structure that made the states the building blocks of the party system and hence prevented the creation of strong, centralized, disciplined national political parties that would have furthered centralization at the expense of territorial-based pluralism and perhaps other kinds of pluralism as well.

The events of the 1960s and 1970s have demonstrated that Diamond's argument was the stronger. As the two men were writing in the late 1950s, the tendency to build strong, centralized national parties was growing. It surfaced in both parties in the 1960s and succeeded to a degree, but only to the extent that the United States Supreme Court interpreted the Constitution in such a way as to enable the national party organizations to impose controls on the state parties by superseding state laws.

In other words, pluralism is not enough because sentiments for pluralism are not enough. Only constitutional barriers will overcome the natural propensity of ambitious men to consolidate power. Even they may not be enough, but at least they give pluralism a fighting chance.

The sources of the pluralist thinking that Grodzins partially reflected can be traced to Harold Laski, whose famous argument in the 1930s that pluralism had come to replace federalism as a means of maintaining liberty was widely quoted for at least a generation.[14] Grodzins himself, recognizing the importance of federalism as a structure, attacked Laski for ignoring these selfsame human realities.[15] Laski, of course, was not only a socialist but a British subject, and his thinking reflected English views that emerged from a setting in which powerful and deeply rooted traditions serve to enhance liberty and certain kinds of pluralism. Perhaps in a country like England tradition is sufficient—though it certainly has not been sufficient to maintain territorial pluralism in the form of strong local government. Once Parliament decided to exercise what, up to the mid-nineteenth century, had been essentially theoretical powers of unlimited sovereignty to transfer powers from the local authorities to the center, the supporters of local control could do nothing about it except try to capture Parliament and reverse the tide, something not likely to happen given Britain's strong centralized, disciplined party system. Such decentralization would require a constitutional revolution animated by an ideological vision strong enough to go against the natural human instinct to hold onto power. That has certainly not happened yet, despite the discussions of the past decade. Laski himself seems to have had second thoughts in light of his disappointment with Britain's Labour government after it came to power in 1945.

For countries without the British tradition, formal constitutional guarantees are vital to the preservation of pluralism. Indeed, they are necessary but not sufficient. Additional institutional barriers are required in the form of checks and balances—most particularly as federal arrangements.

For the United States it can fairly be said that federalism has been of the utmost importance in maintaining pluralism. Federalism has worked in both directions at various times: in the ability of the states to resist federal encroachments and in the ability of the federal government to assault state-fostered or -sanctioned encroachments on legitimate pluralism. What is important about federal arrangements is not the simple matter of power devolved but the more complex matter of power shared, allowing different avenues of recourse for injured parties or for those who wish to protect themselves against injury. This is what Grodzins referred to as the multiple crack, in the double sense of the opportunity to take many blows or cracks at the system and the existence of many fissures or cracks through which to hammer home those blows. This considers the dual possibility of state protection and federal intervention that has made federalism in the United States a major bulwark of pluralism.

But federal arrangements need not be only the American style of federalism, what has been termed modern federation.[16] Other federal arrangements can gain the same ends. Is pluralism not advanced when Puerto Rico enters into a federal arrangement with the United States as a commonwealth (*federacy* is the suggested technical term), allowing it more internal autonomy to preserve its own language and culture than the fifty constituent states? Is liberty not advanced by the fact that Puerto Rico, as part of the United States, is spared the black plagues of revolution, dictatorship, and authoritarian government that are characteristic of most independent Latin American states forced to maintain standing armies, ostensibly for their security?

Students of the European Community will certainly attest that as the member states have developed the EC into a confederation with a high constitutional court responsible for maintaining the common market and common standards of human rights, both pluralism and liberty have been advanced. At the far end of the scale, little Andorra has preserved its liberty for over seven hundred years even though it is a tiny speck between two great imperialistic powers, France and Spain, which for most of that period pursued policies designed to eliminate both liberty and pluralism within their own territories. Their joint rule of the little state through a federal arrangement known as condominium gave Andorra the space it needed to survive and be free while all the independent states around it were absorbed by one or the other of the two powers, losing their liberties and much of their ability to maintain anything like pluralism.

The virtue of federalism lies in its utility in not only maintaining pluralism but also simultaneously containing it. Needless to say, there are many systems of government and political devices for eliminating pluralism. The problem is, How does one contain it while maintaining it? That is where federalism has a special contribution to make. In light of what has been written here, the reasons should be obvious.

In the first place, the governmental compact upon which a federal polity rests can in itself define or delineate what constitutes legitimate pluralism for that particular polity, while its constitution can define the framework within which that pluralism is maintained and contained. Here is where federal arrangements can be of the greatest use—for example, by allowing for different constituent units to maintain different styles of pluralism, thereby permitting people who prefer one kind over another to find their appropriate place and also preventing the spread of certain styles to places where they are unwanted. This was the case in the United States until recently, as the models presented at the beginning of this chapter suggest.

Here too the ability of federal systems to encourage experiments without overcommitment to the results is relevant. Although the nationwide influence of California-style pluralism is real, it is by no means certain that this pluralism is going to conquer the country. In politics, for example, one need only look at the contrast between the mass-based, amateur-dominated politics of California and the amateur-dominated politics of Minnesota to note the differences in political culture and style between the two and the limits of California's influence as long as Minnesota maintains its own political system and party politics. If this is less true in other spheres of human activity, it is because federalism no longer provides sufficient barriers.

It is worthwhile elaborating on this example. If California-style politics has had a serious nationwide impact, it has been on presidential elections, where the styles developed in a minimass society of then 16 million, now 24 million, could be easily translated to a large mass society of 200 to 230 million people. Even there they have been successful only insofar as other factors have led to the decline of state party organizations and political networks as major factors in the conduct of major presidential campaigns. Thus the United States Supreme Court's assault on the federalist basis of pluralism in party organization in favor of the attempt to impose a single national pattern, standard, and way of doing business has been a major contributory factor to the spread of California-style campaigning. The United States Supreme Court and other nationalizing forces that have progressively eliminated these federal devices claim to be speaking in the name of pluralism, but actually they are taking a Jacobin position that in the last analysis is extraordinarily antipluralist. At the time when Harold Laski was writing on pluralism versus federalism, Franz Neumann published an attack on federalism entitled "Freedom and Federalism" that was clearly Jacobin in character.[17] His attack encapsulated the sentiments that came to pervade so many of the Court's decisions. Today it may be said that the hands are the hands of Laski, but the voice is the voice of Neumann.

An Interim Conclusion

Various kinds of pluralism are appropriate in a large, multifaceted polity. If there is any kind that is not acceptable, it is a pluralism that violates the spirit of federal liberty—that seeks to elevate "doin' what comes naturally" at the expense of the bonds of covenant. Implicit here is the argument that without the bonds of covenant there can be no decent civil society. Natural man can function only in the wilderness, where his contact with others is limited and, moreover, where nature itself provides sufficient checks to control his behavior.

Other than that, the argument of this chapter is that liberty is served by having different varieties of pluralism, provided the extended republic is structured to allow those different varieties to find expression and to reach different syntheses in different parts of the polity. Federalism is an excellent way to make that possible. Hence for those Americans who believe that pluralism is a significant dimension of liberty, maintaining a proper federal system should be high on the agenda.

3

LAND AND LIBERTY IN AMERICAN CIVIL SOCIETY

Perhaps the most enduring achievement of the first American regime, the government of the confederation, was the establishment of a national land policy that served to strengthen liberty, equality, and national unity. The very foundation of that regime was tied up with the settlement of the conflicting western land claims of the states, whereby the public domain of the new American West was ceded to the federal government to be held in trust for all Americans as part of the confederation agreement. Once the states ceded their claims to the western lands, all Americans had a common propertied stake in the United States. From that moment on, if not before, the course of American unity was more or less settled.

Beyond that original act, the Confederation Congress enacted two vitally important ordinances designed to establish policy for settlement and organization of those western lands. These ordinances—the Land Ordinance of 1785 and the Northwest Ordinance of 1787—remained the basis for American land policy after the adoption of the Constitution of 1787. The Land Ordinance established the basis for organizing, dividing, and disposing of the public domain. The greatest and most American act of national planning ever undertaken in the United States, it established a system that put an indelible stamp on 80 percent of the American landscape, working to enhance liberty rather than restrict it. The Northwest Ordinance established the principle of carving new states out of the public domain on the basis of free settlement and republican institutions grounded in local initiative and consent. Taken together, these great acts not only reaffirmed the special relationship between land and liberty that had evolved during colonial times, but tied that relationship to the largest goals of American civil society.

It is necessary to pay due attention to the role of land in the constellation of American political ideas and the organization of American political life and to the implications of that role for political action. In its political dimension, land has been used as a major guarantor of the liberties of Americans. Frederick Jackson Turner was the first scholar to recognize this and to suggest some ways it was so in the days of the land frontier. Although Turner's central thesis has been a subject of considerable controversy, his point that land and its use have had particular social and political implications for American society deserves to be taken very seriously.

The Land Ordinance of 1785 established a general land survey system that has been carried from the Appalachians to the Bering Strait. The survey system provided for rectangular surveys dividing the land into townships of thirty-six square miles, six miles to a side. Each township was divided into thirty-six sections, each of one square mile (640 acres). Land was to be sold for a nominal charge of a dollar an acre, with a 640-acre minimum. One section of each thirty-six was to be set aside to support public schools. It was proposed that yet another section be set aside to support religion, with the denomination benefiting to be determined by the majority of resident adult males, but the proposition failed by a narrow vote—not because religion was not to be encouraged but because of the denominational pluralism anticipated among the new settlers. Thus this very first act provided for private ownership of the land, with all that meant for individual liberty; basic public support for education on the grounds that only an educated citizenry could be free; and religious liberty on a pluralistic basis, with no church established or publicly favored. Overall, the act implicitly recognized what the Northwest Ordinance was later to phrase so felicitously: that "religion, morality, and knowledge [are] necessary to good government and the happiness of mankind."

The impact of this Land Ordinance, which was reenacted in 1796 by the Congress of the United States under the new constitution, cannot be overestimated. Those who grew up in the states carved out of the public domain and paid attention to their surroundings are most fully conscious of this impact, since virtually every aspect of the spatial dimension is governed by the land survey to this day, as are many aspects of their governmental structure. Not only is rural government in the American heartland based upon civil townships whose boundaries were determined by the land survey, but the cities from the Great Lakes to the Pacific are also laid out in line with the survey. We see this in the basic division of Detroit into "mile roads" culminating in Eight Mile Road, the city's northern limit, which is also the baseline for the land survey in Michigan. We see it in San Francisco's rectangular grid, which imposes human regularity on its seven-plus hills, and we see it in the cities and towns in between.

The Northwest Ordinance of 1787 added flesh to the skeleton established in 1785 by setting down the terms of settlement in the western lands, setting forth basic civil law for the territories, and also adding the nerves of government. Formally, the ordinance is ordained as a compact (articles of compact in the original text) between the original states and the people founding states in the new territories. As such it is a principal expression of the political compact tradition that was the basis of American revolutionary republicanism. The entire theory of American republicanism is encapsulated in that ordinance and translated into concrete public policy, all related to the link between land and liberty.

Land as a Guarantor of Liberty

Land has functioned as a guarantor of liberty in three ways. (1) The availability of relatively free land in considerable quantity has offered a ready environment for the development of new patterns of land use across successive frontiers while providing relatively equal opportunity of access to each new environment. (2) The widespread ownership of land, with the emphasis on owner-occupied homesteads as the basis of both rural and urban settlement, not only has given the great majority of American families a "stake in society" with the benefits and protections that a landed stake entails, but has functioned to maintain the nation's middle-class character and many of its agrarian values. (3) The very organization of the nation's political system is territorially determined, through units of land ranging from states to precincts. Although rarely recognized as such today, land continues to be used in all three of these ways as a libertarian force vis-à-vis growing governmental power.

The role of land as a prime guarantor of liberty has its roots in the agrarian tradition that remains strong in American life. The American political vision is of a commonwealth that supports and encourages the agrarian virtues of individual self-reliance and family solidarity within the framework of a cooperating community that knows minimal class distinctions, advocates the simple virtues usually associated with religious commitment, and encourages ownership of property by those involved in its use.[1]

The land-oriented roots of America's political vision stem in large part from biblical foundations.[2] The Hebrew Bible that provided the basis for so much of the political vision of the first settlers of British North America on these shores pays particular attention to the uses of land in the construction of the good commonwealth.[3] Those founders of the first colonies who were inspired by a political vision well understood the biblical conception that man is God's steward on earth.[4] More than that, they understood something of the biblical demand for balancing stewardship and private working of the land with provisions for maintaining its equitable distribution, all within the framework of a closely knit community.

The provisions for distributing the land of Israel among the Israelite families, by tribe, formed the basis for ensuring the economic security and personal liberty of each family and the political liberty of the nation.[5] The law of the jubilee year, which required that land alienated from its rightful owners out of economic necessity be restored to the inheriting family, and the law of redemption, which required the entire clan to be responsible for maintaining each family's lands intact in diverse circumstances, were means of maintaining the social and economic basis of personal and national liberty.[6] While the jubilee laws appear to have remained in the realm of utopian legislation, the law of redemption was a vital part of Israelite life. The rise of the monarchy and the demise of the more democratic tribal federation brought with it a drift away from the equitable distribution of the land. The Bible itself reports this and, through the Prophets, criticizes the trend. Still, despite such pressures, tenant farming remained unknown in Israel until Roman times.[7]

Whether discovered directly in the biblical text or via works of political theory such as James Harrington's *Oceana* (whose fundamental feature, the "agrarian" requiring regular redistribution of land, was modeled on the biblical plan), these principles were well known to the seventeenth- and eighteenth-century molders of the American nation.[8] Though no serious attempt was made to transplant biblical land law to American shores, the idea of a regulated division of the land into small freeholds so as to create territorially based communities of yeoman farmers and artisans spread widely throughout the country in various forms.[9] Three basic versions of the biblical vision of the agrarian commonwealth emerged during the first stages of American land settlement.

New England: Communities Created

In New England, the most authentic American repository of the biblically inspired vision of the good commonwealth where "federal liberty" was defined as requiring man to use his freedom to create "a city upon a hill," the agrarian idea was embodied in the network of towns that were linked to form the several colonies. Before any settlers could occupy new lands the colonial legislature would set off a town, fix its boundaries, have it surveyed, platted, and divided into lots, and lay down conditions for its settlement and a fair division of its lands for both public and private purposes.[10] The town system came closest to following the biblical model of land settlement so highly valued by the Puritans. Following biblical demands, each settling family obtained a freehold, but all families were required to live within some organized community as a means of exercising the social controls that Puritans believed all men need to ensure their salvation. At the same time, the principles and practices of territorial democracy gave each town substantial rights of self-government within the boundaries of the colonial charter (and later the state constitution).[11]

As the New England Yankees moved westward, they took their town system with them and, modifying it, created the township structure of the upper Mississippi valley states. Because they were organized around substantially larger farms, these townships were no longer centered on compact settlements that brought families physically close to one another. Still, they preserved the New England idea of a commonwealth of communities, often embracing organized groups that by prearrangement settled en masse in particular townships. West of the continental divide, where the country could not be organized for intensive farming, the Yankee settlers created oasis cities that in some respects were even closer to the original New England pattern, since the environment virtually compelled settlers to huddle together for protection and survival.[12]

The Middle States: Individuality Promoted

A different version of the biblical vision was initiated in the Middle States, most particularly in Pennsylvania. There an initial religious and ethnic pluralism coupled with Quaker individualism led to a greater emphasis on liberty as a means for maintaining privacy, both individual and communal. Hence land organization became a means to guarantee a degree of social separation, individual or communal, depending upon the situation.[13]

The Pennsylvania influence moved westward and southwestward as English and Scotch-Irish Pennsylvanians joined the movement to the interior. The Scotch-Irish, representing the Presbyterian wing of Calvinism as the Puritans represented the Congregational wing, carried the principles and practices of yeomanry into the South, particularly where the plantation style of land use had not taken hold, or could not. East of the Mississippi they settled in the piedmont, mountain, and plateau regions, and west of the river on the marginal piny woodlands. Since they did not need compact settlements for religious purposes in the manner of the Congregationalist Puritans, they gave in to their historically rooted desire for individual liberty and made their farms into bastions of self-sufficiency even at the expense of economic success.[14]

The Pennsylvanians and others from the Middle States who moved westward combined their agrarian attachments with their commercial interests to produce the businessman-farmer who treats his land as a source of pecuniary profit as well as the basis of his way of life. Such entrepreneurs did not seek land to build communities of freemen or to gain isolated self-sufficiency, though in some cases they gained a measure of both. Rather, land to them was a means of guaranteeing their freedom to advance economically by participating in the marketplace. The heart of the American corn belt in the Near and Middle West and such places as the Central Valley of California were settled by people representing or embracing this philosophy of land use. They were the first to move into the cities in search of better marketplaces when opportunities in agriculture became limited (when land became less effective as a means of capitalizing on marketplace opportunities and better ways emerged to take its place). Hence they set the pattern for urban land use during the first era of industrialization in the Middle States, east and west.[15]

The South: Tradition Maintained

Only in the South did there emerge a political philosophy of land use not based on a biblical vision. Where the plantation system became dominant in that section, it made landownership the vehicle for creating a society firmly organized into classes and castes, reinforcing privilege and slavery (or serfdom) rather than equality and liberty.[16] The plantation system not only spread westward from the tidewater areas to the plains (and later, in other forms, to Arizona and California) but, through its various adaptations, managed to survive the demise of its original form at the end of the Civil War to remain in conflict with the southern variant of the family farm imported from north of the Mason-Dixon line.[17] Even in the South, however, government was organized on territorial lines with counties as the fundamental units of local government.

Within those territorial units, the struggle between the two land-use systems has been perennial. This struggle was intensified by the pattern of land allocation in use in the South. Unlike New England, where land was used to create communities, in the South warrants were issued to individuals who were then responsible for locating their own claims on still unsurveyed lands. While this led to numerous confusions and conflicts, it also fulfilled the highly individualistic demands of plantation seekers and yeomen alike.[18]

Territorial Democracy

Whatever the variant of the vision, or lack thereof, open land offered opportunities for equalization, and territorial democracy was the order of the day. Geographically defined units of government, most with permanent boundaries, were established as the country was settled. With their fixed boundaries, these territorial units offered neutral havens for whatever form of settlement or other interests gained a foothold within them. New people settling in (or creating) those units were able to capitalize on easily available land to improve their own economic, political, and social positions within the framework imposed by the area's overall pattern of land settlement.[19] At the same time, certain persistent patterns were fixed in each unit of government by those who settled within it, dividing the country as a whole according to the spread (and in many cases the overlapping) of the several versions of the American vision.[20]

The three systems of organizing the land to guarantee liberty described above both reflected and strengthened basic differences in the political culture of Americans. Each form is characteristic of a particular political subculture in the United States, and each has been adapted to the basic political conceptions and procedures underlying the subculture that created it.[21] The New England system reflected the moralistic subculture characteristic of areas settled and molded by the Puritans and their Yankee heirs. It sought to guarantee liberty by using land to create communities and commonwealths, reflecting that subculture's conception of politics as a vehicle for achieving justice as well as organizing power and political life as means to attain important public goals endowed with special legitimacy. The system that emerged in Pennsylvania and the Middle States reflected the individualistic subculture characteristic of that area of the country. Its emphasis on marketplace activities as the best means for guaranteeing individual liberty and its orientation toward using land to provide access to the marketplace reflected the subculture's emphasis on politics as a process of organizing power on the basis of competing private interests of generally equal legitimacy. The combination of land systems found in the South reflected and reinforced the traditionalistic political subculture characteristic of that region, which emphasized using land to preserve traditional patterns and ties and to guarantee established liberties (which is often the same as guaranteeing private privilege).

The continued existence of these three political subcultures has been of first importance in setting the direction of, and the limits to, any national land-settlement policies. Moreover, the conflict between the subcultures has been reflected in the conflict over various policy proposals through the years. For example, in the late eighteenth century, the New England bias for settling the West through colonization companies, which was reflected in the requirement of the Land Ordinance of 1785 that a minimum sale be 640 acres, was forced to give way to a more individualistic approach. At first this approach represented a compromise between the southern pattern of acquiring land (in any amount) through occupation ("squatting"), the Middle States' approach, which involved individual purchase of set acreages, and the New England system of township survey and division. Subsequently, in the mid-nineteenth century, the Yankees devised the free homestead system, whereby any person who developed a claim of 160 acres by living on it for five years could acquire title for no more than the filing fee. This scheme won over the products of the individualistic subculture while alienating the Southerners.[22]

A similar struggle over urban land settlement policy was avoided on the national plane only because few major national policy decisions beyond those establishing the initial land survey were involved in creating or expanding cities during the initial stages of the industrial frontier. The various subcultural areas created cities in their own images within the context of the Federal Land Survey. Substantial conflicts occurred only in those cities where representatives of the three subcultures came together.[23] Beginning with the New Deal, federal housing and redevelopment programs reintroduced national government policymaking as a significant factor in shaping metropolitan America. These programs also were structured along lines broad enough to encompass the cultural diversity in various sections of the country in their implementation, though, since the sectional differences are expressed through administrative actions rather than through the basic legislation behind the programs, they have remained concealed from the casual spectator.[24]

The Division of the Land

The original division of the land was a political act with extraordinary and continuing political and social consequences, placing its imprint on water and airspace as well as land. Moreover, the way it organized space remains a prime influence on the direction of the flow of human activity and settlement in the various sections of the country and on how space has been reorganized periodically since. Three land division systems—all politically determined—have shaped the original division of American land space.

Metes and Bounds

First in order of time was the more or less localized application of the English system of metes and bounds (or its more formalized, legislature-delineated equivalent in New England) to the Atlantic coastal settlements within the framework of royal charters and land grants during the colonial period. Royal charters authorized the transfer of landownership (or rights) in various ways—through direct grants, proprietary favors, or the corporate decision of actual settlers. Royal and colonial land grants created land reserves for public purposes such as naval timber reserves, parks and common lands, support for the ministry, support for elementary education, and the endowment of colleges. Whatever the primary method of transfer, boundaries of private lands were irregular; hence the boundaries of settlements and the paths or roads that connected them were equally irregular. The states of the East Coast north of Florida, plus West Virginia, Vermont, Kentucky, Tennessee, and parts of Ohio, were subdivided in this way.[25]

The metes and bounds system has been particularly effective in enabling men to divide land so as to maximize privacy and social distinctions, whether individual or communal. In this they are further aided by the terrain to which the system has been applied. The heavily wooded, hilly to steep land characteristic of the original areas of settlement in the East has encouraged irregular boundaries drawn to increase the separation of people and communities. Since the East, particularly the Northeast, had developed a relatively dense and diverse population by the end of the eighteenth century and has increased radically in density and diversity in the intervening years, the advantages of a land division pattern that encourages social distinctions and the maintenance of discrete, if contiguous, local communities seem to have been great. In any case, the system has proved easily adaptable to urbanization and metropolitanization in the Northeast and is visible everywhere except in the heart of the big cities, where the construction of cheap housing for the immigrant poor followed the dictates of raw commercial efficiency with no concern for either privacy or internal social distinctions.[26] What Samuel Lubell has characterized as "the old tenement trail" leads from such neighborhoods to areas in the city or its suburbs where distinctive privacy can be obtained.[27] It is a trail that each successive immigrant group has followed as soon as possible.

The drive for distinctive privacy explains much of the jealous regard for suburban and small-community rights characteristic of eastern metropolitanism. The development of separate political jurisdictions has always been easy in the United States and remains well-nigh universal in this country, but nowhere have those jurisdictions been endowed with such distinct identities as in the East. In that section of the country, not only have their boundaries been drawn distinctively, but their space has been occupied by diverse groups, each of which has tended to shape that space according to its own perceptions and needs.[28]

Rectangular Land Survey

The second land division system in point of time, and the most important historically, was the rectangular land survey systematically conducted by the United States government whose results cover the greater part of the country today.[29] All or parts of thirty-one states are covered by this massive undertaking, which is not yet quite complete, over two hundred years after its initiation. The grid system it laid upon the landscape led, in the first instance, to the laying out of township lines and the establishment of county boundaries from the western border of Pennsylvania to the Pacific Ocean. Its subdivisions formed the basis for all federal land grants and set the framework for most public improvements, including much of the railroad system west of the Appalachians. Since the railroad network determined the location of the cities, particularly west of the Great Lakes, and the cities determined the routes of the airlines and other national transportation patterns created subsequently, its influence persists two centuries later. Farms and ranches—whether embracing forty acres or forty thousand—were established according to the specifications of the land survey. Roads following survey township and section lines created the communications infrastructure of two-thirds of the country. School districts were organized along the same lines to take advantage of federal land grants. Cities founded within its confines were invariably platted so as to coincide, to some significant degree, with its grid, even where they were located to take advantage of natural features.[30]

The basic social characteristic of the rectangular grid system is its openness. The grid pattern is easily understood and highly visible, and strangers can orient themselves to it and pass through it from point to point relatively simply. Thus division of the land by rectangular grid was eminently suited to the openness of the young democracy of the nineteenth century. The grid system remains a powerful force for maintaining openness of various kinds of American society, ranging from ease of entry to feelings of spaciousness. Its role in undergirding settlement in the Near, Middle, and Far West reinforces the qualities of openness for which those sections of the country are noted and which remains pronounced even in the urban and metropolitan settlements that have emerged in those sections.[31] As central cities grew, new plats were added that followed the grid lines, while suburbs were frequently incorporated to include whole townships or sections whose land use and street patterns were dictated by the existing divisions.[32]

It was not until the post–World War II period that basic modifications in the use of the grid system were introduced into the Greater West. Since then, under the influence of planners following the eastern vogue, new suburban subdivisions have been developed within the basic grid that try to replicate the irregular street and property patterns of the East Coast. In general, such subdivisions have been confined to upper-income areas where the drive for privacy at the expense of openness has grown strong.[33] This pattern has been even more pronounced in those parts of the South surveyed under the rectangular system, where the grid pattern never took firm hold even when agriculture was the predominant land use. In most of the greater West, however, the grid system has been urbanized and metropolitanized intact to preserve the openness of the dominant local culture. Privacy in the cities of that sphere is attained through spaciousness of layout and the extensive use of trees and lawns as screens to separate neighbors just enough.

French and Spanish Systems

The third form of land division was encountered by Americans when previously settled areas were annexed to the United States. The annexed sections of French and Spanish America, which made up the bulk of the land in this category, had land systems rooted in their particular Old World patterns of land organization. They had to be harmonized with the American grid so that their inhabitants' property rights were protected while at the same time easing the entry of American settlers. This action was simply a stopgap measure and led to the ultimate imposition of the standard grid over recognized boundaries that followed the less regular forms characteristic of both land systems. Most of the lands involved in the synthesis of systems are located along the country's southern coast, from northern Florida to the Rio Grande, and in the Southwest from the Arkansas River to San Francisco Bay. Hawaii, Louisiana, and Texas are the only states to have preserved land-division systems of foreign origin.[34]

Thus two major patterns of land subdivision have become rooted on the American scene. The older metes and bounds system has been particularly useful as a means of maintaining distinctive privacy, while the rectangular grid system has fostered openness. Policy decisions encouraging either system generally reflect one set of values or the other but rarely make this explicit. Today the opportunity for policy choices has increased somewhat as Americans show greater willingness to alter established patterns on the suburban frontier or in urban renewal areas; hence the need to articulate the values underlying each option has become greater.

Sectionalism and Land Organization

The varieties of land organization and division in the United States have contributed to the development of sectional divisions of considerable social, economic, and political importance. Overall, several distinctive sectional patterns of land organization and division are visible, reflecting differing public value choices and illustrating the way public policy becomes the determining factor in such matters. The patterns have already been alluded to above. Like most public policies in the United States they were—and are—shaped by actions on all three planes of government. Even where they are discussed as national policies, they cannot be considered products of the federal government alone.[35]

The Greater Northeast

The East Coast pattern has been particularly pronounced north of the Potomac and west to the Great Lakes, spilling over into areas surveyed under the rectangular system as a result of the policy preferences of their settlers, to create a sphere of influence best denominated by the greater Northeast. Three sections fall

all or partly within that sphere, each of which has had its own brand of land organization and division.

New England is the section of formally surveyed land encompassed within an all-embracing system of structured towns having irregular boundaries and communication routes to match. The New England towns have preserved their own boundaries and identities as meaningful political units despite intensive urbanization. In fact they may have had to do less to adjust to new urban and metropolitan social and political demands than local governments in most other sections of the country, because of their original design as "small republics" and because of the unbroken contiguity of local governments with municipal powers that they provide within their states. Once consequence of this is that New England remains preeminently a region of small and medium-sized cities that offer substantial opportunites for citizen participation in civic and political life, opportunities that are probably utilized more than in any other part of the country, possibly excluding the "greater New England" of the Upper Midwest.

The Middle Atlantic states preserve the irregularities and privacies of the old system outside their major cities, but the cities themselves have tended to develop street plans with the sameness usually associated with the rectangular system yet without openness, spaciousness, or convenience of movement. Those cities, the dominant forms of land organization in the section for a century and a half, have grown up close to one another; but the section, lacking the all-encompassing character of the New England town system, still preserves at least the façade of distinctive urban and rural differences within a relatively small territorial base. Moreover, the local governmental structure fully reflects that distinction. In this section the combination of privatism and the desire for commercial hegemony combined in the nineteenth century to create very large cities that, in turn, sharpened the urban-rural political cleavage in those states and lessened the opportunities for local civic and political participation.

The states of the Near West (or the Old Northwest) that fall within the sphere of the greater Northeast present just the reverse pattern. The rural areas are clearly organized and divided according to the rectangular grid, but the cities frequently represent irregular modifications of that pattern. Their street systems and lot plats were designed to follow the more casual patterns familiar to those who settled them. Moreover, while the cities have been economically more important than the rural areas for several generations and have exceeded them in population for nearly as long, the rural influence in the section remains strong, particularly in their government and institutions and in the political styles of their residents (except, perhaps, in the very largest cities where immigrant groups have dominated for several generations).

The Greater South

The greater South, stretching from the Atlantic to western Texas and Oklahoma, combined all three land-division systems within its limits in almost equal proportions. The people who created its civilization managed to impress their own patterns of land organization over all three. The United States land survey has counted for relatively little in the greater South. Except for purposes of federal land grants, the rectangular townships were politically meaningless in a system that left local government to the counties, and orderly patterns of settlement meant even less in a land of plantations and squatters. The cities of the greater South are really scattered clearings of various sizes cut in the southern forests, usually linked inseparably with the counties in which they are situated. Although they have formal boundaries as required by law, they are not socially bounded so much as they tend to merge imperceptibly with the forests around them, especially since the onset of suburbanization. Many of those who live and work within them maintain close ties with the countryside through their old homesteads, holding on to them as long as they can make them pay enough to cover their real estate taxes. The result is a combination of privatism and intimacy that encourages social community without equality, a phenomenon that carries over into southern political life.

In this respect, sectional differences between the Upper and Lower South have been relatively minor. Both sections include plantations and small farms, depending upon the variations in their topography. The influence of the grid system is most evident in the Western South, the section west of the Mississippi, which combines western and southern characteristics. Its cities, like its lands, tend to reflect modified grid patterns. However, as in its sister sections east of the river, its cities and counties are physically, socially, and politically inseparable.

The Greater West

The third great sphere, the greater West, stretches from the western Great Lakes to the Pacific and includes two sections, the Northwest and the Far West. It is the sphere dominated by the rectangular survey in city and countryside, and indeed its overall pattern of settlement reflects the impact of the survey system in almost every detail. This is particularly true in the Northwest from Lake Michigan to the continental divide, where the rectangular survey is for all intents and purposes the only form of land division and has the further advantage of being set upon lands that offer no real topographic barriers to its full application. It is also true west of the divide, where the first settlers had so internalized the grid system that they superimposed it on foreign systems in a number of significant places. So strong was their orientation that they refused to compromise with the topography, imposing their own will on it.

The cities of the greater West are oases—often man-made—established on well-nigh empty lands and connected to those lands by the same grid. This oasis effect is most pronounced in the interior. On the west coast a rectangularly defined megalopolis is developing into a single superoasis. In both sections the grid is providing the spatial interstices between and within the metropolitan political units. In a very real sense, the grid was the device used to "tame" the West, to harness a land whose forms and climate resisted human conquest at every turn. No wonder the politics of the greater West often seems to be based on the assumption that there are no serious limits to people's ability to achieve their goals, except those they artificially impose on themselves.

American Land Uses and the Continuing Frontier

Sectional and political cultural differences are fundamental facts of American life. The way they affect the role of land in American politics is tied in to yet another fundamental fact of American life: the continuing American frontier. Since the first settlement on these shores, American society has been preoccupied with successive frontiers of development. As a society, the United States has been geared to the progressive extension of human control over the natural environment and the utilization of the social and economic benefits gained by widening that control (pushing back the frontier line). The dynamism of American society is a product of this commitment to the conquest of the ever-advancing frontier.[36]

Rural-Land Frontier

Like a chain reaction, the conquest of one frontier has led to the opening of another. Since the beginnings of English settlement in North America, the American frontier has passed through three stages. First came the rural-land frontier—the classic American frontier delineated by Frederick Jackson Turner—lasting roughly from the seventeenth century through the nineteenth. It was characterized by the westward movement of a basically rural population interested in settling and exploiting the land and by the development of a socioeconomic system based on agricultural and extractive pursuits in both its urban and its rural components.

American land policy for this frontier stage was heavily influenced by government activity because of the locus of ownership of the public domain. Government decisions on all planes encouraged various forms of public-private partnership directed toward achieving a two-pronged objective. The greater part of the land was to be opened as fully and rapidly as possible for settlement and exploitation, while a smaller share was to be used to finance the public and quasi-public infrastructure that could make civilization and exploitation possible. Government decisions were crucial in both cases, though in both (and particularly the former) much of the task of carrying out the policy was left in private hands. As a general rule, little or no consideration was given to the other dimensions of the natural environment. Whether or not Turner's "safety valve" theory is correct, the availability of land did equalize opportunity and create an environment for innovation.[37]

Urban-Industrial Frontier

Early in the nineteenth century, the rural-land frontier gave birth to the urban-industrial frontier, which began in New England and the Middle Atlantic states and spread westward, then southward much later. In the course of its spread, it transformed the nation into an industrial society—settled in cities and dedicated to developing an industrial base as the primary source of the nation's economic and social progress. The dominant characteristic of the urban-industrial frontier was the transformation of cities from service centers or workshops for rural areas into independent centers of opportunity, producers of new wealth, and social innovators functioning as a result of internally generated forces.

Land policy on the urban-industrial frontier was characterized by an emphasis on private activity, with policy decisions almost entirely the products of an unregulated marketplace. Land, formerly treated as a natural resource of direct value, became a commodity—the locus of profitable activity rather than its source. Lacking even the elemental appreciation of the environment usually found among the pioneers of the rural-land frontier, the builders of cities followed the dictates of the new frontier economics or personal convenience in dealing with their environment. As a result, environmental pollution and destruction probably reached its high-water mark during the heyday of the urban-industrial frontier.[38] Moreover, residents of cities were overwhelmingly tenants, subject to the wishes of landlords as well as employers. In 1900, only a third of the nation's urban dwelling units were owner occupied. The city land environment's direct role as equalizer is less apparent. At the same time, the new cities did help absorb millions of immigrants into American life as equal citizens.[39]

The Metropolitan-Technological Frontier

Overlapping the land frontier at first, the urban-industrial frontier became dominant by the last third of the nineteenth century. By the mid-twentieth century it had given birth, in turn, to the metropolitan-technological frontier, which was characterized by the radical reordering of an already industrialized society through rapidly changing technologies and a settlement pattern that diffused an urbanized population within large, relatively low-density metropolitan regions. The development and application of the radically new technologies of the metropolitan-technological frontier (including such major new forces as the automobile and the airplane, atomic energy, automation, telecommunications, and synthetics) and the suburbanization of the nation's population that accompanied them influenced equally radical social and economic changes to meet their new demands. Like the first two frontier stages, the metropolitan-technological frontier moved from east to west, beginning in the 1920s. It became dominant nationally after World War II, reshaping American life in the 1950s. Americans are at present participating in the political response (one might say backlash) to the social changes wrought by the forces it unleashed in the subsequent decades.

The demands of the metropolitan-technological frontier restored, and may even have increased, the role of government in setting land-settlement policies, reinstituting the public-private partnership characteristic of the first frontier but in a more positively active way. although the development of low-density urbanization clearly followed popular preferences, it was the enactment and implementation of New Deal housing and mortgage guarantee legislation that made it possible. The single-family home became the dominant mode of housing Americans. By 1960 the percentage of owner-occupied housing units in urban America was pushing the two-thirds mark, virtually the same as (if not more than) the percentage of owner-occupied farms at the turn of the century.[40]

Neoagrarianism on the Metropolitan Frontier

In general, land settlement on the metropolitan frontier represented something of a restoration of Americans' agrarian aspirations. The agrarian ideal survived and grew in the minds of most Americans even while the actual process of urbanization accelerated, fostering a crucial ambivalence in their approach to the city. Accepting the necessity and even the value of urbanization for certain purposes, Americans tried to bring the old agrarian ideals into the urban setting and to reinterpret them by establishing a modified pattern of "rural" living within an urban context.

To gain economic advantage, Americans began to flock to cities even in the days of the rural-land frontier, and cities became the pace setters in American life very early in the nation's history. But even as they desired to gain economically and socially by exploiting the benefits of urban concentration, the new city dwellers rejected classic (or Old World) urban styles of living.[41] The characteristically American attempt to have one's cake and eat it too in this case took the form of wanting the economic benefits of urbanization and avoiding the isolation and provinciality of rural life while at the same time preserving as much as possible of the pleasant life-style associated with "country living." The result was the conversion of urban settlements into metropolitan ones whose very expansiveness provides the physical means for combining something like rural and urban lifestyles into a new pattern that better suits the American taste.[42]

As part of the effort to transplant agrarian virtues and pleasures into an urban setting, a whole set of institutions and symbolic actions was developed, partially by design, meant to evoke rural and small-town America and its traditional way of life. Limited and fragmented local government with the concomitant diffusion of land-use policymaking and administration was one of these innovations. The creation of many smaller cities, the bête noire of most professional urbanists, in place of a single large metropolis reflected this desire to maintain the small community, both as an abstract principle and in order to control such crucial local functions as education, zoning, and police, which in a direct or derivative sense embody the traditions of local control. This can be seen in the continued emphasis on political autonomy for suburban communities and in their resistance to any efforts, real or imagined, to absorb them into the political sphere of the erstwhile central city.

Moreover, throughout the nation suburbanites hesitate to use government for more local services than they believe absolutely necessary, for fear that adding more will increase the urban character of the environment. In the fringe areas of cities, large numbers of people resist sidewalks because they represent "the city." Streetlights are frowned upon, sewer systems are resisted, and the maintenance of the neighborhood school is an article of faith. Urban reformers argue against "urban sprawl" on the grounds that it makes urban services too expensive, never realizing that most of the people who opt for the detached subdivisions that compose the "sprawl" do not really want those services in the first place.

It is generally known by now that suburbia has become the equal of small-town America as the symbol of the country's grass roots and the fountainhead of the distinctive "American way of life." This is so regardless of whether suburbia is praised or condemned for its role. The popular literature defending suburbia and that attacking it are both strongly reminiscent of the literature devoted to small-town America two to four generations ago. If some see virtue in the small community—whether it is typified by a predominantly small-town or a predominantly suburban society—others see ignorance, provincialism, decadence, and even corruption.[43]

The sphere of community politics is only one manifestation of this "neoagrarianism." The physical structure of the average American city is another—a crucial one. The standard—one is tempted to use the term "classical"—American city is marked by three great land-use characteristics:

1. There is a sharp separation of commercial and residential areas that not only reduces the city's "urban" appearance but makes possible its functional division into agrarian-style neighborhood "villages." The only commercial intrusions tolerated in these neighborhoods are corner groceries or drugstores, filling stations, and doctors' offices, all of which service the American public's most immediate and persistent demands.

2. A "heart," usually linear in form, of high-rise towers is surrounded by low-rise commercial and residential buildings, set along wide, easily accessible streets, preferably tree lined. The skyscraper has become the archetypical American urban tower, but the tower-and-village form itself is much older, reflected as it is in agricultural and suburban towns that focus on grain elevators and water towers. The immediate drop-off in building height and population density within the city is often more starkly visible than the line between "city" and "country," and the American skyline is unique and highly visible from coast to coast.

3. There is an effort to merge city and country by penetrating the areas of urban settlement with wildlands (or country-style open space) connecting with a network of parks and tree-lined streets that, in turn, merge with the system of private lawns to create a nature-oriented environment in as close to a natural setting as possible. Not every American city lives up to this description, nor do many live up to it in every detail, but the pattern is found in cities (or metropolitan areas) in every section of the country. Moreover, the cities that Americans consider ideal places to live and raise a family in are those that come closest to meeting this ideal image.[44]

The continued emphasis on homeownership and the complex of activities and symbols surrounding it represents still another aspect of agrarianism on the metropolitan frontier that has spread in both cities and suburbs. The owner-occupied home with its lawn and garden is the American urban surrogate for the family farm. Home and home-centered activities represent a major expenditure of energy and resources that, if calculated as work time, would substantially alter the picture of leisure in the United States.

Whereas other nations have responded to urbanization by developing official policies that virtually force their citizens into high-density living patterns, federal, state, and even local policies (other than the property tax) in the United States are heavily weighted in favor of the homeowner and low-density development. Mortgage guarantees, home-financing funds, homestead exemptions, zoning regulations, and many other specific devices have been enacted into law to encourage widespread homeownership. This emphasis is not simply an accidental consequence of the convergence of separately initiated policies; rather the policies themselves were calculated to promote such an end. Except for New York, Chicago, and Los Angeles, apartment living remains the domain of transients, unmarried young adults, newly married couples, and the mobile retired. The recent spurt in apartment construction is apparently designed to meet the needs of those groups rather than to replace the single-family home. Curiously enough, much of the apartment "boom" is a suburban phenomenon, one that is reinforcing the developing self-sufficiency of the suburbs, thus helping to transform them from dormitories that were really no more than extensions of the central city into smaller but self-sufficient cities (American style) in their own right.

The trend toward owner-occupied housing revived such symbolically rural occupations as gardening and "do-it-yourself" home maintenance. The public response to these activities indicates that they are in effect an urban recrudescence of a vital and significant "vernacular" artistic tradition long associated with rural and small-town life. State and county fairs and home-and-garden shows, the public embodiments of the vernacular tradition, outdraw art galleries in annual attendance even in the largest cities, and a major share of adult-education courses deal with home-related activities. The importance of the vernacular tradition in American life is often overlooked, since those generally deemed to be the custodians of the civilized arts tend to be products of the more urbane traditions of Western civilization that originated in Europe.[45]

Similarly, the impact that private maintenance of lawns and gardens has on the aesthetic qualities of American urban areas has generally been ignored by students of urbanization, but it is readily apparent when slum areas, where few such private contributions are made, are contrasted with even the most ordinary suburban tract developments, where lawns and gardens are a social "must." The private expenditure for lawn and garden maintenance far exceeds the public expenditure for parks, beautification, and the like. It represents an important contribution to the "public good" that would be prohibitively expensive if charged against the public purse.

The primary characteristic of land settlement on the metropolitan frontier, then, is relatively low-density occupation of urban lands accompanied by even lower open country densities beyond the metropolitan frontier lines. The generally accepted minimum measure of urbanization is a population density of one thousand or more per square mile, and the measure of suburbanization is five hundred per square mile. Those densities are reached only within tightly defined urbanized areas and are rarely attained even countrywide. In the 1960s, the heyday of the metropolitan frontier, only five small northeastern states had more than 30 percent of their counties within the suburban frontier line. Only twenty-four states (fewer than half) had even one county within the urban density range, and seventeen states did not have even one county with a density of five hundred per square mile. The situation has not changed significantly since then. In 1980 fifteen states did not have even one county with five hundred per square mile, and only twenty-seven had one thousand.

In 1960 not only did 70 percent of all Americans live on under 2 percent of the nation's land area, but open-country densities reached their lowest point in the two generations since the official close of the land frontier. In certain crucial areas they fell below the minimums used to define the regions of the land frontier. West of the Great Lakes, much of the open country had fewer than eighteen people per square mile—the accepted minimum needed to support "civilization" by nineteenth-century standards. Between the one hundredth meridian and the Pacific coast, the frontier line actually reappeared. Vast contiguous territories supporting fewer than two people per square mile and even more territory supporting from two to six (Turner's frontier zone) opened up.

Perhaps even more significant were the density trends in the greater Northeast, where the original megalopolis along the Atlantic coast, and at least one incipient megalopolis in the interior, encompassed two of the nation's three major urban agglomerations of that time. While favorable landforms encouraged the spread of the rural nonfarm population into exurban areas relatively far beyond the cities, but still within feasible commuting distance to urban jobs, really empty land also emerged just behind each megalopolis. Sharp drops in population in north-central

New England, the Adirondacks, and the Appalachians sharply separated almost-urban densities from those of fewer than six and even fewer than two per square mile. As a result, even in the densely populated Northeast, no one lived more than a day's drive from really empty land.

Population density has another dimension. Too great a density produces a kind of human-created wilderness—witness the situation in the "inner city." Exactly what density marks the beginning of that kind of wilderness is not at present known. Under American conditions, it probably lies somewhere between 15,000 and 25,000 per square mile. Popular lore has implicitly recognized that wilderness for what it is, referring to it as "the urban jungle." Psychologists have documented the impact of this ultrahigh-density wilderness on its inhabitants, showing how physical as well as psychological ills result from overcrowding. Politically, the inhabitants of the "jungle" resemble the Indians who inhabited an earlier wilderness in that they are virtually confined to reservations whose boundaries are changed (through devices such as urban renewal) at the pleasure of the local authorities and whose young seek random violence as an outlet, often provoking violent responses from "moderates" on both sides of the reservation line.

By the late 1960s a combination of factors had caused the initial thrust of the metropolitan frontier to diminish and indeed become routinized. Development continued on the peripheries and in the interstices of the suburban areas in most metropolitan regions. Each new development brought with it the same shakedown period and problems that earlier developments had brought, but except in the sun belt, the dynamic was gone. Overall, the country had settled into a period of consolidation similar to that of the 1920s when the urban frontier ended. The discovery of environmental problems at the same time even led to a new rhetoric, if not ideology, suggesting not only that the period of American growth was at an end but that growth itself was bad—that Americans should be content with what they have or even less (a view more appealing to the children of the prosperous than to the poor).

Only the sun belt frontier continued unabated and even expanded, fostering a new sectionalism whose outline, already visible by the early 1960s, began to be filled in with real political content. The result was the emergence of the frost belt–sun belt conflict that, like previous sectional conflicts, was clearly frontier related. In the previous section I suggested that the three stages through which the

United States has passed were substantially separate and discrete. This is quite true when the frontier is viewed countrywide. In particular sections of the country, however, the same processes or stages were frequently more closely interconnected. Thus the Northeast had a long hiatus between the closing of the rural-land frontier and the opening of the urban-industrial frontier and then between the closing of the latter and the opening of the metropolitan frontier.

In the sun belt states, on the other hand, particularly in the Southwest, the three frontiers met. Indeed, the urban and metropolitan frontiers frequently overlapped and were even collapsed into one another. The phenomenal growth of sun belt cities reflects this collapsing of two frontier stages into one. The urban frontier was just reaching the Southwest when the Great Depression came. Urban development halted at that point, only to resume after World War II under conditions of the metropolitan frontier, so that the two were effectively one. This was possible despite the radical difference between the situation in the Southwest and that in the Northeast, where federal policies are set. The reason is that federal policies affecting urban development at the time were essentially neutral, so local and state policies were able to determine the direction of federal programs according to particular local circumstances. What counted in the competition for federal aid were the energy, entrepreneurial skills, and will of each state or locality. Although this may have led to some inequities (a complex question that is by no means clear), it strongly reinforced the frontier process with its healthful encouraging of development. This system was of particular benefit to those sun belt cities that could capitalize upon a combination of circumstances—right location, strong representation in Congress, and an industrial technological base at the cutting edge of the new frontier—to parlay federal programs into a means of strengthening growth.

The only other state where this was true was Minnesota. In the Northeast, Connecticut and New Jersey benefited in similar ways from the merging of the urban and metropolitan frontiers. It was precisely the absence of a firm national urban policy that enabled healthy cities to remain healthy or become healthier, if the frontier conditions in which they found themselves were right. Thus, the sun belt cities and metropolitan areas were still able to benefit in the older way from government assistance in responding to the metropolitan frontier. The results are visible all around, beginning with a phenomenal growth that paralleled the great age of city formation in the Northeast in the last generation of the nineteenth century. This subsequently led to the frost belt reaction—a reaction that can be accepted as quite reasonable in the context of American politics but that need not be evaluated by objective standards as other than a matter of competing interests.

At the same time, the city-suburban sectionalism that separated the declining minority in core city areas from the expanding areas on the metropolitan periphery began to diminish in two ways. Most metropolitan regions lost their center-periphery structure and were transformed into matrices built around multiple centers with pockets of development and underdevelopment, growth and decline, scattered throughout the region. Inner-city "jungles" became wildernesses through abandonment by choice as well as forced displacement, opening them to new uses, while "inner ring" suburbs began to decline as well. Nonwhites began to move into suburbs of all kinds in increasing numbers, stimulating private efforts to redevelop neighborhoods close to the stronger nodes within the region, most of which are far more successful than parallel direct government efforts. These private efforts do indeed benefit from government assistance of the old style, now known as "leveraging" private investment.

On the other hand, the 1960s thrust of most federal policies continued. Even if many Great Society programs were abandoned, the principles that lay behind those programs were not. Efforts at greater federal intervention in metropolitan regions were just as pronounced, though less successful as they ran into obstacles of one kind or another. Despite rhetoric to the contrary, the programs proposed by the Carter administration all represented attempts at redirection referred to as "reversal of urban decay" and "conserving existing communities."

The Rurban-Cybernetic Frontier

In 1976 the post–World War II generation came to an end. Nothing symbolized this better than the election of Jimmy Carter, the first American president to have come of age since World War II, who ran on a platform suggesting that the issues of the post–World War II generation were no longer central in American life. As the new generation began, the third stage of the American frontier no longer seemed compelling. At the same time, despite the "limits of growth" rhetoric, there was every sign that a fourth stage was beginning—a rurban or city belt–cybernetic frontier generated by the metropolitan-technological frontier.

The rurban-cybernetic frontier first emerged in the Northeast, as did its predecessors, as the Atlantic coast metropolitan regions merged into one another to form a six-hundred-mile-long megalopolis (the usage is Jean Gottman's)—a matrix of urban and suburban settlements in which smaller suburban and exurban places came to share importance if not prominence with the older central cities.[46] It was a sign of the times that the computer was conceived at MIT in Cambridge and developed at IBM in White Plains, two medium-sized cities in the megalopolis that have become special centers in their own right. This in itself reflects the two primary characteristics of the new frontier.

The new locus of settlement is in medium-sized and small cities and in the rural interstices of the megalopolis. The spreading use of computer technology is the most direct manifestation of the cybernetic tools that make such city belts possible. In 1979 the newspapers in the Northeast published frequent reports of the revival of the small cities of the first industrial revolution, particularly in New England, as the new frontier engulfed them. Countrywide, first the media and then the United States Census focused on the shifting of population growth into rural areas. Both developments are as much a product of the newest technology as of the older American longing for small-town or country living. Both reflect the urbanization of the American way of life no matter what life-style is practiced, or where.

Though the Northeast was first, the new rurban-cybernetic frontier, like its predecessors, is finding its true form in the South and West, where these city belt matrices are not being built on the collapse of earlier forms but are developing as an original form. The present sun belt frontier—strung out along the Gulf coast, the southwestern desert, and the fringes of the California mountains—is classically megalopolitan in city belt form and cybernetic, with its aerospace-related industries and sun belt living made possible by air conditioning and the new telecommunications.

Government Intervention, Land, and Liberty

Two points should be clear: first, that there has been a close relationship between landownership and use and individual liberty in the United States since its beginnings. The second point is that this relationship has not been one of anarchy. Instead, it has involved the careful design of government policies—local, state, and federal—to encourage using land to advance individual liberty within a context that also preserves the public interest. Thus, dealing concretely with the question of land and liberty also requires us to consider what kinds of government policy should be developed to foster the relationship and which governments should be involved in designing and implementing those policies.

The rule in the United States has been that when it comes to land policies, the more local the better, albeit always within some intergovernmental framework that recognizes that the states have eminent domain over the American national territory and that the federal government was and remains the largest single landowner in the United States. Thus day-to-day matters of land use have been and remain the responsibility of local government. Only recently have a few states involved themselves in land-use questions as part of the governmental response to the environmental movement. Until the enactment of recent environmental legislation, the federal role was essentially confined to its function as landowner and to assisting Americans in acquiring and developing land through assistance in infrastructure development, grants-in-aid, or financial credit assistance.

Nevertheless, the federal land survey legislation also provided a model for the relationship between government, land, and liberty. It did so by establishing the notion that even where government intervention was necessary and government planning was part of that intervention, it would be backstopping and facilitative in character, designed to enable individuals to use land to enhance their liberty but in such a way as to preserve the public interest. The inclusion of a public dimension in such matters by design, and the development of designs that harmonize public and private interests as far as possible, provide ways for conflicting interests to be adjudicated when conflicts arise. In economic terms, this is an effort to control externalities for the public weal. It is the antithesis of planning as socialists and statists use the term.

The results of this form of federal planning have been lasting and, overall, beneficial. In the twentieth century, local zoning developed along the same lines and was based on the same principles. This is why in the United States zoning is the land-use tool par excellence, as distinct from the European approach, which involves much more intensive land-use controls. Zoning as a principle involves setting parameters to control externalities in the public interest while allowing individuals freedom to exercise their property rights. It is a means of dealing with collective goods in such a way that individual rights have maximum protection. I have already suggested that the desire to control zoning served as a stimulus for establishing suburban governments on the metropolitan frontier. In that sense the American approach to land policy has stimulated both individual liberty and civil community: the sense of a local public that is composed of citizens, not merely consumers, who take an active interest in the health of their community because they understand their stake in it.[47]

The problem of growth is not simply physical; it is how to accommodate the newness and transience that is the American frontier condition. It is difficult to deal with that problem in the best of circumstances. On earlier frontiers, when the sense of citizenship and civic pride was a part of the common coin of the realm and the lack of externally provided alternatives was apparent to all, civil community could be and was maintained, even by transients. Studies of nineteenth-century communities reveal that cadres of active citizens were no less susceptible to moving around than are those of today, but they were not distracted by commitments to external corporations or governments and a self-perception as consumers rather than citizens.

Future Land Uses and American Values

One pronounced characteristic of the latter phases of the metropolitan frontier was the emergence of a concern with the entire environment of which land is a part. As each new frontier stage has extended human occupation farther into the larger or overall land-air-water environment, with the present stage well into all three environmental dimensions, public response to contemporary challenges in the realm of land settlement increasingly considers the total environment. This is where the real issues of land and liberty are now being confronted. That most of the expert proposals for dealing with the total environment tend to ignore American desires in the matter of land settlement—desires that have survived many changes in American life—has made meeting those challenges more difficult. The very fact of their survival has puzzled these experts. Only recently have certain social scientists begun to show that many of the "instincts" of the American people have a basis in reality, even in the efficient provision of services.[48] The real task before Americans is to develop land policies that support those desires and the values they represent while maintaining (or creating) a decent environment within which they can develop.

It is still too early to delineate with surety all the imperatives or even the propensities of the rurban-cybernetic frontier, but some are already visible. Perhaps foremost is the new sectionalism, the reemergence of an older basis of American politics to replace the politics of class, reflected at its height in the New Deal and the political realignment of which it was a part. This politics of class attacked the division of urban America into "two cities," the "Wasp" and privileged versus the "ethnic" and denied. It persisted through the metropolitan frontier years in no small measure because even after affluence and influence came to Wasps and ethnics alike, it was reinforced by the transformed politics of race. As blacks moved from the southern backwaters remaining from the old rural-land frontier to the world of the metropolitan frontier, their problems took on an economic prominence previously submerged by the legally enforced caste system.

The politics of class divided the country into liberals and conservatives, a division that most concede has become very blurred in recent years. The blurring of what were once relatively clear-cut differences is a reflection of the emergence of the new frontier with its new problems and politics revolving once again around "have" and "have not" sections whose economic interests are often diametrically opposed. Significantly, this renewed sectionalism is tied to the end of the economic dominance of the Northeast. The "sun belt–frost belt" division is only one aspect of this new sectionalism; presidential contests have revealed how sharp are East-West divisions as well. The reallocation of House seats in the wake of the 1980 census has sharpened divisions as they are translated into new power balances in Congress and the Electoral College. These sectional divisions are reflected in life-style differences as well.[49]

The issues associated with what current idiom denominates "life-style" for the moment have contributed to a great weakening of the political party system and a rise of single-issue politics. While these manifestations may be less long-lived than the conventional wisdom suggests, it is very likely that a continued concern with life-style issues will be a major propensity of the rurban-cybernetic frontier, and at least some resolution of the conflicts associated with those issues will become a major imperative. This problem is intensified as the city belt dimension, with its emphasis on smaller communities, will encourage recrudescence of the kind of territorial democracy that potentially allows different life-styles to flourish without clashing, while the cybernetic dimension, with its propensity to foster a global village tied together by telecommunications, will work in the opposite direction.

In a society in which the props of citizenship have been eroded, the problem is intensified. The only solution is to build civic community in the cities of the United States—metropolitan or otherwise. Building civic community is a most difficult task, since it involves a revival of citizenship. Norton Long has written extensively about the problem of local citizenship, quite properly suggesting that it is the basis for truly healthy cities.[50] As correct as Long's analysis may be, it is not likely that classic forms of local citizenship can be revived in the United States. There is no polis in the offing in America, not even in healthy cities. At best we can hope for civil community, a community of limited liability based upon a modest sense of citizenship.[51] This is difficult enough, since it means cultivating a renewed sense of the need for communities to rely on their own resources, human and material, as well as a renewed will to be citizens rather than consumers. The creation of civil community can reestablish the possibility of properly negotiating with the federal government in matters affecting the city. More important, it will provide a basis for building cities that are not merely service units making consumers happy but political entities that produce participating citizens. Appropriate patterns of landownership have a key role in this effort.

Most indicators point to a continuing and even growing American commitment to low-density urbanization on this new frontier, with complexes of small and medium-sized cities physically contiguous but preserving their own social, economic, and political patterns replacing the big central city-suburban fringe pattern of the metropolitan frontier. In sum, land still serves, and has the capacity to serve, its traditional political function in America: as a guarantor of the liberties of Americans. Although land is hardly free anymore, it still is more plentiful than in most countries, and in both the peripheries of the reborn frontier and the growing untapped hinterland it continues to offer most Americans broad choices of environment as well as providing opportunities for developing new patterns of land use. Widespread homeownership, with its concomitant emphasis on homely outdoor pursuits, has maintained traditional patterns of widely diffused landownership to give most Americans not only a stake in society but even ties to the land itself. Finally, territorial democracy not only remains the major vehicle for political expression in the United States but, in light of the growing interest in restoring state and local government to a more central place in the American government constellation, may even be on the threshold of regaining some of its original meaning.

PART TWO

COVENANTS

4

THE DECLARATION OF INDEPENDENCE: THE FOUNDING COVENANT OF THE AMERICAN PEOPLE

The Declaration of Independence is the most concise and thorough statement of the basic political philosophy of the American people. Nearly fifty years after writing it, Thomas Jefferson remarked: "Neither aiming at originality of principles or sentiments, nor yet copied from any particular and previous writing, it was intended to be an expression of the American Mind."[1] Abraham Lincoln—perhaps America's leading political thinker and archetypal hero—repeatedly affirmed that all his political principles were based on the Declaration, which for him was at one and the same time a noble accomplishment, a great promise, and a demanding set of goals.[2]

The Declaration stands where it does within the American political tradition because it is the covenant that transformed the disparate colonists into an organized people, the American people. With all the many worthwhile words that have been written or spoken about the Declaration, this function has not been made as explicit as it should be. Early orators who spoke in praise of the Declaration, living as they did within a recognized covenant tradition, needed only to treat the covenantal character of the document through use of the appropriately resonating phrases. Even Lincoln, who already had to call attention to the centrality of the Declaration as a cornerstone of American political principles, could benefit from those shared resonances.[3]

Today the resonances have been lost because we have lost the awareness of the covenantal tradition. Yet the tradition itself persists in more ways than we often recognize. Thus a recovery of the Declaration of Independence as covenant is important for restoring awareness too.

The Declaration is the covenant that firmly established Americans as an organized people, bound by a shared moral vision as well as by common interests. A covenant is a morally informed agreement or pact based upon voluntary consent and mutual oaths or promises witnessed by the relevant higher authority, between peoples or parties having independent, though not necessarily equal status, that provides for joint action or obligation to achieve defined ends (limited or comprehensive) under conditions of mutual respect that protect the individual integrities of all the parties to it. Every covenant involves consenting, promising, and agreeing. Most are meant to be of unlimited duration, if not perpetual. Covenants can bind any number of partners for a variety of purposes, but in their essence they are political in that their bonds are used principally to create bodies political and social.

Covenant, Compact, Contract

Covenant is tied in an ambiguous relationship to two related terms, compact and contract. On one hand, both compacts and contracts are in a sense derived from covenant, and sometimes the terms are even used interchangeably. On the other hand, there are very real differences between the three that need clarification.

Both *covenants* and their derivative, *compacts*, differ from *contracts* in that the first two are constitutional or public in character and the last is private. As such, covenantal or compactual obligation is broadly reciprocal. Those bound by one or the other are obligated to respond to one another beyond the letter of the law rather than to limit their obligations to the narrowest contractual requirements. Hence covenants and compacts are inherently designed to be flexible in certain respects as well as firm in others. As expressions of private law, contracts tend to be interpreted as narrowly as possible so as to limit the obligation of the contracting parties to what is explicitly mandated by the contract itself.

A covenant differs from a compact in that its morally binding dimension takes precedence over its legal dimension. In its heart of hearts, a covenant is an agreement in which a higher moral force—traditionally God—is a party, usually a direct party to or guarantor of a particular relationship, whereas when the term compact is used a moral force is only indirectly involved. A compact, based as it is on mutual pledges rather than the guarantees of a higher authority, rests more heavily on a legal though still ethical grounding for its politics. In other words, the compact is a secular phenomenon. This can be verified historically by examining the shift in terminology that took place in the seventeenth and eighteenth centuries. While those who saw the hand of God in political affairs in the United States continued to use the term covenant, those who sought a secular grounding for politics turned to the term compact. Though the distinction is not always used with strict clarity, it does appear consistently. The issue was further complicated by Rousseau and his followers, who talk about the social contract, a highly secularized concept that, even when applied for public purposes, never develops the same level of moral obligation as either covenant or compact.

Covenant is also related to constitutionalism. Normally a covenant precedes a constitution and creates the people or civil society that then proceeds to adopt a constitution of government for itself. Thus a constitution involves implementing a prior covenant—effectuating or translating a prior covenant into an actual frame or structure of government. The constitution may include a restatement or reaffirmation of the original covenant, as does the Massachusetts constitution of 1780, but that is optional:

> The body politic is formed by a voluntary association of individuals. It is a social compact by which the whole people covenants with each citizen and each citizen with the whole people, that all shall be governed by certain laws for the common good. It is the duty of the people, therefore, in framing a Constitution of Government, to provide for an equitable mode of making laws, as well as for an impartial interpretation and a faithful executive of them, that every man may, at all times, find his security in them.

Since earliest times, covenants have followed a formula that has been passed down from generation to generation and epoch to epoch essentially unchanged.

This form has been described by students of ancient Near Eastern history as containing the following elements:
1. a preamble naming the parties to the covenant;
2. a prologue, historical or ideological, establishing the setting or grounding of the covenant;
3. the operative section of the covenant, including stipulations or what is agreed;
4. provisions for public reading (proclamation) and deposit of the text for safekeeping;
5. the divine witness to the covenant; and,
6. the advantages of performance (blessings) and sanctions for nonperformance (curses).[4]

Examining the Declaration, we find these classic covenantal patterns repeated.

1. *The preamble, or statement of who is doing the covenanting:*

   In Congress, July 4, 1776, by the Representatives of the United States of America, in General Congress assembled.

Note that the heading of the Declaration affirms the practice of democratic principles by announcing that the document is the product of a "congress" of individuals who are "representatives" of the people living in the thirteen former colonies. In America the word "congress" refers to an assembly of elected representatives or delegates. This *electoral representativeness* is the source and basis of their authority to issue the Declaration.

The heading also contains one of the first uses of the term "the United States of America." It affirms the important fact that the thirteen states declared their independence as a united body, as an American entity of a still unspecified kind. This is significant for the future argument over the true character of the federal union.

2. *A prologue to establish the setting or grounding of the covenant:*

   Preamble

   When in the Course of human events, it becomes necessary for one people to dissolve the political bands which have connected them with another, and to assume among the powers of the earth, the separate and equal station to which the Laws of Nature and of Nature's God entitle them . . .

Although the writing style of Jefferson's day differed from that of today, the capitalization of "Course" may imply a sense that history is progressive, that it moves along a course toward human betterment. This view of history was widespread during the eighteenth century and had its roots in the biblical concept of history. Many ancient societies viewed history (or time itself) as cyclical—as involving an eternal return to beginnings—and as largely outside human control. The Bible views history as generally progressive, having a beginning (creation) and an end (the messianic era and the end of days), and as subject to significant human control in the partnership with God established by the covenant between them. Indeed, the very idea of "revolution" depends upon the belief that people can improve their lot by making their own history. By the eighteenth century this view of history had become closely associated with the modern idea of "progress"—the belief that the growth of science and knowledge, along with the spread of education, would foster the rational enlightenment and moral excellence necessary to create and maintain good societies—but it also remained rooted in biblical religion, its original source. Both combined to influence the Americans in their revolution.

In this opening paragraph, Congress declares that the Americans are no longer transplanted Englishmen (or Britons) but are a separate *people* entitled, like all peoples, to political independence. The idea that mankind is by nature divided into "peoples" is the basis for nationalism. The idea of nationalism goes back at least to the thirteenth century .. when the first nation-states—Israel, Ammon, Moab, and Edom—emerged on the world scene, but it became dominant in shaping political life only in the modern era, beginning in the seventeenth century. Although the American founders prided themselves on their commitment to individual choice and claimed that people have a natural right to choose or consent to their national identity rather than simply remaining bound to the nation of their birth, it is obvious from this passage that they saw the human race as being naturally and appropriately divided into "peoples" who were the building blocks of the international order, such as it was, and who thereby had rights as peoples, especially the right of self-determination.

The Declaration declares that Americans are a *single* "people" (see also *Federalist* no. 2). A people is referred to in the Declaration as "they" or "them." At the time, this was the common grammatical usage in connection with collective nouns, but it went out of style in the United States at about the end of the nineteenth century. (It remains the norm in Great Britain to this day.) The present-day substitution of "it" for "they" represents a loss of nuance in the sense that a "people" is now made to seem as if "it" were a monolithic whole having a life apart from the human beings who compose it. The form "they" conveys a clear sense of a people as a compound of many unique individuals, groups, or entities. In this sense the plural usage is federal or covenantal in character, reflecting the establishment of unity through union, a compound, rather than through amalgamation.

According to the Declaration, "peoples" and "nations" are equal under the laws of nature and God, but with the implicit caveat that they are equal when they can exercize the "powers" to which they are entitled. The "Laws of Nature," then, extend to peoples and recognize power as natural and legitimate.

The dual phrase "the Laws of Nature and of Nature's God" reflects an attempt to strike a balance between the secular (or what was then called the Deistic) belief in a self-regulated universe operating according to its own laws, and the more traditional religious belief in God as the governor of the universe. In line with the eighteenth century's emphasis on reason rather than on faith or revelation as the proper basis of human knowledge, the Declaration appeals to both reason and faith—in that order:

> a decent respect to the opinions of mankind requires that they should declare the causes which impel them to the separation.

Aside from the tactical value of proclaiming to the world—enemies and potential allies alike—that the Americans were serious, this phrase reflects the founders' belief in the "new political science" as derived from Hobbes, Locke, Harrington, and Montesquieu. This "new political science" held, among other things, that legitimate political authority derived partial validity from "the opinions of mankind," which in turn deserved "decent respect."

As used in the Declaration, "opinion" means *opining* or considered thought, not the kind of instant, off-the-cuff reaction gathered in today's so-called "public opinion" polls. The difference is crucial. The human capacity for self-government rests to no little extent on the ability of individuals to respond to issues on the basis of careful and considered reflection, not heated passions or momentary impulses. The founders believed that almost every person is, by nature, capable of listening to reason and of formulating rational opinions. Hence their considered opinions deserve a "decent respect" and can be used, to a degree, to validate human action.

Underlying this idea of opinion is the even deeper belief that through reason and observation people are capable of discovering true knowledge about the proper forms of government and human conduct, and that therefore it is possible to make rational distinctions between good and bad, just and unjust governments. It is in this respect that the founders viewed political knowledge as "political science."

Present-day positivist social science tends to hold that such knowledge is impossible because goodness and justice are merely expressions of individual or group "value" preferences that are based not on objective reason, but on subjective passion and self-interest. Therefore goodness and justice are simply relative "values" that have different but equally valid meanings among different individuals and societies at different times. We can conduct a public opinion poll to learn what people *believe* is good or bad, but we cannot know what *is* good or bad. According to this view, then, the founders were motivated by their personal preferences about the good, which were based not on any real knowledge of the good, but on passion and self-interest. Hence the Declaration of Independence is little more than a high-sounding rationalization of their selfish interests.

Yet if all values are relative, then, for example, it is ultimately impossible to say anything good or bad about slavery or Adolph Hitler. It is possible only to say that one likes or dislikes Hitler in the same way that one likes or dislikes corn flakes for breakfast. To the founders, this view would have gone against reason and common sense. The choice between democracy and fascism is not a choice between Cheerios and Rice Krispies, but a choice between justice and injustice—indeed, life and death. Like all proper covenants, the Declaration is a covenant of life; it is designed to transform mere life into the good life. What follows defines the basis for the good life reflected in the Declaration.

3. *Stipulations and operative elements:*

—We hold these truths to be self-evident, that all men are created equal, that they are endowed by their Creator with certain unalienable Rights, that among these are Life, Liberty and the pursuit of Happiness.

Here, in the few succinct words of the Declaration's most famous phrase, the whole foundation of American political life is sketched out. That foundation is rooted in certain fundamental "truths" that are taken to be "self-evident," that is, axiomatic and immediately accessible to reason and common sense in a manner not unlike the way phenomena of nature are immediately accessible to sight and touch. The founders held that these self-evident "truths" are grounded in reason and experience—especially human experience rightly understood—which allow us to say that these "truths" are more worthy of our attention than others.

The problematic phrase "all men are created equal" has been both a keystone of American political life as well as a major bone of contention. The idea of equality has become a potent force in modern life. The Declaration's position rests in part on the Judeo-Christian view that all people are equal before God and in part on the teachings of the "new political science," which argued that all people are equal because they share the same basic nature.

Of course, at the time of the writing of the Declaration, certain people such as slaves were not treated as "equals," even though individuals such as Jefferson, Abigail Adams, and Judge Samuel Sewall of Boston had broad visions of equality. In 1774 the Rhode Island Assembly had condemned slavery as a denial of natural rights and liberties. Jefferson had included an attack on slavery in the first draft of the Declaration, but it was removed at the insistence of southern delegates, who refused to approve the Declaration in that form.

What is important is that the idea of equality is nevertheless stated so broadly and forcefully in the opening of the Declaration, thereby placing it at the center of the revolutionary enterprise and obliging Americans to come to terms with it. As such, it stands as a goal toward which American political life ought to be moving, as a standard against which the conduct of that political life can be judged, and as a voice of reason or a thorn in the side for those who cling to unenlightened opinions about inequality. Hence since 1776 the concept has undergone considerable expansion, both in terms of incorporating more and more people within its scope and in terms of emphasizing more and more ways people ought to be equal, or at least more nearly equal.

Note also that equality stands as the first self-evident truth, thereby suggesting that equality is a necessary, though not sufficient, condition for the preservation of life, liberty, and the pursuit of happiness. It is not sufficient, because people can be equal in the way, for example, that slaves and prisoners can be equal to each other. But it is necessary for liberty, because without equality some people could be said to have a natural or legitimate authority to rule others in the way that monarchs asserted a natural or God-given right to rule subjects and that slaveowners claimed a natural right to control slaves because of their alleged inferiority. Hence, if all people are equal, each person has a rightful claim to self-determination and is under no prior natural or divine obligation to obey any other person without first giving his or her consent. Because this is the essence, though not the whole, of liberty as Americans understand it, we can see why "equality" comes first in the Declaration.

The second of the great "truths" is that people have been "endowed by their Creator with certain unalienable Rights." This means that, just as one is born with two lungs and a heart, each person is also born possessing certain natural rights that belong to him or her by virtue of God's creation or nature's endowment. Therfore these rights can be said to precede government. They are not granted or given by government, and most important, they cannot be taken away or surrendered. The purpose of government is to guarantee them.

Of course a person or a government may, in fact, deny another the exercise of his or her rights, just as one person may murder another, thereby destroying the right to life. But the Declaration's point about inalienable rights is that no one has any legitimate authority to do so, and that no matter how much a person may be enslaved by another, the slave still retains his or her natural rights even while unable to exercise them. In a sense the arbitrary denial of a person's exercise of rights is a crime against nature. The firmness with which this idea of rights is held in the United States is reflected in the fact that there is hardly an American who has not, at one time or another, declared, often angrily: "I know my rights."

Life, of course, is the basic right, and a highly important one, especially in light of the brutal and casual ways governments throughout history have often treated it. For the founders, the purpose of government is to protect and enhance life, not to destroy it. Government does not have an inherent right to take life.

Historically, the right to life has raised several difficult problems for Americans. Does government have the right to take the life of a criminal, especially one who has taken another's life? Until recently, the opinion was overwhelmingly that it did. While that is still the case, the matter is being questioned in many quarters. Does government have the right to conscript (draft) people into the military and order them to risk their lives? Traditionally, Americans have been much more comfortable with the idea of a volunteer army, but they have endorsed conscription when they have considered it necessary. Does a person with an incurable disease have the right to end his or her life (or have it ended) by having life-support machines and measures cut off? (Can government limit one's right to decide what to do with one's own life?) Modern medical advances have raised many new right-to-life questions, including, paradoxically, the "right to die." In 1976 California enacted the first such "right to die" law on the grounds that it permits people to die naturally and with dignity. On the other hand, it is an accepted principle that government can intervene in such matters. Do women have a right to abortion? Does a husband or mate have a right to participate in such a decision? Does a fetus have a right to be born? These questions have provoked the greatest divisions in American society since the slavery issue. All of the foregoing are endorsed by Americans under the terms of the right to life.

According to the Declaration, mere life is not enough. Humans are endowed with an inalienable right to a life of "liberty" or freedom. Although liberty has been given many definitions, Americans have usually understood the kernel of liberty to include freedom from arbitrary external controls, restraints, interference, and obligations and freedom to exercise maximum control over one's own destiny.

However, this does not mean absolute liberty for everyone to "do their own thing," which would result in pandemonium and mass destruction. Rather, what is meant is a kind of "federal liberty"—not the liberty to do whatever one pleases, but the liberty to act in accordance with the Constitution. Or, as James Wilson defined it:

> [There is a] kind of liberty which . . . I shall distinguish by the appellation of *federal liberty* . . . . When a confederate republic is instituted, the

communities, of which it is composed, surrender to it a part of their *political independence* . . . . The states should resign to the national government, that part, and that part only, of their *political liberty*, which, placed in that government, produces more good to the whole, than if it had remained in the several states. While they resign this part of their political liberty, they retain the *free and generous exercise* of all their other facilities, as states, so far as it is compatible with the welfare of the general and superintending confederacy. (Emphasis mine)

Since we are condemned by nature to live with one another, it is necessary to restrict certain liberties in order to preserve liberty. The intention of the Declaration is to point us always in the direction of liberty by recognizing first that the construction of good government must begin with the presumption of liberty and proceed from there. Therefore, government restrictions on individual liberty must be justified on rational grounds as necessary for the greater preservation and enhancement of everyone's liberty. Finally, restrictions on liberty must be within the framework of the political compact and enacted by the people or their representatives.

The last inalienable right is "the pursuit of happiness." The meaning of this right for the founders is not entirely clear. Some suggest that they understood this to mean the right of everyone to pursue, within the limits of everyone else's liberty, their own version of happiness. Others, accepting the freedom implicit in the above, suggest that the founders believed there was such a thing as true happiness but that it could be attained only through free pursuit. Still others see the phrase as applying to political happiness only.

—That to secure these rights, Governments are instituted among Men, deriving their just powers from the consent of the governed . . .

The attitude toward government expressed here is continuously positive. Government is treated as necessary and useful—a positive good designed to secure human rights. It is not just a necessary evil. At the same time, the potential for evil in governments is recognized in the phrase "just powers," which implies that government, once in existence, can take power unjustly as well. Here indeed is the great political problem of humanity. People have inalienable rights on an equal basis, but since they are otherwise unequal in many respects, they can secure their rights only by banding together and creating a proper government based on a mutual agreement—a covenant or compact.

In other words, power is recognized as a reality. The only question is how to organize and harness it for the common good. A government, to function, must be able to exercise power, including the ultimate power of life and death. This leads to the possibility that government will abuse this power. If government does abuse its powers, it is no longer legitimate and can be rejected by the parties to the compact; hence the emphasis on "just powers."

The theory that government is instituted by covenant or compact was so widely acknowledged in revolutionary America that it could be presented in the sophisticated form used here, as "the consent of the governed." In the United States, governments were constituted and reconstituted through covenants and compacts from the first foundings of settlements in the seventeenth century. For Americans, then, the compact theory is much more than a convenient myth; it is a reflection of real experiences.

Furthermore, by "consent" the Declaration means consent that is both freely given and informed. Consent cannot legitimately be extracted by force. The Declaration also implies that consent is a continuing process. It is not a one-time act of the founders, to be simply accepted by their descendants, but involves a continuing process of participation by which citizens constantly give or withhold their consent. This idea of consent, that "the people shall judge," is the heart of democracy. Although it is based in part on the idea that "the opinions of mankind" deserve "decent respect," a continuing problem for any democracy is that the people be able to judge well rather than poorly. Hence the idea of consent also implies a certain responsibility on the part of the citizen to be informed and of the government to be informative rather than secretive.

> —That whenever any Form of Government becomes destructive of these ends, it is the Right of the People to alter or to abolish it and to institute new Government, laying its foundation on such principles, and organizing its power in such form, as to them shall seem most likely to effect their Safety and Happiness.

Here is the right to renegotiate the compact—to establish a new constitution—even through revolution. Revolution is not the preferred way, but it is certainly a legitimate way. Who can undertake the renegotiation (or revolution)? The "people" in the sense used at the beginning of the Declaration—not dissatisfied individuals or groups. (Individuals or groups may secede from particular civil societies by migrating—like the migrants to America or, later, the emigrants to the West.)

Change cannot lead to the abolition of government, only to the replacement of one form (or system) with another. (Form as used in the eighteenth century is roughly equivalent to the term *system* as it is used today. Both in turn are roughly equivalent to Aristotle's use of the term *constitution*.) The change can be radical—meaning that it can get to the root of the matter—since it can involve laying the foundation for the new form on new principles as well as organizing the powers of government in new forms.

Note that there is no best form specified. Every people must develop a form of government specifically suited to them. As long as the form chosen provides for the securing of the people's rights (safety) and allows them to pursue happiness in a manner fitting their needs, it is deemed suitable. The borrowing of one people's constitution by another is rarely if ever successful.

Note that the measure of a good constitution or form is whether it is likely to provide a particular people with "safety" and "happiness." The former has to do with sheer security, the preservation of life and limb, while the latter is a matter of the quality of life. Government can do much to secure the former; it can only provide a proper climate for the latter.

> Prudence, indeed, will dictate that Governments long established should not be changed for light and transient causes; and accordingly all experience hath shown, that mankind are more disposed to suffer, while evils are sufferable, than to right themselves by abolishing the forms to which they are accustomed.

Here the Declaration is double-edged. On one hand, it makes a valid political observation that, as a matter of fact, people are prone to tolerate bad government rather than to act to change things. On the other hand, it suggests that this caution is a good idea for the sake of the peace and happiness of mankind. Note the use of the plural "they" in connection with "mankind."

> But when a long train of abuses and usurpations, pursuing invariably the same Object, evinces a design to reduce them under absolute Despotism, it is their right, it is their duty, to throw off such Government, and to provide new Guards for their future security.

Given the general desirability of caution before changing governmental forms, the Declaration then indicates under what conditions revolutions can legitimately be mounted and even must be. A "long train of abuses and usurpations" leading to "absolute Despotism" makes action necessary. What follows is a justification of the American Revolution in light of the principles above.

The Legitimacy of the American Revolution in Light of the Foregoing Principles

> —Such has been the patient sufferance of these Colonies; and such is now the necessity which constrains them to alter their former Systems of Government. The history of the present King of Great Britain is a history of repeated injuries and usurpations, all having in direct object the establishment of an absolute Tyranny over these States. To prove this, let Facts be submitted to a candid world.
>
> He has refused his Assent to Laws, the most wholesome and necessary for the public good. [*Excessive use of the royal veto to limit power of colonial legislatures*]
>
> He has forbidden his Governors to pass Laws of immediate and pressing importance, unless suspended in their operation till his Assent should be obtained; and when so suspended, he has utterly neglected to attend to them. [*Failure to act is as much a betrayal of the principles of good government as bad action*]
>
> He has refused to other Laws for the accommodation of large districts of people, unless those people would relinquish the right of Representation in the Legislature, a right inestimable to them and formidable to tyrants only. [*Royal action cut off the westward movement of the American people*]

He has called together legislative bodies at places unusual, uncomfortable, and distant from the depository of their Public Records, for the sole purpose of fatiguing them into compliance with his measures.

He has dissolved Representative Houses repeatedly, for opposing with manly firmness his invasions on the rights of the people.

He has refused for a long time, after such dissolutions, to cause others to be elected; whereby the Legislative powers, incapable of Annihilation, have returned to the People at large for their exercise; the State remaining in the meantime exposed to all the dangers of invasion from without, and convulsions within.

He has endeavoured to prevent the population of these States; for that purpose obstructing the Laws for Naturalization of Foreigners; refusing to pass others to encourage their migration hither, and raising the conditions of new Appropriations of Lands.

He has obstructed the Administration of Justice, by refusing his Assent to Laws for establishing Judiciary powers.

He has made Judges dependent on his Will alone, for the tenure of their offices, and the amount and payment of their salaries.

He has erected a multitude of New Offices, and sent hither swarms of Officers to harass our people, and eat out their substance.

He has kept among us, in times of peace, Standing Armies, without the Consent of our legislatures.

He has affected to render the Military independent of and superior to the Civil power.

He has combined with others to subject us to a jurisdiction foreign to our constitution, and unacknowledged by our laws; giving his Assent to their Acts of pretended Legislation:

For quartering large bodies of armed troops among us:

For protecting them, by a mock Trial, from punishment for any Murders which they should commit on the Inhabitants of these States:

For cutting off our Trade with all parts of the world:

For imposing Taxes on us without our Consent:

For depriving us in many cases, of the benefits of Trial by Jury:

For transporting us beyond Seas to be tried for pretended offences:

For abolishing the free System of English Laws in a neighbouring province, establishing therein an Arbitrary government, and enlarging its Boundaries so as to render it at once an example and fit instrument for introducing the same absolute rule into these Colonies: [*References to the Quebec Act, which gave the French-Canadian protection in their religious and cultural life at the expense of English conceptions of free government and individual rights*]

For taking away our Charters, abolishing our most valuable Laws, and altering fundamentally the Forms of our Governments:

For suspending our own Legislatures, and declaring themselves invested with power to legislate for us in all cases whatsoever.

He has abdicated Government here, by declaring us out of his Protection and waging War against us.

He has plundered our seas, ravaged our Coasts, burnt our towns, and destroyed the lives of our people.

He is at this time transporting large armies of foreign mercenaries to compleat the works of death, desolation and tyranny, already begun with circumstances of Cruelty and perfidy scarcely paralleled in the most barbarous ages, and totally unworthy of Head of a civilized nation.

He has constrained our fellow Citizens taken Captive on the high Seas to bear Arms against their Country, to become the executioners of their friends and Brethren, or to fall themselves by their Hands. [*References to British practice of impressing seamen*]

He has excited domestic insurrections amongst us, and has endeavoured to bring on the inhabitants of our frontiers, the merciless Indian Savages, whose known rule of warfare, is an undistinguished destruction of all ages, sexes and conditions.

In every stage of these Operations We have petitioned for Redress in the most humble terms: Our repeated Petitions have been answered only by repeated injury. A Prince, whose character is thus marked by every act which may define a Tyrant, is unfit to be the ruler of a free people.

Nor have We been wanting in attention to our British brethren. We have warned them from time to time of attempts by their legislature to extend an unwarrantable jurisdiction over us. We have reminded them of the circumstances of our emigration and settlement here. We have appealed to their

> native justice and magnanimity, and we have conjured them by the ties of our common kindred to disavow these usurpations, which would inevitably interrupt our connections and correspondence. They too have been deaf to the voice of justice and of consanguinity. We must, therefore, acquiesce in the necessity, which denounces our Separation, and hold them, as we hold the rest of mankind, Enemies in War, in Peace Friends.

The foregoing list of charges should be read for a better understanding of what Americans consider to be the principles and practices of good government rather than for their precise historical accuracy. In that respect they represent a negative statement of the stipulations of the covenant. As part of the polemic purpose of the Declaration, it was necessary to attribute to the king many acts really initiated by Parliament. Moreover, some of the "grievances" were as much products of the interests of the dominant circles in America as the consequences of English imperial policy. What is important is that the list conveys a sense of what governments should and should not do. Eleven years later, the Constitution of the United States included provisions designed to prevent many of the "abuses" and "usurpations" listed above.

The last paragraph, containing an oblique reference to the attempts by Parliament to legislate for the colonies, goes to the heart of the matter. Note how delicately the relationship between the two separate yet related peoples is portrayed in order to establish clearly the fact of separateness (which is a result of "the circumstances of our emigrant and settlement") as well as "common kindred."

4 and 5. Publication and Divine Witness:

> WE, THEREFORE, the REPRESENTATIVES of the UNITED STATES of AMERICA, in General Congress, Assembled, appealing to the Supreme Judge of the world for the rectitude of our intentions do in the Name, and by Authority of the good people of these Colonies solemnly publish and declare, that these United Colonies are, and of right ought to be, free and independent states; that they are Absolved from all Allegiance to the British Crown, and that all political connection between them and the State of Great Britain, is and ought to be totally dissolved . . .

The final paragraph begins by calling upon God to witness this act and its meaning and concludes by indicating the Americans' firm reliance on the protection of divine providence. Congress explicitly publishes and declares its actions. In fact, Congress provided elsewhere that the Declaration be read publicly in the square behind the Pennsylvania statehouse (today known respectively as Independence Square and Independence Hall) and throughout the newly independent United States. It concludes with:

> and that as Free and Independent States, they have full Power to levy War, conclude Peace, contract Alliances, establish Commerce, and to do all other Acts and Things which Independent States may of right do—And for the support of this Declaration, with a firm reliance on the protection of Divine Providence, we mutually pledge to each other our Lives, our Fortunes and our sacred Honor.

6. *Blessings and curses:*

The blessings of freedom and independence, presented in some detail, represent the advantages of performance, while the sanctions are the risk of life and fortune and sacred honor.

The ambiguity of the final paragraph froms the basis for all subsequent arguments over whether the United States declared independence as a unit or simply declared together the independence of the separate states. Later interpretations of the character of the compacts creating the Union (which led to the Civil War) depended upon the different understandings of this paragraph. For practical purposes, the Supreme Court of the United States finally ruled in 1936 (*U.S. v. Curtiss-Wright Export Corp.*) that the United States declared its independence as a unit and that the states were from the first instance bound together as a single nation in matters of foreign affairs and defense.

Appropriately enough, the best explanation of this paragraph is that it summarizes a federal act leading to a federal result. What we have here is a tripartite covenant of people. *Free and Independent States*, and the *United States of America* witnessed by God. The American people, their union, and the states were born at the same moment, through the same act—and they were born free.

5

THE PRINCIPLES AND TRADITIONS UNDERLYING AMERICAN STATE CONSTITUTIONS

Over the years, considerable attention has been given to the political theory of the United States Constitution and its implications for American government and politics. Studies of the document itself, the Constitutional Convention of 1787, *The Federalist*, Supreme Court interpretations, and executive and legislative actions of constitutional import abound, as well they should. State constitutions, however, have been studied almost exclusively from a reformist perspective—to recommend the elimination of presumed deficiencies. Relatively little attention has been given to the political theories and philosophic assumptions underlying the fifty state constitutions and their colonial predecessors.

Even when students of American government, as well as reformers, have examined state constitutions from the perspectives of history, institutional organization, interest accommodation, and the inclusion or exclusion of specific provisions, they have generally bypassed the important functions of state constitutions as overall frames of government for polities that are in most cases larger and better developed than most of the world's nations; practical public expressions of political theory and the purposes of government; and reflections of public conceptions of the proper roles of government and politics. The tendency has been to assume either that the philosophic assumptions of the state constitutions are the same as those of the United States Constitution or that state constitutions are wordy patchworks of compromises having little rhyme or reason. Neither assumption is accurate, and even those constitutions that can be said to be bundles of compromises reflect the political struggle between representatives of competing conceptions of government within particular states. Moreover, compromise itself reflects a larger theory of politics based upon bargaining and negotiation as opposed, for example, to command or armed conflict.

This slighting of state constitutional theory is ironic because the framers of the federal Constitution were influenced by their experiences with their respective state constitutions and the preexisting conceptions of constitutional government in the original states. Between 1776 and 1798, the first fourteen states (including Vermont) framed and ratified some twenty-five constitutions. Yet only recently has the classic Massachusetts constitution of 1780, still in force with 106 amendments, been studied for the purpose of understanding its political theory.[1] This constitution is one of the most explicitly philosophic of all the state constitutions and had a significant impact on the framing of the United States Constitution as well as the constitutions of a number of other states settled by pioneers from Massachusetts and other heirs of the Puritan tradition.

More recently, Donald S. Lutz has examined the underlying political theories of all the early state constitutions of 1776–98.[2] The results show some significant similarities as well as differences among these constitutions and between them as a group and the United States Constitution. Generally, for example, these early state constitutions were more communitarian in orientation than the federal Constitution and placed more emphasis on direct, continuing consent of popular majorities. The debates over the framing and ratification of these constitutions also show that political theory is not the exclusive domain of an intellectual elite in America. Instead, the "common people" can be found to have made important and informed contributions, even if not always expressed in the formal language of philosophy.[3]

This reflects the close connection between theory and practice that might be expected of a republican polity. Ideas that did not have operational implications were simply not acceptable to American thinkers and doers. Thus American political thought is generally best expressed in practical ways through, for example, Supreme Court decisions, state papers (e.g., Hamilton, Gallatin, Lincoln), arguments such as *The Federalist Papers*, and constitutions.

Three Constitutional Traditions

Although all the constitutions of the United States share a certain common foundation and set of overall philosophic assumptions, there are also important differences and variations on basic themes, derived in part from competing conceptions of constitutionalism in the founding era and the federal right of constitutional choice. In the first place, by 1787 three general conceptions of constitutionalism had emerged in the new nation.[4]

One was based on older, *Whig* republican forms brought to American shores by the first British and northwest European colonists and further developed in the intervening four or five generations. The Whig tradition emphasized a communitarian polity and the importance of republican virtue. Individualism was tempered, and legislatures as representatives of the community could intervene and regulate behavior in ways that would now be regarded as infringements of individual rights. At the same time, the Whig tradition placed great emphasis on direct, active, continuous, and well-nigh complete popular control over the legislature and government in general, through such devices as small electoral districts, short tenures of office, many elective offices, sharp separations of power, and procedures approaching constituent instruction of elected representatives.

In facing the task of framing a national constitution, however, a new republican or *Federalist* conception of constitutionalism emerged, primarily through the work of James Madison.[5] While the Federalist idea agreed with the Whig tradition that all powers of government be derived from the people, Madison added the pregnant phrase, "either directly or indirectly." This reflected the Federalist effort to cope with the problems of establishing an extended and diverse democratic republic compounded of constituent polities—particularly the problem of majority tyranny. The Federalist conception of republican remedies for republican diseases placed greater emphasis on balancing individual and group interests and refining the interests and opinions of the people through such devices as large electoral districts, indirect senatorial elections, longer tenures of office, limited numbers of elective offices, and a system of separated but shared powers. The Federalist view also saw commerce as a partial way of solving the problem of republican virtue in a large republic.

At the same time, as the Federalist conception was emerging, Alexander Hamilton developed yet another approach, which may be termed the *managerial* conception. Although it too shared the view that governmental powers should be derived from the people, Hamilton emphasized the idea of virtual rather than actual representation.[6] This view of representation is also reflected in Hamilton's preference for lawyers as legislators. The managerial view conceptualized politics as a matter of executive leadership and rational administration within a hierarchical system. Accordingly, it emphasized more centralized national power under a strong president. Principles of commerce, moreover, were central to this conception of constitutionalism, since the polity was designed to support and strengthen the commercial classes.

Whereas the United States Constitution became the repository of the Federalist view, many of the state constitutions retained much of the earlier Whig conception, as illustrated by such constitutional features as frequent elections to fill many offices. The managerial view, which was substantially repudiated with the election of Thomas Jefferson to the presidency, remained an undercurrent in American constitutionalism. In the late nineteenth century it reemerged as a potent force in the public administration school, developed in part by Woodrow Wilson and refashioned in part by ideas imported from Germany.[7] The managerial tradition in the states emphasized "streamlined" state government headed by a strong governor leading an integrated executive branch whose department heads he appointed and whose civil service was organized hierarchically and selected by merit only. Legislatures were treated more as impediments than anything else, although properly appointed—so the theory went—they would faithfully do the governor's bidding. Much of the struggle over state and local government reform in this century has reflected clashes between managerialism in the Hamiltonian style, usually referred to as governmental modernization, and the persistence of earlier theories of republicanism embodied in the constitutions of many of the American states.

The patterns of state constitutionalism, however, have been further compounded by the federal right of constitutional choice. Each state is free to adopt its own republican constitution. As a result, the geographic, ethnic, religious, socioeconomic, cultural, and historical diversity of the states has meant that each has assembled a constitutional package based on its own conceptions and interpretations of Americans' common republican assumptions as filtered through their Whiggish, Federalist, and managerial variations, plus the particular and at times peculiar conceptions of government prevalent in each state. Some have done it succinctly, as in the 6,600 words of the Vermont Constitution of 1793, which is still in effect with only fifty-two amendments. Others have gone to great lengths, as in the 583,000 words of Georgia's ninth constitution adopted in 1976. Thus, while the American constitutions have had common roots and a common trunk since 1776, they have branched out in different directions in order to meet the particular needs and wants of each state's interested citizens.

There are a number of other significant differences between the United States Constitution (and the government created by it) and the state constitutions (and the governments created by them). The federal Constitution is one of limited, delegated powers. As such, it reflects what the American people sought to accomplish as well as to avoid through union, and what they could agree upon as the principal tasks of the general government, particularly nationwide defense and commerce. But it does not reflect all of what the American people wanted to accomplish *in general* through government because, beyond the federal Constitution and its bundle of powers designed to serve the states and people in common, other rights and governmental matters were left to the people as citizens of the states.[8] Thus all powers not delegated to the United States are reserved to the states or to the people. As plenary governments, the states automatically possess all powers not specifically denied them by the United States Constitution or their citizens.

State constitutions are potentially far more comprehensive and often have been—for better and worse. Consequently, a state constitution must be explicit about limiting and defining the scope of governmental powers, especially on behalf of individual liberty. Each state constitution has a bill of rights—often called a declaration of rights—which usually appears at the beginning of the document. It has been noted that these declarations enumerate more rights in more detail than the United States Bill of Rights. What has been overlooked is why. Most immediately, their place at the beginning of the constitution is intended to announce that the protection of rights is the first task of government, indeed, its raison d'être. In many cases, however, these represent a restatement of the political compact or covenant through which the state is called into existence by its people. The Massachusetts Constitution is a case in point.

The body politic is formed by a voluntary association of individuals. It is a social compact by which the whole people covenants with each citizen and each citizen with the whole people, that all shall be governed by certain laws for the common good. It is the duty of the people, therefore, in framing a Constitution of Government, to provide for an equitable mode of making laws, as well as for an impartial interpretation and a faithful execution of them, that every man may, at all times, find his security in them.

This difference is one of the principal manifestations of the differences in underlying theory between the federal and state constitutions.

The clear spelling out of the powers and limits of government is generally expressed in state constitutions through:

–an explicit declaration of rights (almost invariably broader than the first ten amendments to the United States Constitution);

–a thorough delineation of the structures, powers, and procedures of the three branches of government (in some cases, including the precise apportionment of the legislature, provisions setting the salaries of elected officials, and specific limits on legislative sessions);

–detailed provisions limiting and directing the power of the state and its subdivisions to tax, borrow, and spend;

–provisions defining the state's obligations and powers in various functional areas such as education, highways, banking, corporations, business regulation, and elections;

–specific provisions governing the disposition and exploitation of the state's lands and natural resources;

–delineation of the powers of the state to create local governments and explicit denial of its power to alter them, once created, without local consent.

In addition, these constitutions often include precise descriptions of the state's boundaries. Most state constitutions also have unique provisions reflecting local circumstances. Among them are tax exemptions for aspects of farming in agricultural states; regulation of feudal land tenure in New York (which inherited certain problems in this regard from the days of the Dutch); a provision that English be taught in all schools in Nebraska (where at one time some immigrant groups eliminated English as the language of instruction); a prohibition of outlawry in

Texas; the right to fish in California; and the right to sell door to door in Minnesota (a Populist measure designed to enable farmers to eliminate the middleman). More recent innovations include "right-to-work" provisions that outlaw the closed or union shop in some states; guarantees of the right to bargain collectively in others; and provisions barring racial and sexual discrimination in a growing number.

The state constitutions establish constitutional polities made up of formally subordinate civil communities (counties, cities, townships, boroughs, etc.) having varying degrees of home rule. While the United States Supreme Court has made a point of specifying the *unitary* character of the states as polities, many, if not most, states are constitutionally *unions* of their counties or towns under their own constitutional theories and were held to be such by their jurists until the twentieth century.[9] In contrast to a unitary state, a union provides for the maintenance of the integrity of the constituent units through their participation in the state government and local home rule. In the American states, constitutional home rule is frequently used as a device to maintain the states as unions. This is another aspect of state constitutionalism that also deserves exploration, particularly in light of the United States Supreme Court reapportionment decisions of the 1960s, which directly, if unthinkingly, assaulted the very foundations of this aspect of state constitutionalism.

While the federal government has expanded its powers into spheres unanticipated in earlier generations, the states continue to perform myriad direct, day-to-day functions ranging from alcoholic beverage regulation and alimony arrangements to pothole repair and zoning regulation by plenary right (usually referred to as their police powers)—all of which affect and reflect the health, safety, welfare, and morals of their citizens. They also administer most of the federal programs that affect their citizens. Thus the states remain significant determinants of the quality of life of the American people. The way each state frames and allocates powers through its constitution reflects certain conceptions of government and understandings of the two faces of politics—power and justice. That is, state constitutions are important determinants of who gets what, when, and how in America because they are conceptual and at times very specific statements of who should get what, when, and how.

The detailed specificity of state constitutions affects the way they shape each state's governmental system and patterns of political behavior. Unlike the openendedness and ambiguity of many portions of the United States Constitution, which allow for considerable interpretative development through judicial, legislative, and executive action—especially Supreme Court action—state organs, including state supreme courts, generally hew closely to the letter of their constitutions because they must. One result of this is that state attorneys general play a special role in state constitutional interpretation, since they are generally required to give advisory opinions on the constitutionality of the actions of state government departments that depart in any way from established routine. Another consequence is that formal change of the constitutional document occurs more frequently through constitutional amendment—whether initiated by the legislature, special constitutional commissions, constitutional conventions, or direct action by the voters—and in a number of states, through the periodic writing of new constitutions. As a result, state constitutions have come to reflect explicity the changing conceptions of government that have developed over the course of American history, particularly under the pressure of successive waves of reform.

State constitutional development and interpretation are also affected by the political cultures of each state.[10] This is most readily evident in the differences between the North and South and the character of their constitutional development. While the United States as a whole shares a certain common political culture, there appear to be three major political subcultures in the country—individualistic, moralistic, and traditionalistic—rooted in the particular constellation of ethnic and religious groups and socioeconomic conditions that make up each state.[11] Differences in political cultures give each state constitution its own character, while similarities of political culture among various states also give their constitutions certain common threads achieved, in part, through borrowing ideas back and forth.

Finally, while the national Constitution is subordinate only to the people of the United States, the state constitutions are limited by the national Constitution in substantial ways, as well as subordinate to the peoples of the states. This sets certain parameters on state constitution making within which each state has to work out its own constitutional arrangements. In addition, most of the states have other documents with constitutional status. The original thirteen had colonial charters that may still have constitutional relevance in fixing land titles and boundaries, while the states carved out of the public domain are to some extent constitutionally bound by the congressional enabling acts that preceded their admission to the Union.

Six Constitutional Patterns

There appear to be six constitutional patterns among the American states. These patterns are rooted in the original constitutional conceptions of the founding era plus differences among the types and goals of pioneers who first settled the northern, middle, and southern colonies of the New World. Subsequent migrations carried the constitutional ideas of these sections westward and in some cases resulted in significant changes as settlers mixed, confronted new environments and sets of governmental problems, and framed their constitutions at different times, thereby incorporating conceptions of government prevalent when they were written.

The Commonwealth Pattern

The commonwealth pattern derives largely from the constitutions of the states of greater New England. They are basically philosophic documents designed first and foremost to set a direction for civil society and to express and institutionalize a theory of republican government. Based on seventeenth- and eighteenth-century Puritan and Whiggish ideas about constitution making, this pattern is the oldest in America. It emphasizes the constitution as a covenant establishing a civil society and setting forth its frame of government. These constitutions, as brief or briefer than the federal document, concentrate on setting forth the philosophic basis for popular government, guaranteeing the fundamental rights of the individual, and delineating the elements of the state's government in a few broad strokes. Frames of government in the classic American sense, they have shown great longevity and, at least in the case of Massachusetts, greater longevity than the United States Constitution.

Except for Vermont, none of the New England states has had more than two constitutions in its history, and Vermont has had only three, the last being adopted in 1793. Their fundamental documents have not been treated lightly. Like the federal Constitution, they have not been altered to reflect every new constitutional fad but have remained general documents reasonably adaptable to different times and needs.

Eight states outside New England whose political character was formed by New Englanders have followed the commonwealth pattern. All are still operating under their original constitutions. Although the youngest among them—those admitted as states in the latter half of the nineteenth century—have somewhat longer constitutions than their sisters formed earlier, as a rule they are also relatively short. Their greater length is accounted for in the somewhat more detailed restrictions placed on the institutions of state government and in the granting of constitutional status to state educational and welfare institutions.

Minnesota's constitution is a good example of this variation of the commonwealth pattern.[12] Adopted in 1858 when Minnesota attained statehood, it is about 40 percent longer than that of Massachusetts, but it still ranks among the shorter constitutions. The additional material in the Minnesota Constitution consists of more explicit delineations of the powers and duties of state officers and clear provisions for schools, taxes, banking, highways, and legislative apportionment.

The Commercial Republic Pattern

A second pattern has prevailed in the middle states (the northern states just south of New England and the states to the west of them that they have influenced, including most of the very large ones). These states have built their constitutions upon a series of compromises required by the conflict of ethnic and commercial interests and ideals created by the flow of various streams of migrants into their territories and the early development of commercial cities.

The patterns in all are much the same. As each stream of migrants has been able to demand a government modeled after the one its people knew "back home" or a fundamental law that would protect its socioeconomic interests, the state's constitution has been replaced or revised accordingly. Most of the states in this category have had three to six constitutions apiece. These constitutions tend to be longer than those written in the commonwealth mold, primarily because the compromises written into them have had to be made explicit and presented in detail to soften potential conflicts between rival elements that have sharply divergent views of what is politically right and proper.

Illinois is an example of this tradition.[13] Illinois was organized as a state by southern settlers in 1818. They endowed the state with a brief document that reflected the South's approach to constitution making. Then, in the 1830s, large numbers of New Englanders began to arrive in the state. As they consolidated their settlements, they wanted to adapt the Illinois government to their own needs. To do so, they needed to change the state constitution, particularly in regard to local government, public education, and public welfare. In the 1840s they successfully bargained with their fellow citizens from southern and middle states backgrounds to reach a compromise embodied in the constitution of 1848.

This compromise was seriously strained by the Civil War, which almost rent Illinois as it did the Union. In order to settle outstanding differences and restore harmony, the state adopted a new constitution in 1870 that maintained the compromise of 1848 but restructured the institutions that embodied that compromise to allow for minority representation in each part of the state. Between 1870 and 1970, none of the several attempts to adopt a new constitution succeeded, precisely because leaders of the state's important interests were afraid to upset the balance of forces established by the compromise. New interests were accommodated by constitutional amendments, initially granting home rule to Chicago in 1904, and a spate of modernizing amendments in the late 1950s. The cleavages of the Civil War era had sufficiently diminished by the late 1960s to enable a new constitutional convention to shape a document (ratified in 1970) that is considered one of the most up-to-date in the country.

The Southern Contractual Pattern

The southern states developed a third pattern of constitution making, one that began with a general penchant for changing constitutions and was enhanced by the need to do so because of the disruption of constitutional continuity caused by the Civil War. Except for North Carolina and Tennessee, none of the eleven states of the former Confederacy has had fewer than five constitutions, most of which embodied the constitutional changes of secession, reconstruction, and the restoration of white supremacy. Alabama, for example, adopted a constitution upon its admission to the Union in 1819, a revised document when it seceded from the Union in 1861, and still another when it sought to be restored to full rights in 1865. Then it adopted two constitutions during Reconstruction (1868 and 1875) and finally a constitution ratifying white supremacy in 1901. Yet the Civil War is not solely responsible for the South's relatively casual attitude toward its fundamental charters. Of the five southern states that did not secede, only West Virginia has had fewer than four constitutions.

Constitutions of the southern contractual pattern are unique in other, related ways. They are the only group to formally acknowledge the supremacy of the United States Constitution (a product of Reconstruction). At the same time, most of them contain (and retain) many provisions—particularly regarding elections, civil rights, and legislative apportionment—that have been invalidated by United States Supreme Court decisions. In general, the southern contractual pattern has looked upon state constitutions as instruments designed to perpetuate a particular social system based on slavery or racial segregation. As political instruments, southern state constitutions are designed to diffuse the formal allocation of authority among many offices in order to accommodate the swings between oligarchy and factionalism characteristic of southern state politics. Perhaps because of the fluctuating balance of factions in many of the southern states, their citizens have also been more tempted to write into their constitutions materials normally included in ordinary legislation.

Texas is a prime example of this pattern. The Lone Star State's first constitution, adopted in 1836, established the Republic of Texas. Then Texas adopted a new constitution in 1845 to join the Union, another in 1861 to join the Confederacy, a fourth in 1866 to rejoin the Union, a fifth in 1869 to satisfy radical Republican Reconstructionists, and a sixth in 1876 to restore white supremacy and Democratic control and to limit state government, in part, by fragmenting power and establishing many independently elected offices. Indeed, the constitution includes an explicit statement of the principle of limited government. The Texas constitution is long, somewhat unwieldy, not highly venerated, and contains 233 amendments. Efforts to substantially revise the constitution failed at the polls in 1975.

The Civil Code Pattern

Louisiana is the one state that operates within a constitutional pattern of its own. Because of its original French background, its constitutions have been more like the basic civil codes of European countries—long, detailed, and not particularly revered. The Pelican State has had eleven constitutions since 1812. Its tenth, adopted in 1921, contained some 256,500 words, over six times as many as the average state document. As of 1965, it had been amended 439 times. The Louisiana constitutional tradition provides, in effect, a continuing referendum on all basic governmental decisions in the state and its localities. In 1974, however, 36 percent of the registered voters turned out to adopt (by 58 percent) a modernized constitution containing only 29,704 words.

The Frame of Government Pattern

The fifth pattern is to be found exclusively among the less populated states of the Far West. In these states the constitutions are primarily frames of government. They explicitly reflect the republican and democratic principles dominant in the nation in the late nineteenth century when their first constitutions were written, then go on to specify the structure of state government and the distribution of powers within it in the style of the times. These constitutions tend to be businesslike documents of moderate length that reflect the relative homogeneity of the states themselves. Indeed, among those states, only Oklahoma has a population of over two million, and it has the longest constitution of the group, reflecting in part its southern antecedents.

Montana is a good example of this frame of government pattern. It was admitted as a state in 1889, and its original constitution reflected the frame of government approach when it was at its height. In 1972 the state adopted a constitution after what experts in the field consider to be a model process of constitution writing and ratification. Although the new constitution incorporates many of the recommendations of constitutional reformers, it also appears to remain faithful to the frame of government pattern, adapting it to late twentieth-century ideas.

The constitutional tradition of the Treasure State has tended to emphasize limited government except on certain matters of economic development. After

World War II, Montana emerged from almost a century of well-nigh colonial status under the control of the Anaconda Company and, later, Montana Power. In part the new constitution of 1972, which replaced the state's original document of 1889, symbolized the new independence of the state and the assertion of power by the general citizenry.

The Managerial Pattern

Alaska and Hawaii, the two newest states, reflect a sixth constitutional pattern, one developed in the second half of the twentieth century. Their constitutions come closest to fitting the model designed by today's constitutional reformers. This reform model emphasizes conciseness, broad grants of powers to the state executive branch, and relatively few structural restrictions on the legislature. Their constitutions also feature articles dealing with local government, natural resource conservation, and social legislation. In all of this they reflect the Hamiltonian managerial model, albeit without being aware of it. While, as a model, it is as old as the republic itself, only in the twentieth century has it entered the mainstream of American constitutional development, and only in the newest states could it serve as the basis for constitutional foundations.

Alaska's constitution of 1956 must serve the nation's last land frontier and to some extent preserve it at a time when it is experiencing great pressures of modern economic development. Since statehood, Alaska's constitution has been amended fourteen times, in part to correct some of the excesses of the managerial approach.

Directions

Constitutional design is the way connections are made between political ideas, political culture, and institutional development for the most practical purposes. To understand constitutional design in the states and to enhance Americans' constitution-making capabilities, we must properly examine and articulate the explicit and implicit political theories and philosophic assumptions of the American state constitutions manifested by the three constitutional traditions, as they have found expression in these six patterns.

The object of such efforts should be to reconstruct the inner logic of the state constitutions so as to understand their basic theoretical conceptions of government, its proper role in society, and the very purposes of the constitutions. In this respect, each constitution must be treated as a package made up of diverse elements, including compromises, which together shape a fundamental role for government in the state. In some cases these ideas are expressed more or less explicitly in the constitution; in most, however, they are implicit, because most Americans are not readily given to abstract theoretical or ideological statements about government. Instead, state constitutions appear to reflect a "logic in use" that needs to be "reconstructed."[14] This logic is based on certain familiar and common understandings of government held by Americans but is worked out or put to use according to the particular goals and conceptions of each state's constitution makers. In turn, this logic revolves around a number of value concepts, such as consent, representative government, and rights, which cannot be defined precisely but whose use in each state constitution results in a certain definition or understanding of the concept.[15]

For example, the concept of the separation of powers appears in every state constitution. Yet very few state constitution makers or citizens would be able to define the concept in the abstract or develop a theoretical justification for it. The concept is used because it is part of the common constitutional coin of the realm, so to speak. Its role in governance is relatively clear-cut. In terms of the political theory of each constitution, however, we must explore its logic in use.

To understand the theoretical assumptions of each constitution it is necessary to look at each provision and concept in five ways: by itself as stated in the constitution; in relation to the other provisions of the constitution; in relation to earlier constitutions or founding documents; in comparison with similar provisions in other state constitutions; and in relation to its actual interpretative use.

The following themes and concepts are particularly important.

Covenantalism. Throughout American history the concepts of covenant, compact, contract, and constitution have been closely related, though each has a different shade of meaning.[16] The Massachusetts Constitution, for example, declares itself to be "a social compact, by which the whole people covenants with each citizen, and each citizen with the whole people." Covenantal and compactual constitutions tend to rest upon some prior consensus or communal understanding of political life in which government is seen as a positive instrument for bettering the commonwealth. Other constitutions, however, appear to be framed in a more contractual vein in which explicit terms must be mandated in order to permit the various competing and individualistic forces to live together within the state. In some cases the contract involves a broad spectrum of the state's citizenry; in others it amounts to a contract among the elites for the purpose of maintaining the privileges of certain groups at the expense of others.

Fundamentality. Some constitutions are treated as basic, fundamental laws of the land while others are more like extraordinary statutory codes. Related to this is the length of the constitution, its character of detail, and the specificity of those details.

Conception of government. Does the constitution see government as a positive, energetic force in the life of the state or as a "necessary evil" to be limited and hemmed in as much as possible?

Purpose of government. Is the purpose of government to advance certain common statewide goals, to mediate among contending groups otherwise free to pursue their self-interest, or to maintain some status quo? Is government designed to serve the common citizenry directly or indirectly, or is it aimed primarily toward certain groups?

Scope of government. What is the range of government action provided for in the constitution, and in particular, what policy fields and mechanisms receive the most attention?

Consent and representation. How and in what ways does the constitution provide for the consent of the people and the representation of different interests in state government? To what extent does the constitution rely on simple majority rule, extraordinary majority rule, or dispersed majorities?

Separation of powers. How are powers allocated among the branches of state government and the constituent units of each branch and in what detail? Is power pulverized in the process or well coordinated and orchestrated into a cohesive system? This will necessarily involve an examination of the specific powers and duties of each branch and the limits on each.

Federalization. In turn, how are powers allocated between the state and local governments? To what degree does the constitution mandate a unitary government or a more federal arrangement among local governments?

Rights. What are the fundamental rights of the people according to the constitution, and what do these rights add up to as a package?

Federal parameters. Finally, how does the state constitution regard and cope with the limitations imposed by the United States Constitution?

6

CONFEDERATION AND FEDERAL LIBERTY

One Genus, Two Species

Conventional accounts of American history treat confederation and federation as two very different ways of dealing with the problem of political organization. Indeed, within the limited context of American history this approach can be understood as reflecting the sense of profound transformation brought about by the United States Constitution of 1787. In a larger sense, however, the American experience shows federation and confederation to be two species of the same genus—federalism—each seeking in its own way to combine liberty with appropriately effective government.

As we commemorate the two-hundredth anniversary of the American founding, it behooves Americans and students of politics everywhere to reexamine the American experience under confederation as well as federation, and most especially the principles underlining the confederal experiment, to try to understand exactly how both species were given their modern form in the new United States. Such a reexamination is especially appropriate at this time because the serious revival of confederal options around the world since World War II inevitably leads us back to the original American experience. In the century following adoption of the Articles of Confederation, there were other confederal experiments in Europe and Latin America, all of which foundered in the face of the nationalistic tendencies of the modern epoch, which emphasized the linkage of nation building and state building on a centralized basis or, at a minimum, along the lines of federation. In the postmodern epoch, on the other hand, constitutionalized transnational political organization based on shared economic and cultural foundations has become more acceptable, leading to a renewed interest in the possibilities of confederation.[1]

The modern character of the American confederation and its connection with federalism should be noted at the outset. One of the reasons for ignoring the close relationship between the confederal and federal experiences of the American confederation is that students have treated it as if it were simply a late example of a premodern league rather than a perpetual union of states. Indeed, this view was developed directly and explicitly by the authors of *The Federalist* as part of their polemic against the Articles of Confederation and on behalf of the new federal Constitution. One can understand their reasons for trying to identify the existing confederation with the ancient and medieval European leagues, which were premodern expressions of the federal principle. However, we need to question the accuracy of what they did. Their descriptions of the weaknesses of those leagues are generally accurate, and their attribution of some of those selfsame weaknesses to the American confederation was also justified; but in the heat of the political battle they went beyond that. Whether they properly classified the American confederation with those leagues needs to be examined more closely.

The polity established by the Articles was a "Confederation and perpetual Union," as described in its preamble, whereas the Constitution of 1787 was designed to "form a more perfect Union." Therein lies the similarity and the difference. The confederation established by the Articles was perpetual and had virtually unlimited power within its sphere. It was far more than an alliance, since when a state acceded to it it could no more withdraw than can a state from the federal union. Moreover, in international law, the United States of America was an independent entity constituted by its states and not simply a committee of them. It was a confederacy (Article I) that came into existence only after ratification by all the member states. Were it merely a treaty or alliance, it could have come into existence for those states ratifying it immediately upon their ratification. In fact, it hardly can be said to have "come into existence," because in reality the Articles represented a formal constitutionalization of what had been established in 1775 by "the United States in Congress assembled," an entity that continued to function from 1775 to 1781 even while the Articles were pending ratification.

Here I suggest that confederation and federation as developed in the United States after 1775 were both modern devices. As such, American-style confederation, no less than federation, was a different form of political organization from the earlier leagues. That is one reason the study of the American confederal experience does not lead us away from federalism but improves our understanding of federalism as a genus and the application of federal principles and arrangements in the real world.

What Constitutes Liberty?

The central interest of both federation and confederation, and indeed of true federalism in all its species, is the issue of liberty. All forms of federalism begin with the assumption that government in some form is necessary and that the development of appropriately effective government is a major human task. In this respect federalist theories are realistic. The other "given" of federalism is that humans are born free and that good government must be grounded in a framework of maximum human liberty. The task of constitution makers is to develop a regime for each people that secures liberty even while recognizing and allowing for government in its coercive aspects.

To say that liberty stands at the center of federalist striving is to open the door to the question of what constitutes liberty in the federal context and how federalists deal with the problematics of liberty. On one level, these questions lead to what may be the decisive difference between confederation and federation. Federations are communities of both polities and individuals and emphasize the liberties of both. The American federation has placed even greater emphasis on the liberty of individuals than on the liberties of its constituent polities, an emphasis that has grown more pronounced over the generations. Confederations, on the other hand, are primarily communities of polities, and they place greater emphasis on the liberties of the constituent polities. It is the task of the constituent polities to protect individual liberty, more or less as each defines it, although in confederations of republics they must conform to at least minimum standards of individual liberty in order to preserve the republican character of the whole. The minimum guarantee of individual liberty in the Articles can be found in Article IV, which gave the "free inhabitants in each of these states . . . all the privileges and immunities of free citizens in the several states," "free ingress and regress to and from any other state," and "all the privileges of trade and commerce"—in other words, basic civil and commercial rights.

Thus, to understand a confederation it is necessary first to understand what constitute the liberties of its constituents and how those constituents see confederation as protecting those liberties. American pluralism has strayed far from the concept of group liberties to become almost exclusively individualistic. This is not surprising, given the character of American society. No doubt one of the reasons it was possible to convince a majority of Americans voting by states to abandon confederation for federation was because, even in the Revolutionary era, the states were not able to command a level of identification stronger than that of individual self-interest and the growing common perception that Americans were Americans, first and foremost.

Had the states been perceived by a majority of their citizens to be primary organic communities, as John C. Calhoun later argued, there is little doubt that the Constitution of 1787 would have been rejected on behalf of state liberties. As it was, the real challenge to that document revolved around the protection of individual liberty (the need for a bill of rights in the federal Constitution). Not that the principle of state liberties was totally rejected—the political liberties of the states were deemed very important, as witness the Tenth Amendment—but they were not primary in the American scheme of things.

Because of this special character of American pluralism, Americans have a very difficult time understanding issues of group rights. That made federation easy for them. But for much of the world group rights—variously defined as national, local, or ethnic liberties—are of the essence. For them confederation may be the most viable way to attain the combination of liberty, good government, and peace that federalism promises.

On another level, both species of federalism must deal with the perennial problematics of liberty. Whether articulated or not (and in the United States, it usually is not), the foundation of their effort rests on the distinction between natural liberty and federal liberty. Natural liberty is unrestricted, the freedom of the state of nature, whether understood in Hobbesian or Lockean terms. In the end it is the liberty that leads to anarchy, or the war of all against all. According to federal principles, proper liberty is federal liberty, that is, liberty to act according to the terms of the covenant (*foedus*) that calls the body politic into existence. Every proper polity is established by a pact among its constituents that is covenantal insofar as it rests upon a shared moral sensibility and understanding and is legitimate insofar as it embodies the fundamental principles of human liberty and equality. Behavior that does not fit within those terms is, in effect, a violation of the covenant and a manifestation of anarchy. Hence it can be stopped and its perpetrators punished by the appropriate institutions of government.

In sum, federal liberty is liberty established by agreement. The content of any particular agreement may and will vary. Thus John Winthrop could understand true liberty as that flowing from the covenant between God and man in which God dictated the terms of the agreement and man pledged to accept them.[2] On the other hand, James Wilson of Pennsylvania, one of the authors of the Constitution of 1787, could understand federal liberty as a strictly secular expression of the compact establishing civil society.[3] Today, when the Supreme Court of the United States holds the state and federal governments to standards of behavior based upon the United States Constitution, even when the implementation of those standards places heavy restrictions on individual behavior, in effect it does so on the grounds that the Constitution is a compact entered into by the people of the United States that, inter alia, delineates what constitutes federal liberty within the American system.

This discussion would not be complete if we did not recall that one of the basic tensions informing American civilization is the tension between natural and federal liberty. Admiration for the former has been expressed in various ways in American history, from the eighteenth-century ideal of the "noble savage" to the "natural man" of the nineteenth century, to "doin' what comes naturally" in the first half of the twentieth, to the "let it all hang out" of our times. Indeed, natural liberty was clearly dominant in the land from the mid-1960s through the 1970s.

Federal liberty found its first expression in the theopolitical stance of the Puritans and has retained favor among those applying religious standards and moral expectations to the American people and their polity—including the eighteenth-century revolutionaries, the antislavery forces of the antebellum years, the Populists and Progressives of the late nineteenth century, and those who fought the civil rights battles of the 1950s and 1960s. All of the foregoing believed that people were not naturally free to commit certain wrongs but as citizens or residents of the United States, living under its constitution, could be required to act or refrain from acting in ways that violated the terms of that constitution.

The Articles of Confederation had as the focus of their concern the federal liberty of the constituent states. Hence they had what was at once a more limited and far broader definition of federal liberty to work with, restricting the freedom of the constituent states in those few fields where it was deemed necessary for a uniform confederal standard while allowing each in its own way to determine what constituted federal liberty for its own citizens.

Federation and Confederation

Returning to the differences between federation and confederation, we may begin with the classic distinction—that in federations the federal government can reach out to its citizenry directly as well as through the constituent polities, while in a confederation the confederal government must reach individual citizens only through the constituent polities. This definition is accurate as far as it goes, but it is not complete. We must add the point made above that a federation is more concerned with preserving individual liberty, while a confederation places greater emphasis on preserving local liberties of its constituent polities.

A third characteristic distinguishing federations from confederations is that the former have a common law of some scope that is enforceable throughout the federation, while the latter tend to leave matters of law to the constituent polities except as explicitly provided in limited areas determined to be of such general concern that they must be governed by a common law. This is a matter of the greatest importance; some might even say it is the heart of the matter. Federation is possible only where a sufficiently comprehensive common law binding all citizens of the constituent units is possible. By the same token, confederation is a viable means of establishing federal ties in situations where the parties to the bargain can tolerate only specific and limited common laws.

The Articles provide for a common law of war and peace and a common foreign relations. Implicit in the Articles is a common republicanism that is so taken for granted that it finds expression only in the prohibition against granting titles of nobility in Article VI. The Confederacy also had full powers over coinage, weights and measures, and postal services.

The most ambiguous elements in the Articles are those relating to interstate commerce and the general welfare. On the one hand, it is clear from Article IV that the United States is to be a single entity for commercial purposes, but without eliminating the powers of the states to protect their own respective economies, as suggested obliquely in Article VI. Similarly, there are two references to the general welfare, one in Article III as one of the ends of the Confederacy, and the second in Article VIII with regard to the revenue-raising powers of the new Congress. Both references are general and openended.

A fourth dimension must be added, having to do with the ends of the polity. Every polity is devoted to the attainment of certain ends, to the achievement of justice as it is conceived by those who constitute it. In this respect the extent to which the general government possesses power, though crudely related to the defined ends of the polity, is not determinative of those ends. One of the perceived problems of the American confederation is that the confederal government was not adequate to achieve the ends for which it was instituted. I have already mentioned two elements involved in determining the ends of federal polities—liberty, however defined, and good government, however defined. In both cases federal polities, because they are constituted in a formal way by a pact or articles of agreement, are likely to be more explicit about their understanding of these and other ends to which they are devoted. These ends are generally stated in the preambles to their constitutions, but they may also be stated or explicated in the body of the constitutional document(s). As a general rule, confederations have more limited ends than federations. With respect to the United States, the principal difference between the Constitution of 1787 and the Articles of Confederation was one of means rather than ends. In this respect the Preamble to the 1787 Constitution specified that what is proposed is the establishment of "a more perfect union," not a new one. What was changed was the means for effectuating the union, which required the expansion of the powers granted to the federal government even in order to obtain already agreed-upon ends.

The major shift with regard to ends was from an emphasis on the liberties of the individual states to the establishment of liberty, justice, and domestic tranquility for the people of the United States. Article III of the Articles sets forth the ends of the Confederation:

> The said states hereby severally enter into a firm league of friendship with each other, for their common defence, the security of their Liberties, and their mutual and general welfare, binding themselves to assist each other, against all force offered to, or attacks made upon them, or any of them, on account of religion, sovereignty, trade, or any other pretence whatever.

Contrast it with the Preamble to the Constitution of 1787:

> We, the People of the United States, in Order to form a more perfect Union, establish Justice, insure domestic Tranquility, provide for the common defence, promote the general Welfare, and secure the blessings of Liberty to ourselves and our Posterity, do ordain and establish this Constitution for the United States of America.

I would not want to minimize this shift. In a certain sense it is of the essence; but it is not, as some would have it, the exchange of a loose league for a consolidated union. There is more of a shift in emphasis than in underlying form. I do not wish to enter here into the question of how effective or ineffective the Confederation was; that dispute is well known. One thing is clear, however. While we cannot and never will know whether the potentialities within the Articles of Confederation could have been developed to deal with the problems of a growing United States, the confederal government was not simply a failure. It had a number of accomplishments, not the least of which involved the extension of its powers into new spheres, whether with regard to the organization of western lands (after all, the Confederation Congress established the basis for admitting new states into the United States), in banking (the Confederation Congress established the first bank in the United States as its instrumentality), or in the initiation of support for educational and eleemosynary development.

Following Madison, the distinction between the two regimes can be summarized as follows: the Constitution of 1787 provided a government that was partly national and partly federal to replace the Articles of Confederation, which established a regime that was partially federal and partially a league. The first combination came to be known as federation; the second came to be known as confederation. The tension built into the former is between the national and the federal elements, while the tension built into the latter is between the federal and the league elements. Since federal arrangements always involve one or another set of built-in tensions, the character of the tension of each particular arrangement is the major clue as to the species of federalism involved.

The difficulties—often fatal—of confederation flow from this basic tension. In our consideration of whether confederation can be a viable federal option, we must raise the question whether (or under what conditions) the confederal tension can be sustained in a polity on a long-term basis. This is a real issue in the European Community today.

The American Rationale for Confederation

The American Confederacy and the Articles of Confederation that established and guided it must be understood as a Whig mechanism, an extension of the commonwealth principles that informed constitution making in most, if not all, of the individual states. It has the classic dimension of an Old Whig or Commonwealthman polity, American style. It is covenantal rather than contractual, since for the enforcement of its provisions it relies principally on the states' moral commitment to making the Articles effective. It not only required consent but emphasized it in the Whig manner by requiring the constant renewal or reaffirmation of consent at almost every step in the governing process. In this respect it relied on another Whig principle, republican virtue, as the mainstay of the polity, since it was implicit that only if republican virtue flourished would the states live up to their moral commitment.[4]

The Whig reliance on republican virtue was tied in with its emphasis on homogeneous polities in which community would exist to foster republican virtue and a shared public interest. That is one of the major reasons the United States as a whole could be no more than a confederation in the Whig scheme of things. It was too diverse to properly foster or maintain either. (That is why in the debate over the ratification of the Constitution of 1787 the Federalists concentrated their attack on the notion that the states could be sufficiently homogeneous, arguing that they also were too large.) For the Whigs, the states had that capacity, which was another reason each state was to vote with one voice in the Congress and was to be responsible for implementing (appropriately adapting) the acts of Congress.

In Whig tradition, the Confederacy's principal institution was the legislature, formally titled "the United States in Congress assembled." It in turn was tied as closely as possible to the people or, more accurately, the polities it represented, following the Whig pattern of exercising control first over governmental power and then over the governors who wield it. The members of the Congress were delegates chosen and supported by those who sent them, and they sat for limited terms only, again a classic Whig control device also found in most of the early state constitutions. There was heavy reliance upon consensual action by several bodies in order to implement programs, particularly the United States in Congress assembled and the individual states but also Congress and its Executive Committee, with minimum sanctions to bring about cooperation among them and a heavy emphasis upon each accepting its moral responsibility (or consenting) to do its share.

The practical deficiencies of the Whig approach to governance soon became apparent in the states as well as the Confederacy. A great part of the triumph of the Federalists over the Whigs lay in their genius in creating better mechanisms of governance, through which Whig principles could be embodied in Federalist institutions. Ultimately it was this synthesis of Whig principles and Federalist institutions that created the golden age of American federalism. We should have learned from the Confederation years and the period since 1965 that to the extent that one or the other is abandoned, the country suffers; but more on that below.

The existence of the Confederacy was taken for granted from the first. There was never any debate as to whether the states should be united. The debate centered on the character of the union, not its existence. For all intents and purposes, the union came into existence no later than 1775; indeed, the very process of declaring independence reflected the degree to which the United States of America already existed. In this sense the union began with the people of the several states seeing themselves as Americans in certain respects from the first and as linked to one another as Americans across state lines.

This is another way the American Confederacy was a Whig confederacy, a confederacy of commonwealths that was to embody commonwealth ideals, not like the European leagues or even the United Netherlands, which was a union of provincial oligarchies. There is no question as to the republican and popular character of either American regime or its constitution. The United States was born free under its first constitution as much as under its second. Indeed, the argument in later years was that it was born even freer under its first than under its second. This is an argument I do not accept, but it is testimony to the ideals embodied in that first American constitution. In other words, the fundamental principles of American government were established under the Articles—that the United States was to be a commonwealth of commonwealths resting on popular and republican bases, able to function only through the cooperative interaction of its components in a nonhierarchical way and committed to partnership to advance common goals for the general welfare.

The great acts of the Confederal Congress reflected this overall thrust. Those acts included the acquisition of the western lands as the common property of the United States, provision for their settlement and organization as future states of the Confederacy, the initiation of a national banking system, the provision of a common defense force, and the negotiation of treaties of peace and alliance with the European powers having interests in North America. These and other acts of the Confederacy all involved the application of the aforementioned principles in concrete ways. Their success is attested by the fact that they were continued or reenacted under the new federal Constitution and continued to provide a basis for American development long after the Confederacy gave way to the new regime.

Whig Principles and Federalist Mechanisms

The history of the adoption of the Constitution of 1787 can be examined from the perspective of how the Federalists constructed a stable and lasting extended republic by taking the essence of the Whig rationale and standing it on its head to overcome its weaknesses. Cutting through the polemics surrounding the struggle over ratification of the Constitution of 1787, we can begin to understand the degree to which the second United States Constitution represented a supplement to the first, a synthesis of old principles and new practices as well as a departure. While the Constitutional Convention produced a well-articulated Federalist theory in contradistinction to the Whig theory, it is important to note that the former was not the exclusive theory of all members of the convention or even of those who were most active in drafting the new constitution. I am suggesting that, the radical Federalists aside, the theory behind the United States Constitution incorporated certain Whig principles to some degree while transcending them in the invention of the mechanisms of government for which the Constitution is justly famous.

The two most original elements of Federalist theory are the idea of the extended republic as a means of controlling the evils of class and faction and the idea of the separation of powers as a means of providing energetic yet controlled government. Both were simultaneously extensions and transformations of Whig theory. The Federalist theory of the extended republic followed the confederal precedent of the Whigs, but rather than relying on expectations that shared understanding of the common weal in politically homogeneous polities would promote good government, the Federalists realistically recognized the problems of class conflict and factional struggles and sought to control them through the device of a large federal republic that would dilute their intensity. So too the principle of dispersing power among various units that must function cooperatively or concurrently was not foreign to the Whigs. The crucial addition of the Federalists was the invention of the tripartite separation of powers based on the presidency and a separate executive branch, a judiciary headed by a supreme court, and a bicameral legislature with one house representing the people and the other the states. Those who held Whig principles had little difficulty adjusting to this invention, which, as a mechanism, offered clear advantages over the kinds of power sharing that lay at the root of the Whig system, especially since that earlier division between Congress and the states was incorporated into the new constitution, albeit on somewhat different terms. Indeed the Whigs had already come to the tripartite division in their own state constitutions.

The matter of the extended republic was somewhat more difficult for the Whigs to assimilate. It represented a greater theoretical departure. The Whig premise was that only where those who held the power of government were subject to direct oversight by the citizenry were they likely to be properly controlled. Each extension of government beyond local control presented its own complications for the Whigs. Governments serving larger arenas had to be fenced in with more restraints, albeit moral restraints more than mechanical ones, other than the narrow bag of Whig tricks such as selecting representatives for the shortest possible terms of office with maximum possible rotation and bound as closely as possible to those who selected them.

Now here was James Madison standing that theory on its ear and arguing just the reverse: that the extended republic offered greater republican stability not so much because of better formal divisions, but because it prevented the division of society into two classes, the few creditors and the many debtors, which had been the case in small republics since time immemorial. This was an argument to be conjured with precisely because it addressed the great question of liberty that preoccupied the Whigs. To the extent that the Constitution of 1787 was based upon this argument, it did represent a radical change.[5]

For our purposes, the great change the Constitution of 1787 wrought was to constitutionalize power and its limits, to set forth clearly the expanded powers of the federal government, but also to clearly limit them through mechanisms and institutions designed to keep a potentially powerful government under control. The federal system had become more national in its thrust but was counterbalanced by becoming more explicitly federal in its organization, in contradistinction to the Articles, which were more federal in their thrust but more like a league in the organization they established.[6]

In accomplishing this, the new constitution moved the American people from a reliance upon covenantal principles—that is, moral obligation as a means of ensuring compliance with agreed-upon arrangements—to compactual ones, in which the means of compliance and the penalties for noncompliance were specified and enforceable. To say this is to oversimplify to some extent. But allowing for that oversimplification, in the main it is the best way to describe the fundamental transformation of principle from the first constitution to the second.

The claim that the United States is indeed a polity founded by covenant can be sustained only in light of the document itself. The Declaration of Independence was the covenant that established the American people and set forth the basic principles to guide them as a people. The Articles of Confederation must be read in light of the Declaration of Independence, since many of its silences or ambiguities relate to the widely understood and widely accepted principles of the Declaration. In that respect it is an operational gloss on the covenant itself and, like it, relies on moral commitment for the enforcement of obligations. Thus both the Declaration and the Articles make references to the Deity, the first "appealing to the Supreme Judge of the World" and the second recognizing that "the Great Governor of the World" inclined "the hearts of the legislatures" of the respective states "to ratify the said articles of confederation and perpetual union." Both references should be understood as more than piety. As in every covenantal document, they are designed to invoke moral obligation. God is made a witness to the proceedings and to the consent freely given to the result. The Constitution of 1787, on the other hand, is long on sanctions or, more accurately, grants of power to Congress to enforce its terms, but it contains no reference to Heaven. It is thoroughly secular in its means and ends, a compact rather than a covenant.

On one level, the failures of the Articles of Confederation attest to the limits of covenants without operative sanctions in human society. Nevertheless, a strong measure of Whiggery survived to help inform the new federal Constitution and direct it toward larger ends than those the radical Federalists proposed as appropriate for the more perfect union. The Whig influence was felt in somewhat contradictory ways, and not necessarily ways that met the expectations of the old Whigs of the revolutionary generation; but that is all too often the way of human affairs, and we need not be surprised at that result.

The resurgence of Whig influence came simultaneously with the struggle over ratification, which in one sense, of course, the Whigs lost. Fearful of the extensive powers granted the federal government under the new constitution and unwilling to fully trust procedural devices and intricate mechanisms to restrain federal power, the Whigs insisted on the addition of a bill of rights to the new constitution, which was done as soon as the new government was organized. The idea of a bill of rights was classic Whig doctrine, though in the case of the federal Constitution Whigs seemed to have imbibed Federalist principles by demanding one that was enforceable and not simply a declaration of principles designed to generate moral obligation on the part of the governors toward the governed, as was the case with the declarations of rights in the state constitutions. Thus, in the adoption of the Bill of Rights itself the new synthesis began to be manifest.

Even more far reaching was the decision on the part of the Anti-Federalists, most of whom were Whigs, to accept the new constitution and actively participate in the organization and administration of the new government. By accepting the results of the struggle over ratification, those who shared Whig principles in one way or the other almost immediately gained substantial power within the new federal government and were able to use that power to interpret the new constitution in a manner consistent with their Whig ideas.[7]

Perhaps one of the best examples of this was Albert Gallatin's introduction of cooperative federalism as the accepted form of intergovernmental relations in the time of Thomas Jefferson's presidency. Rather than exploit powers granted the federal government to enable it to operate directly within the states in pursuit of federal goals, Gallatin developed ways and means of federal-state cooperation whereby the federal government and the states undertook joint programs. In doing this, Gallatin restored the important Whig control device of cooperative action, albeit within the framework of the federal Constitution, which relied less upon goodwill than heretofore and more upon latent federal powers. Gallatin's efforts were to influence the course of American government and administration from that time forward.[8]

In short, the adoption of the Constitution of 1787 did not simply substitute Federalist principles for Whig principles, but created a new tension between the two sets of principles that has played itself out through federalist institutions and a federal, as distinct from a confederal, regime. That tension remains with us.

For the first two generations under the Constitution, the United States resembled a confederation almost as much as a federation, as those who espoused a confederal approach shaped a federal constitution to their ends.[9] In the third generation, those who tried to push the confederal approach too far precipitated a civil war, with the inevitable backlash toward federal union. After the corresponding excesses of Reconstruction, however, the federal balance was restored for two more generations, only to be upset in the direction of centralization once again. It was during those generations that Americans lost sight of the principles of the founding generation, both Federalist and Whig. Both covenantal and compactual theories of the polity were rejected in favor of the then more fashionable organic and evolutionary (Darwinian) theories. Concomitantly, hierarchical views of the state came to replace the idea of the federal commonwealth. Progressives and reactionaries, socialists and capitalists, reformers and standpatters were swept up by the new styles. Only among the midwestern and western Progressives did the Whig outlook continue to prevail, while the Federalist outlook came to be confined to politicians with a stake in the system as it existed.

It was only in the post–World War II generation that we began to rediscover the teachings of the Federalist founders, principally through the work of Martin Diamond, and only toward the end of that generation did we begin to pay attention to the Whig founders. We are still engaged in the latter exploration. Only insofar as we understand the ideas and actions of both sets of founders will we be able to understand the origins of the American federal commonwealth and to steer the ship of state in the right direction.

Conclusions

Confederation, as conceived and practiced by the American people between 1775 and 1789, was not merely an imitation of earlier European leagues. Rather, it was an attempt to develop a species of popular government within the federal genus that would reflect the extension of Whig principles to a polity expanded to a size beyond that of any in history other than the autocratic Russian empire. As such, it merits serious consideration for what it can teach us about the problem of federal arrangements in extended republics.

Although the result, the United States of America as a confederation, was rejected after less than half a generation (incidentally, the minimum time needed for a regime to consolidate itself) and replaced by a presumably radically different approach to the organization of government, in fact what emerged was a synthesis between the Whig and Federalist approaches, based upon a perennial tension between the two. That tension has accompanied the American people in their experiment with self-government ever since, at times more self-consciously and at times less. The roots of that tension lie in the effort to combine federal liberty with good government. The tension itself has been a creative one that deserves to be fostered. The best way to do so is to begin by understanding the premises of both Whig and Federalist thought underlying the American political system, as well as the federal mechanisms used in the governance of that system.

7

DEVELOPING AN AMERICAN THEORY OF FEDERAL DEMOCRACY

Since the late Martin Diamond brought the American academic and intellectual communities back to a concern with the political meaning of the Constitution of the United States of America (its full and proper title) and the founding of the American federal republic (whose regime he described as a democratic republic and which I describe as a federal democracy), the question of the federal character of the Constitution has been central to the discussion.[1] Diamond himself emphasized the importance of this federal dimension, and much of his writing focuses on it. Taking his definition of "federal" from late medieval sources and his interpretation of the Constitution from *The Federalist*, Diamond concluded that the federalism of the Constitution was constitutionalized decentralization rather than true federalism, which had been tried under the Articles of Confederation and found wanting. For Diamond, federalism—read constitutional decentralization—was an absolutely essential element of the American democratic republic. In that sense he was a true friend of federalism.

While Diamond was formulating his argument, the late W. W. Crosskey was challenging the federal character of the Constitution in a different way.[2] His was a lawyer's argument, that the Constitution had to be read as a contract and that when so read, with full understanding of the eighteenth-century linguistic usage, it could only be understood as having established a modestly decentralized unitary state. Whereas Diamond's argument was political in the classic sense—his dispute with contemporary political science, for example, was over the political importance of institutions (including constitutions) and foundings—Crosskey's was utterly apolitical, as if, just because many of the delegates to the Philadelphia convention were trained as lawyers, they sat in the Pennsylvania State House and, as lawyers, negotiated a binding contract among several parties that was to be unambiguous in language and inflexible in interpretation.

A different kind of intellectual assault on the fundamentally federal character of the Constitution came from more conventional quarters: political scientists of various kinds who accepted the position, unchallenged until recently, that the Constitution was unmistakably federal—indeed unambiguously so—but who had concluded that federalism was obsolete or unjust or both. This is not the place to go into the intellectual history of their views. Suffice it to say that they derived from two sources: Jacobin-Marxian ideas that, in political science jargon, were embodied in the conception of the reified state organized according to the center-periphery model, and managerial theories that emerged in the twentieth century as part of the "scientific management" approach to the organization and direction of large organizations.[3] For some, these two sources were combined to generate an unmitigated endorsement of centralization on all fronts: the presidency, constitutional law, government administration and finance, and the party system on the grounds of both justice and efficiency. For others, all that was sought were organizational changes whose consequences were centralizing, in the name of greater efficiency.

In the latter case, proposals for change endorsed federalism in principle even when undercutting it in practice. Perhaps the most extreme expression of the former view was William Riker's conclusion to his book, *Federalism*—that to believe in federalism was to believe in racism.[4] In any case, the answer of those people to the question, How federal is the Constitution? would be, Too federal for our times.

Since the presentation of those theories, the federal character of the Constitution has been reexamined by Vincent Ostrom, Martin Landau, and Heinz Eulau, among others, who have suggested that it is not only quite federal indeed but properly so in terms of political and administrative theory.[5] They not only see the federalism of the constitution as a "given" but also understand it as a precursor of what today is known as cybernetic theory. Like their colleagues in the previous grouping, all are more concerned in their analyses with the results of the Constitution than with the framers' intentions. In this respect they differ radically from Diamond and Crosskey.

The argument in this chapter is in line with the work of Diamond and the last group of political scientists. It departs from Diamond in its emphasis on the authentically federal character of the Constitution, suggesting that concentration on European philosophical sources alone is misleading—that biblical-Reformation-Puritan religious/theological sources were at least as important, if not more so, in shaping the framers' understanding of federalism.

The Basis of the Argument

Several points must be made at the outset:

1. The Constitution was written by a committee.
2. It was written as a political document, not as a legal contract.
3. As such, its terminology reflects current fashion as well as precise usage and strives for ambiguity where that was deemed politically necessary.
4. The framers of the Constitution drew upon more than one major source of ideas for their understanding of federalism.
5. *The Federalist*, valuable as it is as a work of political thought and exposition of the Constitution, is not the whole commentary on the subject.

Contrary to the fashion—or to wishful thinking—among certain schools of constitutional interpretation, there is no "founder" in the American constitutional founding. The document was truly the product of a committee—perhaps the best committee ever assembled, but still a committee. Moreover, it was a broadly based committee, representative of a wide range of views regarding the appropriate regime for the fledgling United States of America (a strong name applied to a relatively weak confederation of states). The convention committee included people as different as Alexander Hamilton (whose role as constitutional interpreter was more important than his role in the convention itself), who wanted as strong a unitary state as he could get, and George Mason, who did not really want to change the Articles of Confederation in other than marginal ways. All the evidence points to a wide spectrum of views with regard to federalism, which converged by both necessity and inclination toward the honestly federal Connecticut compromise (of which more below).

Although the legal profession was nominally overrepresented in Philadelphia, it is common knowledge that legal training has been a major gateway into politics in American civil society at least since the beginning of the eighteenth century. The men at Philadelphia were political leaders—politicians, if you will—above all else. They were engaged in the greatest of political exercises, the design and construction of a regime, and they were political artisans of the highest order. The business of the members of the convention was the business of politics, the judicious mixture of fidelity to principle and felicitous compromise. Artful use of language is a major means of combining the two. Thus the language of the Constitution is crystal clear where possible and ambiguous where necessary, and the document must be read in that spirit. Nevertheless, until our own generation, one thing of which there was no doubt was that the Constitution articulated a truly federal system of government. Even the opponents of its ratification, who held (as Diamond did 180 years later) that the term "federal" when applied to regimes properly applies to what we today call confederations, never challenged the federal character of the new regime after the adoption of the Bill of Rights.

The federalism of the Constitution was crystal clear, just as the division and sharing of powers was left ambiguous. For men like Hamilton, the opportunities for centralization offered by the Constitution's ambiguity on the division of powers may have been the difference in their willingness to accept its federalism; and the same may have been true for those on the opposite side of the matter. Thus Americans were bequeathed what Woodrow Wilson later described as the "cardinal question of American politics." Crosskey's work is extraordinarily valuable in helping us understand eighteenth-century usages and hence what was clear to the framers and what was left ambiguous, but I believe he is wrong on the contract issue.[6]

Twentieth-century students of the Constitution, usually relying totally on *The Federalist* and selected Anti-Federalist publications, have concluded that the framers of the Constitution were more or less exclusively products of classical education, of Hobbesian-Lockean political science, and of Enlightenment philosophy. No one would deny the existence of this "line of tradition" as a major factor in the founding of the United States of America, but there was another line of tradition actively represented in the founding as well—the biblical-Reformed-Puritan tradition.

Both traditions address the idea and practice of federalism. The first tradition did indeed understand federalism as confederation—a strictly political affair that involved a permanent league of states in which sovereignty, indivisible by its nature, remained with the constituent units. The second, however, came to federalism through theology—their theology was known as federal theology, from *foedus*, "covenant," referring to the grounding of all human relationships in the original covenant between God and man described in the Bible and in subsequent subsidiary pacts. By the mid-eighteenth century, this tradition viewed federalism in theopolitical terms. Its federalism was not bound by classical notions of the polis, the perfectly complete polity that could at best be leagued with others; it functioned within the biblical framework of constituent polities held together by a shared common law and institutions—a concept much more like the federalism that emerged from the Constitutional Convention.[7]

The Biblical-Reformed-Puritan tradition of federalism was spread throughout British North America, but in particular it took root and became the dominant tradition in New England. Connecticut was the first North American polity to be founded on fully federal principles, religious and political. It was literally a federation of four original towns, subsequently expanded. The constitution of that federation, the Fundamental Orders of Connecticut (1639), is a full statement of the tradition from its biblical base onward. One hundred and fifty years after the founding of Connecticut, its sons, heirs to a long federalist tradition, proposed the Connecticut compromise and saved the Philadelphia convention.

In a paper prepared for the Workshop on Covenant and Politics of the Center for the Study of Federalism, Donald Lutz demonstrated the power and ubiquity of this Biblical-Reformed-Puritan tradition in the writing and adoption of the Constitution.[8] He, with his mentor Charles Hyneman, explored all the known political writings of Americans in the era. As part of his analysis, he enumerated the sources cited in connection with that process.[9] While *The Federalist* relies exclusively on classical sources (a point of great significance in others' analyses of the work), overall Lutz found that the Bible was by far the most-cited source.[10] Indeed, the book of Deuteronomy alone, with its discussion of the Mosaic constitution for Israel, is cited more than any other source.

Lutz's work (and that of students of eighteenth-century political history) throws an entirely different light on the subject, showing that we can no longer assume the Constitution is solely a product of Locke and the Enlightenment. Perhaps if *The Federalist* had been written to persuade New Englanders or Scotch-Irish Presbyterians (instead of already-secularized New Yorkers, with their individualistic political culture), its authors might have turned to biblical sources as part of their polemic.

That is why *The Federalist* cannot be considered the sole authoritative commentary on the Constitution. Great as it is, its authors had more than one ax to grind. At the same time others also wrote, preached, and argued the constitutional issues. Diamond, relying exclusively on *The Federalist*, could properly conclude that Publius pulled some sleight of hand in appropriating the term "federal" for the new Constitution, but for the people of Connecticut and the rest of the Calvinists in America, Publius was hardly changing definitions in midstream.

It is ironic, then, that the campaign for ratification of the Constitution did bring about a reversal of definitions. If "federal" meant confederation for so many Americans before 1787, it came to mean federation after 1789. Yet just as it had a broader meaning earlier, so does it continue to have a broader meaning today.

Federalism continues to be one of the most important issues of the American political system. Indeed, in our time it has become one of the most important political issues throughout the world. Over three-quarters of the human race now live within federal systems or systems utilizing federal arrangements. Yet federalism, however important, is one of those issues that have all too often fallen under the rubric of a subjective MEGO—*Time* journalese for "my eyes glaze over," what that magazine's editorial staff writes across boring copy destined for the wastebasket. The origins of American federalism as we know it are to be found in the institution of a constitutional process that not only was crucial for the history of the United States of America, but was also crucial in demonstrating that there could be constitutional change through procedures other than violent revolution and abandonment of the principles of democratic republicanism.

The result of that process, the United States Constitution of 1787, today is the cornerstone of the American polity. This was not always or immediately the case. For example, George Mason, the architect of Virginia's constitutional tradition, was not pleased with the results of what he played a major role in initiating. His critique of the results of the 1787 Constitutional Convention, while in my opinion ultimately wrong—that is to say, the notion of rejecting the constitution drafted in 1787 would not have served the American people in good stead—has many important elements that we should keep before us as we move into the third century of the American federal union. Many elements in that critique have turned out to be correct. George Mason did have the foresight to see dangers that lay ahead, dangers that to some extent have been realized. Even if Americans continue to prefer the results the American people chose rather than the result he wished them to choose, they can learn from his critique.[11]

A Federalist Rejection of Federation

We must recall that George Mason was an Anti-Federalist who was for federalism. We have noted the brilliant stroke of political genius that led the Federalists to appropriate the term in 1787, so that George Mason—who considered himself far more of a federalist than they—became known as an Anti-Federalist. Realizing that George Mason saw himself as a federalist, that his critique was not against federalism but against a constitution he saw as undermining federalism, makes it very important for us not only to understand his critique, but to learn something about federalism by virtue of the fact that he could legitimately consider himself a federalist as much as could the Federalists.

George Mason was a federalist who opposed federation. He was for confederation. George Mason rejected federation for federalist reasons. He thought that it would bring too much consolidation of government—that it would create too strong a general government, covering too large a territory to preserve what he understood to be proper republican government and the attendant political and civil rights of the citizens. In considering confederation a proper form of federalism, he suggested that federalism was not simply what we take it for granted as being in the United States today. Americans today assume that federalism is what the United States is. Of course that is one kind of federalism, a federation. It may even be the best kind; but it is not the only kind.

When George Mason first raised his objections to the Constitution of 1787, the term federal referred to what we call confederation. Indeed, in *The Federalist* Madison had to refer to the new government being proposed as "partly federal and partly national"—national meaning consolidated—for that reason. But the Federalists knew that Americans were committed to federalism; they were committed to the federal principle. They already knew that whatever union was formed would have to be based upon some variety of federalism, so they seized the term for themselves. They took this creature that they had invented, which they refer to elsewhere in *The Federalist* as a compound republic—in other words, compounded of constituent units—and called it federal, thus seizing the term for themselves.[12]

What Is Federalism?

Conventional accounts of American history treat confederation and federation as two very different ways of dealing with the problem of political organization. Indeed, within the limited context of American history, this approach can be understood as reflecting the sense of profound transformation brought about by the Constitution of 1787. In a large sense, however, the American experience shows that federation and confederation are two species of the same genus—federalism—each seeking in its own way to combine liberty with appropriately effective government. Today there are actually six or seven different species of federalism functioning in the world (table 7.1).

If these different species of federalism exist, we should know something about what they have in common—what differentiates them from other forms or genera of government as well as what differentiates them from each other. When we find out what it is that federation and confederation and the other species of federalism share, we will understand the essence of federalism and know what each species must preserve and translate into the realities of everyday political and governmental life if we are to achieve the goals for which federalism was designed.

In a word, federalism has to do with the combination of self-rule and shared rule.[13] It combines political entities that desire to continue to rule themselves but also want to share in an enduring political community. For those who follow the teachings of the Bible, Hobbes, Locke, and other classic natural rights theorists, all legitimate civil society is federal—that is to say, is constituted by its members, who have covenanted or compacted with each other to form a body politic while preserving their respective integrities as individuals, so that they rule themselves

Table 7.1 Taxonomy of Compound Political Structures

Political	Economic	Religious	Principal Characteristics
Union	Multidivision corporation	Episcopal church polity	Clearly bounded territorial constituent units regain "municipal" powers concentrated in the common government
Consociation	Guild system	Ethnic congregations (in centralized or heirarchical church)	Nonterritorial constituent units share power concentrated in common overarching government
Fueracy	Conglomerate		Constituent units empowered through bilateral charters concluded with overarching government
Federation	Economic community	Presbyterian church polity	Strong self-governing constituent units linked within strong but limited overarching government
	Conglomerate, if the constituent units are represented in the overall management structure		
Federacy	Customs union	Autocephalic church (linked polity of larger hierarchical church)	Asymmetrical permanent linkage between two self-governing units, with the larger having specific powers denied the smaller, in exchange for which it retains internal self-rule. Bonds can be dissolved only by mutual consent

Associated state			Same as federacy but bonds can be dissolved unilaterally by either party
Condominium	Joint stock company		Joint rule or control by two units over a third or over some common territory or enterprise
Confederation	Common market	Congregational union or federation	Strong self-governing constituent units permanently linked by loose, limited-purpose common government
League	Free trade area	Congregational convention	Loose but permanent linkage for limited purposes without common government but with some joint body or secretariat
Interjurisdictional functional authorities	Joint enterprises	Board of missions	Joint or common entities organized the constituting units to undertake specific tasks

---

while at the same time being a part of civil society and functioning together to share rule collectively. It is this particular characteristic that lies at the root of any theory of federalism. Any theory that purports to be federal yet does not relate to this effort to combine self-rule and shared rule is fallacious or inadequate.[14]

To some extent federalism is a bit like trying to have one's cake and eat it too. Martin Diamond used to give what he called the Jimmy Durante definition of federalism. In the movie classic "The Man Who Came to Dinner," Durante comes to visit the central figure in the movie—the man who keeps breaking his leg in the country home of his quasi-friends outside New York City—and in his madcap way he sits down at the piano and starts to bang out a song whose opening line is "Did you ever have the feeling that you wanta go and the feeling that you wanta stay?" That is federalism. On one hand you want to go, to be independent. On the other hand you want to stay; you want to be a part of something larger than yourself.

A second element in any federal theory is that federalism involves noncentralization—the constitutional distribution of powers among multiple centers of authority held together through some constitutional vehicle that constitutionalizes noncentralization. In essence, authority is to be divided while power is to be shared. Again, that is an aspect of self-rule and shared rule.

Federalism is not the same as decentralization. In a decentralized political system there is a center that decides what is to be centralized and what is to be decentralized; therefore, what is decentralized can be recentralized by decision of the center. Federalism is a model for noncentralization that constitutionally guarantees there shall be no single center. On this Federalists and Anti-Federalists were agreed. The federal government was to be a framing institution, not a single power center. The states were to be the constituents of the federal system—the United States of America (the name is a federal name; we say it so easily that we do not stop to think about it)—not the peripheries around the center.

The founders' terminology reflected this. Take the matter of the seat of the federal government. The term capital implies the top of the power pyramid or the center of power. Washington was not described as the nation's capital until the twentieth century. It was referred to as the seat of the federal or general government—the latter was the preferred term—just as Americans still talk about county seats and refer to the building housing the seat of state government as the statehouse. There is a great difference between the seat of government, which is one place within a network of equal places, and a capital, which reigns at the top or occupies the center.

Third, federalism has to do primarily with relationships and only secondarily with structures. Because of what happened in the nineteenth-century discussions of American federalism surrounding slavery, states' rights, secession, and segregation—when federalism was reduced to a careful and almost hairsplitting analysis of what was legally possible under the United States Constitution and what was not—Americans became preoccupied with federalism as structure. However justified tactically, that was a conceptual error whose consequences were to mislead subsequent generations down to the present.

What constitutes the legitimate exercise of federal power and what is a legitimate exercise of state power are important questions. I do not mean to diminish or denigrate them. But treated as they were then, they remained at the level of structural considerations. Structure is very important, but as a way of expressing relationships, not for its own sake.

Mason versus Madison: The Confederalist Argument and the Federalist Response

George Mason was fearful of the proposed federal constitution because he thought it would so change the relationship between the states and the federal government by establishing direct links between the federal government and the individual citizens that it would reduce liberty. His opponents argued that it is precisely this change in relationships that was necessary if liberty were to survive. James Madison, Mason's northern Virginia neighbor and his great opponent on this issue, argued that only in an extended republic, where the pettiness of individual states is somehow moderated by the multiplicity of interests that come together within a federal framework, will liberty be preserved. Mason's position was that creating such an extended republic would rob the small republics of their power to foster community; and without community, liberty cannot be preserved.

Theirs was a historic debate; the perennial contention about relationships and the structures that flow from them. It is a debate, I would submit, about federal democracy.

Though Madison's position won, the American system that emerged from that confrontation is a federal democracy in which something of George Mason is preserved as well. Indeed, for the first 145 years after the adoption of the Constitution of 1787, Mason often seemed to have won over Madison in fact, if not in theory, as his approach to federalism animated the relationships between the states and the federal government within the formal framework established by James Madison. Why? Because the relationships were more important than the structures.

Different Models of Polity

Today political scientists and others are attracted to mapping all political phenomena on continua—there is a continuum for everything. Among them is a centralization-decentralization continuum, with federalism at one end and a centralized unitary government on the other. Toward the middle are decentralized unitary and centralized federal governments, all on one continuum. This kind of conceptualization is one of the reasons the United States is having trouble maintaining federalism today. When one starts with an erroneous model, one gets an erroneous result.

Since federalism is quite different from decentralization, it is not at all on the same continuum. This difference can be demonstrated most easily when we contrast federal polities with other forms of political organization. In all the history of study, speculation, and empirical research about political systems, political philosophers and political scientists have come up with essentially three models of polity: the hierarchical model, the organic model, and the federal model. From Plato and Aristotle or the Bible before them right down to the latest work published in the journals of political science, implicitly or explicitly we find those three models of political organization and governance.

In the very first essay in *The Federalist*, Publius presents the constitutional ratification issue to the American people by stating that it is given to them to determine whether they shall have a government established by "force," "accident," or "reflection and choice." "Force" is a polemical way of identifying a hierarchical system, since such systems are essentially established by force. Political philosophers and scientist alike see hierarchical systems as having been established first by conquest, whereby the conqueror imposes a power pyramid on a community or on a body politic. "Accident" is a polemical reference to polities that have developed organically—in other words, whatever happened to happen, happened, and the people get the system that results. Finally, there are those political systems that have been established by the deliberate acts—"reflection and choice"—of those who are to be the citizens of the polity, who come together and by some act of covenanting or compacting establish a body politic. This is the highest form of political constitution according to *The Federalist*. There are various combinations and permutations and variations of the three models, but there are only three models.

The Hierarchical Model

The classic example of the hierarchical model is ancient Egypt.[15] It is no accident that the pharaohs built pyramids to mark and commemorate their persons,

Theory of Federal Democracy

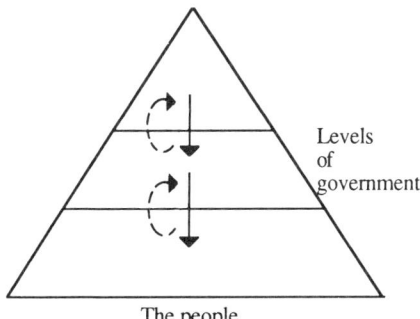

Figure 7.1 The hierarchical model.

because the Egyptian system was a power pyramid (fig. 7.1). The pharaoh was on top; indeed, he was a god or demigod. He governed through a hierarchy of control, and the whole pyramid rested on the Egyptian people. That is the way of power pyramids. France, a modern democratic republic, is a good example of the hierarchical model. It is a state that was established by conquest as the Count of Paris expanded his domains and, accordingly, ruled hierarchically from Paris, the capital.

Whenever people talk about the American system as a system of levels of government, they have implicitly adopted the power pyramid model. Nobody talked that way about the United States in the nineteenth century; that terminology was not introduced until well into the twentieth century, after students of politics began to absorb theories derived from traditional management and organization theory, with its hierarchical emphasis on chains of command. Management as we know it, modern management, is derived from the military models developed by the French and the Prussians, which were hierarchical. Woodrow Wilson, father of the study of public administration in the United States, based his great essay "The Study of Public Administration" on the German model. So too did his colleagues in the late nineteenth century—for good reason, because if one wants a managerial system, there is something to be said on behalf of that structure. But those ideas were then transposed from good management sense to a kind of managerialism that saw the whole world as properly organized in that way, and

Americans began to talk about the United States as having levels of government: the federal government on the top, the states as the middle level, the local governments as the lower level. Implicitly, there were the people back underneath the pyramid again, just as in the days of ancient Egypt.

This model has given us a terminology that rolls off our tongues today; we do not even think about it. Yet it is a model that challenges the very fundaments

Figure 7.2   The American system of government.

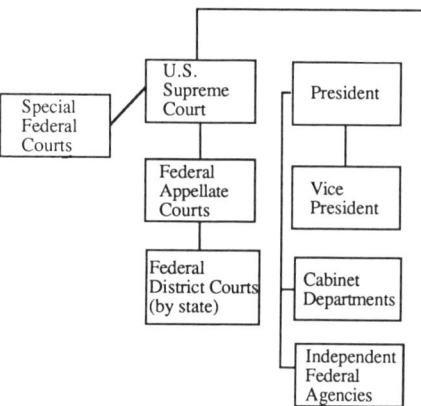

Theory of Federal Democracy   155

of federal democracy. If we take a nineteenth-century textbook on American government and look at a chart of how the American system is organized, we find something like figure 7.2. Notice that the people are on top; the United States Constitution is the mediating instrument between the people and their institutions; and the federal and state governments are presented as equals. Look at a government textbook today, and what do we see? That power pyramid: the federal

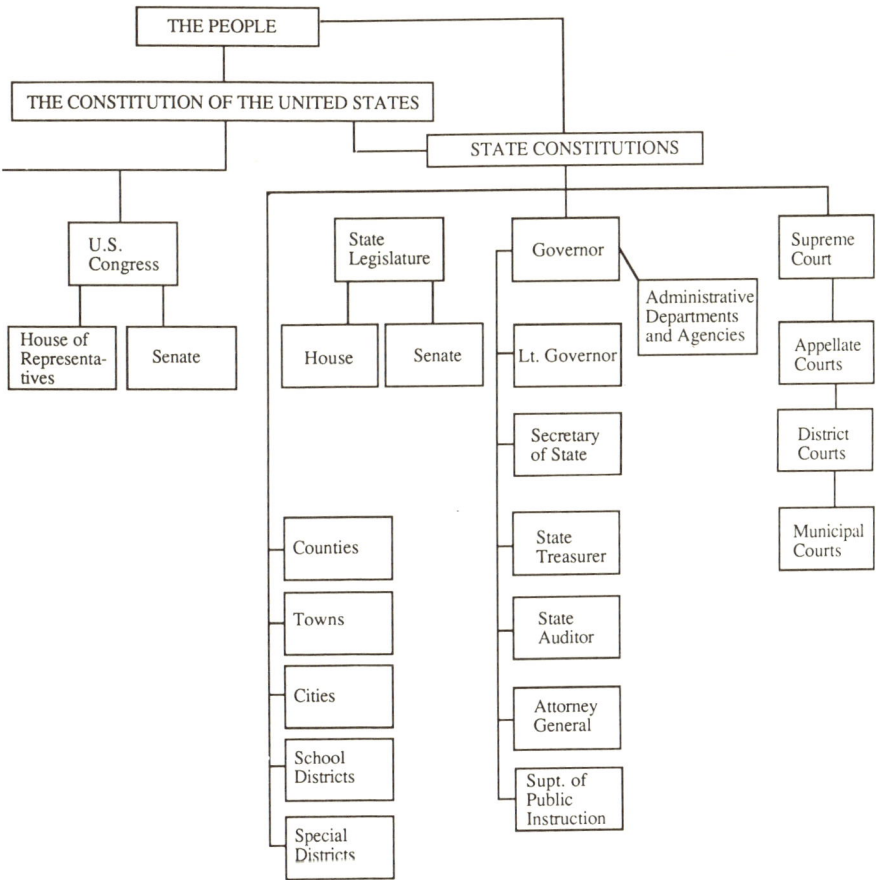

government on top, the states in the middle, local governments underneath. The charts never mention the people or the Constitution. The people are there, all right—but in that hierarchical structure, the Constitution is hardly there at all.

Today we know the consequences of that reconceptualization. In the 1960s and early 1970s, we had to contend with the imperial presidency. That was only natural. If there is a government pyramid, there has to be an apex. If there was to be somebody at the apex of an American pyramid, it was going to be the president; he had become the center of attention, the focus of all the media. And so Americans began to believe that not only was the federal government superior to the states, but the president was superior to Congress. Presidents began to believe their press releases. So John F. Kennedy and Lyndon Jonson got the United States into the Vietnam War by presidential manipulation, and Richard Nixon gave Americans Watergate by exercising what he called "executive privilege." These were only two of the most visible and painful consequences of the imperial presidency, following the patterns of the hierarchical model.

The Organic Model

The classic example of the organic model is to be found in ancient Mesopotamia, whence it spread to Greece and Rome.[16] It was reflected in Mesopotamian religion, in which the gods were conceived as members of a common council, an elite governing the universe. Each had his or her favorite people, whose task it was to support their special god or goddess. The gods were at the center of the universe, and the people around the periphery. This system was a little more open than that of ancient Egypt, in the sense that it was an oligarchy instead of an autocracy; there was no single person or god at the apex—they were all sitting around the same table, as it were. Marduk, the senior god, who became known as Zeus in Greek and Jupiter in Roman mythology, presided at the head of the table, but he did not sit at the top of a pyramid. Thus the center-periphery model (fig. 7.3) is that of classic Western polytheism.

Britain, particularly England, is a good example of the organic model. It developed by expanding its territory with the merger of petty kingdoms through marriage, creating a new center within which the elites gathered, with each having a share in the larger whole. The organic model is constructed so that the

Theory of Federal Democracy

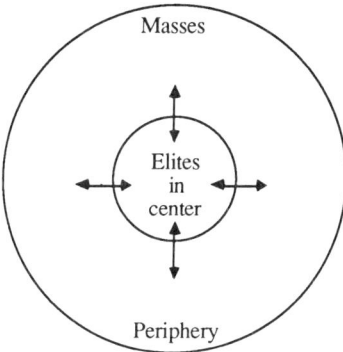

Figure 7.3   The center-periphery model.

center makes the crucial political decisions. In Britain Parliament (which technically includes king, Lords, and Commons) is the sovereign center, as per Walter Bagehot's classic description: if Parliament chose to legislate a man into a woman or a woman into a man, it would have the sovereign power to do so. (This was said before doctors could do that surgically.) Parliament is representative of the estates and territories of Britain.

Over time, as England developed organically, access to and participation in the center was expanded. The introduction of representative government in both France and Britain institutionalized what became, in time, the democratic republican dimensions of both polities, but France still remained a pyramid and Britain a center with a periphery. In Britain, if you are not in London you are nowhere, and in France, if you are not in Paris you are nowhere. Today the peripheries are represented democratically in the center, but it is still the center that decides. We have a current example of this before us. Prime Minister Margaret Thatcher has decided to reduce the power of local government in Britain. If she can carry a majority in Parliament, she can do so. There are no constitutional barriers, regardless of the opposition of the local authorities.

The Federal Model

How would we describe the federal model if it is not a power pyramid or a center and periphery? The federal model is best described as a matrix (fig. 7.4). Think

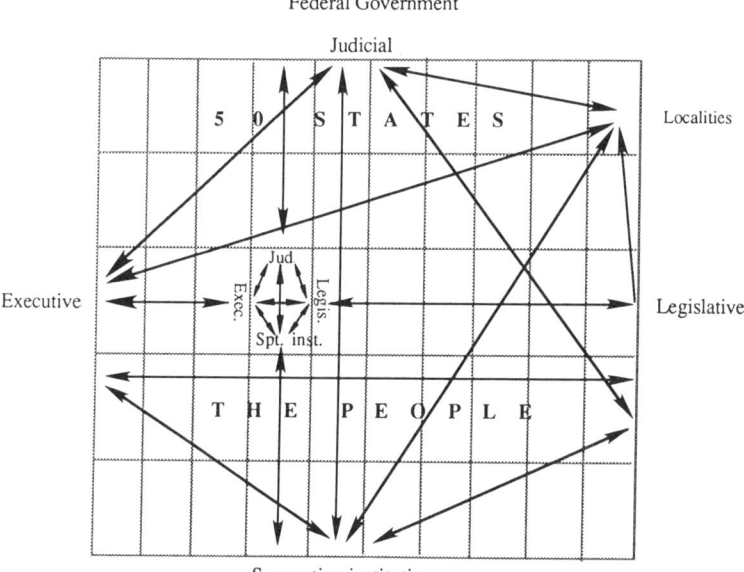

Figure 7.4 The federal model.

of it as a big square or rectangle for which the federal, or general, government is the framing institution constituted by its basic constituent units, which may be further divided into local governments. What we have is a congeries of arenas—boxes inside boxes, of different sizes, smaller and larger.

What does this suggest? In a power pyramid, inevitably, the higher one is, the more important. In a center-periphery model, the more central one is, the more important. In contrast, smaller or larger does not alone dictate importance. Sometimes small is more beautiful, sometimes large. The federal matrix suggests that for certain purposes smaller arenas are more important and for others larger arenas are, but that smaller or larger does not a priori determine or define importance. Hence it is in the federal matrix that it is possible to develop the best combination of self-rule and shared rule, of having one's cake and eating it too, of wanting to go and wanting to stay. It offers the best possibility for the synthesis of George Mason's argument that without community there is no liberty and

James Madison's argument that without an extended republic where multiple competing interests can prevent polarization of civil society into two classes, liberty cannot survive.

In a federal matrix, the largest arena is designed to undertake those tasks and protect those rights that must be addressed collectively to achieve and preserve the purposes of the polity, while smaller arenas can provide appropriate scale or community. That again is the essence of any federal arrangement and is at the heart of federal theory.

The matrix, then, is both a matrix of power and the matrix of arenas. Just as the hierarchical model finds expression in our time in theories of administration and management which emphasize the importance of the chain of command, and the center-periphery model finds expression in theories of elite-and-mass, which emphasize the necessity to concentrate power in certain elites in order to govern effectively and to deal with the masses, the federal model finds expression in cybernetic theories of human organization. Cybernetic theory states that the best way to organize life is through multiple channels, intelligent redundancy, fail-safe mechanisms, and cells linked together so that not every cell has to function perfectly for the system to work. Martin Landau, one of the leading professors of public administration of our time, has suggested that the founding fathers two hundred years ago anticipated cybernetic theory and that the federal model is, indeed, the governmental equivalent of a cybernetic model.[17]

Take another look at the matrix. Think of it as a grid through which political and governmental power courses like electricity. For some purposes the people load certain elements in the grid with greater power, and for others they load different elements. In the United States, foreign affairs and defense are loaded on that element that frames the whole, the federal government. The heavy loadings for education are in the local arenas, and those for highway construction are in the state arenas. These loadings can be shifted in a variety of ways, depending on what is more likely to achieve the various goals the publics in a particular system set for themselves. High-level career patterns and salaries reflect this distribution. The pinnacle of power in highway administration is to become head of the state highway department in one of the great states of the Union. The most important positions in elementary and secondary educational administration are those held by the superintendents of the major school systems—and not necessarily the big-city school systems; the superintendent of an important suburban school system may at times be at the top of the profession.

This matrix is federal because it is established by the coming together of individuals or individual polities as equals to establish the political order. From the beginning, the federal model involves the active consent of equals. Classically, a covenant involves both separating and uniting. Indeed, in the Semitic languages of ancient Western Asia, where the idea of covenanting first emerged, making a covenant is referred to as "cutting a covenant." In the Bible, ancient covenanting involved a ritual in which the parties binding themselves took an animal, sacrificed it by cutting it in half, and then passed between the two halves, after which they would bind the pieces back together. In other words, the cutting is to assure that both parties recognize their separate integrities as partners to the covenant, and the binding is to demonstrate that they are partners and are truly linked.[18] Federalism involves covenanting and the partnership that flows from it. It is a model in which people, institutions, or polities covenant or compact together to form a large whole in which their own equality and integrity are preserved, along with the establishment of the new framing entity. Federalism, in the last analysis, involves a linkage between this covenant and the partnership it creates.

Americans know of this linkage from their historical and constitutional experience, even if only subconsciously. It is what united George Mason and James Madison as federalists and republicans. Both Mason and Madison accepted this fundamental theory, even as they diverged in recommending how it should be applied. Mason's critique, as I have suggested, was that the only federalism that would work to preserve the values of federalism would be small-republic federalism or confederation. Only where there could be face-to-face community or something close to it could the civil and political rights of citizens be preserved. Otherwise, there would be federal encroachment on local liberties, willy-nilly. If the largest arena was too large, it would lose touch. If it lost touch, it would be transformed, sooner or later, into a power pyramid; that has been the history and the fate of so much of the human race.

Madison argued differently. Both were right. As we look at the more than two hundred years of experience with federalism in the United States, we can see how right Mason has been in so many ways and how we need to reform the system as it works to regain what we have lost through overemphasis of the federal government's role. Americans who have been born into the way of James Madison and who genuinely believe that, on balance, what he proposed was necessary and right must also be aware of George Mason's critique of the United States Constitution. We must try to include in the substance of the federal system those elements that Mason wanted us to consider as much as the elements that concerned Madison.

8

THE CONSTITUTION AND THE BLESSINGS OF LIBERTY

The Preamble of the Constitution of the United States lists six ends to which the Constitution is addressed: union, justice, domestic tranquillity, defense, general welfare, and liberty. The last is presented most fully—to whit, to "secure the blessings of liberty to ourselves and our posterity." Taken together, those six ends define the goals of republican government. To best achieve those ends the American founders recognized that simple republicanism was not enough, that what was required was a compound republic, what we today call a federal system. The history of the founding generation of the United States of America is in no small measure a history of finding the way to such a compound republic—what the Preamble refers to as a "more perfect union"—the first item on the list.

For the founders, republicanism meant popular government, what Daniel Webster and Abraham Lincoln later defined as "government of the people, by the people, and for the people." Almost immediately most of them began to see that republicanism of that kind had to be democratic republicanism. Hence, once the Constitution was established, the thrust of the American political experience has been in the direction of strengthening the democratic aspects of the American compound republic.

Let us look once again at the six ends of the Preamble and read them as a list, placed in a certain order by design. I am not claiming that the framers deliberately

The Constitution and the Blessings of Liberty

did so. I simply do not know whether they did or not. But whatever their intention, what emerges is a certain hierarchy of ends. The first step in the achievement of the substantive ends is forming a more perfect union. That will make it possible to establish justice, which in turn will ensure domestic tranquillity. Domestic tranquillity makes it possible to provide for the common defense, and a country both tranquil and secure by definition promotes the general welfare at one level and can devote itself to further efforts to that end. The highest of these ends is not simply liberty but the blessings of liberty, which encompass justice, tranquillity, security, and welfare. The ends presented in the Preamble represent, in a sense, a rephrasing in greater detail of the ends presented in the Declaration of Independence—life, liberty, and the pursuit of happiness.

Union—a compound republic—is thus a means to larger ends, but so important a means that it becomes an end in itself. Lincoln emphasized this at the time of the Civil War when he spoke of " the constitution, the union, and the liberties of the people" and argued that it was first necessary to preserve the union in order to preserve the other two. Lincoln well understood that for Americans the blessings of liberty depended upon the more perfect union, that is to say, the compound republic.

Our task is to examine the relation between liberty and American federal democracy as reflected in the Constitution of the United States. We begin with two fundamental questions: What kind of liberty is to be fostered in order to bring blessings? And how is it best fostered? We must begin our inquiry by understanding that, as Donald Lutz has persuasively argued, the Constitution of the United States is an incomplete document in that it rests on the constitutions of the individual states.[1] Thus any consideration of the larger question of the Constitution and liberty is connected with the more specific question of this chapter because the United States is a compound republic and its constitutional system is built accordingly.

What Kind of Liberty?

The American founders certainly did not confuse liberty with anarchy. Their writings are peppered with comparisons between the two whose conclusions were unequivocal. Indeed, fear of anarchy was one of the major propellants toward constitutionalism for most of the American leadership, Federalist and Anti-Federalist alike. This fear was enhanced by the very fact that they were making a republican revolution and that historically both revolutions and republics had been noted for bringing about anarchy.

Just as they rejected anarchy, so too did they reject natural liberty. Elsewhere in this volume, I have discussed natural liberty as one of the basic myths of the American experience, the idea that in this new world of nature, humans are also freed from the shackles of society to become "natural men."[2] For the most part, the hidden or not so hidden assumptions behind the myth of natural liberty were that human society is corrupting while human nature is unequivocally good, and therefore humans must be emancipated from the chains of society so their better natures can flourish unimpeded. Although this myth was presented most systematically by Jean-Jacques Rousseau, it can be found back at the very beginning of the age of the discovery and exploration of the Western Hemisphere. There were those who saw the Native Americans as natural men and hence as living happily in paradise. It was not difficult for them to take the next step and to hope that Europeans arriving on the shores of the New World could emancipate themselves from the bonds of society and regain their true natures as well.

A variant of this myth with a somewhat less optimistic view of human nature accepted that humans were not totally good by nature but saw in the human confrontation with the challenges of nature the true testing ground for "real men." This version of the myth allowed first barbarism and even savagery, treating them as part of the process of winnowing the wheat from the chaff or separating the gold from the dross. Perhaps the archetypal expression of this view was to be found in the myths of the voyageurs and the mountain men, individuals who set out for the wilderness, leaving civilization far behind, and had to survive by honing their skills as men. Failure to do so almost inevitably meant death at the hands of nature, while success produced the hero who, by being in harmony with nature, rose above the constraints of human law to a loftier morality. This myth developed into the larger myth of the western hero, who, tempered in the wilderness, could then come back to civilization to restore good and do justice beyond the limits of the law.[3]

In the twentieth century, after the land frontier was closed and opportunities no longer existed for natural men to venture forth into vast stretches of truly wild nature, the myth of the natural man took two turns. For the first half of the century, fliers who were aviation pioneers or test pilots were viewed as carrying on the tradition of the natural man. In a sense, Chuck Yeager and his colleagues were the last of these natural men. After them, as Tom Wolfe points out in *The Right Stuff*, came the astronauts who were more like pampered gladiators.[4] (His book is a wonderful study in contrast and conflict between the "natural man" test pilots of Edwards Air Force Base and the indulged astronauts.)

More recently there has been a reversion to the first variant of the myth, with individuals in society seeking to return to nature not by confronting the wilderness but by dropping social conventions and "doing what comes naturally"—"letting it all hang out." The first represented a mild expression of the attack on surviving Victorian conventions at the time of World War II, which was part of the move to loosen the forms of society in the first postwar generation, whereas the latter was one of the mottoes of the student revolt of the 1960s, which sought to abandon social convention altogether.

I repeat, natural liberty was not what the founders had in mind. Even Jefferson, who was much closer to assuming the natural goodness of man than the vast majority of his colleagues, believed that people had to live together in community in order to develop civilization, which, if simple enough, was a good thing. Others, John Adams for example, drawing upon their Puritan heritage, had no confidence in the innate goodness of humans, even if they no longer believed in their innate depravity. They could see the "old Adam" in all people and viewed their task as building a political order that would contain those human passions that led to depravity and, where possible, channel them into more productive lines of activity, thereby strengthening what Lincoln later called "the better angels of human nature."

One of the basic tensions underlying the American experience is between the myth of the natural man and the countermyth of fallen man, brought to American shores by the Puritans. The Puritan view was summed up by the old couplet taught to children in Massachusetts schools, "In Adam's fall, we sinnéd all." For some, this view was fully Calvinist in its emphasis on total human depravity except for the few elect, chosen of God by predestination. For others "the old Adam" was less than total. Rather, humans had to know that they were swept by passions that led them to evil inclinations and that those inclinations were all too easily translated into behavior.

In the Puritans' view, humans had to be curbed by social bonds, not released from them. Rather than viewing nature as redeeming and society as corrupting, they saw nature as corrupt and a properly religious society as having the potential, if not to redeem (since only God could do that), at least to keep corruption within bounds. Thus the laws of Massachusetts and other Puritan commonwealths provided that no citizen should be allowed to settle beyond the reach of civilization, lest he lapse into savagery. It was the obligation of the polity to enact legislation to preserve and strengthen morality and the task of the magistrates to enforce that legislation.

In a sense, the American Constitution was the product of a reconciliation of these two views, achieved in part through their synthesis. Rejecting both myths, the founders saw humans as mixed in their natures, having both good and bad inclinations. The difference between them was the difference between Jefferson and Adams, with some following Jefferson in expecting man to be infinitely perfectible if he lived under the right institutions, and others viewing man as being of limited perfectibility but capable of improvement through the right institutions. In both cases there was a convergence around the necessity for proper institutions. That is why Martin Diamond could refer to the American Revolution as "a revolution of sober expectations."[5]

What emerged out of all of this was an understanding of liberty as what, following John Winthrop and James Wilson, we may refer to as federal liberty. Federal liberty, in the modern sense, is the liberty to be a partner in establishing the covenant founding civil society and then the liberty to live according to the terms of the covenant. Both dimensions of the definition are important. Totalitarian societies, both religious and secular, have emphasized the second half alone. That is to say, in claiming their citizens are free people, they define freedom or liberty as the liberty to obey the rules of the church or polity, which are unilaterally imposed, in some cases in the name of God and in others in the name of some other transcendent historical authority, power, or force. True federal liberty requires that humans be partners in making the covenant defining right and wrong and the rules of the game that flow from that definition before they can be expected to live according to them, and that processes be provided for reexamining the terms of the covenant and, if necessary, changing the rules. Even in those cases where God is considered a partner or guarantor, that must be so. That is what constitutionalism is all about.

In the American political tradition, federal liberty has taken two forms. One, first enunciated by John Winthrop, deals with the relationship between individuals and civil society, and the other, first defined by James Wilson, deals with the relationship between the states and the federal government under the Constitution of the United States. Winthrop, one of the founders of Puritan Massachusetts, enunciated his famous doctrine of federal liberty in 1645:

> There is a two-fold liberty, natural (I mean as our nature is now corrupt) and civil or federal. The first is common to man with beasts and other creatures. By this, man, as he stands in relation to man simply, hath liberty to do what he lists; it is a liberty to evil as well as to good. This liberty is incompatible and inconsistent with authority and cannot endure the least restraint of the most just authority. The exercise and maintaining of this liberty makes men grow more evil and in time to be worse than brute beasts: *omnes sumus licentia deteriores*. This is that great enemy of truth and peace, that wild beast, which all of the ordinances of God are bent against, to restrain and subdue it. The other kind of liberty I call civil or federal; it may also be termed moral, in reference to the covenant between God and man, in the moral law, and the politic covenants and constitutions between men themselves. This liberty is the proper end and object of authority and cannot subsist without it; and it is a liberty to that only which is good, just and honest. This liberty you are to stand for, with the hazard (not only of your goods, but) of your lives if need be.[6]

Developed in the seventeenth century, Winthrop's full definition reflects a republican predemocratic understanding of the political order. Recognizing this, we still can draw upon its essence to understand the federal liberty of the individual in a democratic civil society.

James Wilson, one of the delegates to the Constitutional Convention from Pennsylvania, Scottish born and educated, was a product of the Scottish Enlightenment. In other words he came out of the same Reformed Protestant tradition as the Puritans, but he identified with its more secularized expression as developed in Scotland in the mid-eighteenth century. In defining the appropriate relationship between the states and the federal government, he drew upon the same concept of federal liberty for a secular setting. (Wilson himself was a believer who saw natural law as coming from God and at least partially revealed in the Bible.)

For Wilson, federal liberty was the means of sharing the attributes of sovereignty, with both the states and the federal government deriving their powers by delegation from the sovereign people through constitutional compacts in such a way that each remained an instrument of the people while at the same time checking the other. His argument was that just as individuals entering a political compact gained greater liberty by surrendering part of their natural rights in exchange for a limitation on the liberty of others to do them harm, so too did the constituent states gain more by surrendering part of their freedom of action to a general government in return for being partners in a larger whole. "Federal liberty then is the liberty to enter into a covenant or compact through which each party surrenders certain of its natural liberties in order to gain more from the new partnership created, to whose rules the parties are then obliged to follow."[7]

A complete definition of federal liberty requires a synthesis of Winthrop and Wilson to include the two dimensions of morality and self-interest. American constitutionalism rests upon that synthesis. This is not immediately apparent in reading the Constitution of the United States.

Two Constitutional Traditions

It is well accepted that one of the great goals of the Constitution was to establish a large commercial republic. This, indeed, is the essence of the Federalist theory of constitutionalism. Commerce is presented as an alternative to republican virtue as a means of maintaining republican government. Self-interest rightly understood is presented as the motivation for the self-restraint necessary to maintain republican government, and "ambition countering ambition" (in the words of *The Federalist*) is the basis for controlling the excesses of human energy. The original Constitution provides substantive protection for only a very few liberties, relying instead on the procedural guarantees built into the system of government it establishes. The protected liberties are of three kinds: those involving the physical liberty of the person, such as the right of habeas corpus; those involving the freedom of the marketplace, such as the guarantees of the right of contract and protections of patents and copyrights and provision for a uniform rule of bankruptcy; and those emancipating individuals from the effects of family and religious ties, such as the bans on bills of attainder and religious tests for office. The Bill of Rights further extended this effort to use the federal constitution to protect individual rights and liberties, with nine of the ten amendments being exclusively devoted to that subject.

All told, the federal constitution is oriented toward creating and protecting a national marketplace, both political and economic, and toward protecting that marketplace and access to it by all citizens as individuals. This thrust has been continued in almost every subsequent constitutional development, whether by formal amendment or United States Supreme Court interpretation. The Civil War amendments were designed to open both aspects of the marketplace to blacks and, by extension, other nonwhite groups. Most of the other amendments deal with terms of suffrage and are also designed to extend access to the marketplace—to women and, most recently, to older teenagers. To participate in the marketplace, one need only subscribe to the rules of the game, which, in the federal constitution, are political rather than moral. The Constitution goes so far as to specify that no religious test shall be used in connection with federal officeholding and that what is required is that every state, as well as the federal government, maintain a republican form of government.

Were the federal constitution to stand alone, one could conclude that morality and government were entirely separated in the new American constitutional order. This is not, in fact, the case. Since both the federal constitution and the government it creates are incomplete and need the states to be complete, we must also look at the state constitutions to see what kind of liberty they are committed to protecting and fostering. Certainly in the revolutionary period most of the state constitutions were designed to foster commonwealths rather than marketplaces— that is, polities that were both republican and committed to a shared moral vision. It is not unfair to say that the federal constitution could emphasize individualism and the marketplace precisely because the founders could count upon the state constitutions to emphasize community and commonwealth.

The idea that a proper republic should be a commonwealth grew out of the Whig tradition developed in Britain and British North America in the late seventeenth century, which reached its apotheosis in the states at the time of the American Revolution. The original American state constitutions also followed the Whig model. It was only after the adoption of the federal constitution that there slowly developed a synthesis between the Federalist and Whig constitutional models that began to influence state constitutional development. Jacksonian ideas of democracy were democratic adaptations of Whiggism rather than deviations from it. It was only in the post–Civil War period that the synthesis began to reshape state constitutions, most particularly the constitutions of the newly admitted western states.[8]

Liberty, under the commonwealth model, was concerned not simply with individual rights but also with the preservation and fostering of community. Thus communal liberties, though never as important in the New World as in the Old, had a place within the commonwealth model along with individual liberties. The federal constitution, while making no such provision directly, tacitly recognized the importance of communal liberties by leaving the states free to protect and foster them as they pleased. The New England and southern states did so unequivocally. Even in matters of religion and state, Massachusetts and Connecticut went so far as to maintain established churches into the nineteenth century, and New Hampshire did not drop its last religious tests until the end of the Civil War generation. In other aspects of life, the New England states continued to use the authority and powers of government to maintain a certain moral order—where they can and where there is consensus, they still do. The western states settled by New Englanders reproduced a limited version of the New England pattern.

Until the Civil War, the southern states, whether original or new, were organized to maintain what Abolitionists called "slavocracy" and rule by the "slave power"—social systems resting on slavery and concentrating power in the hands of a plantation-centered elite. After the war and Reconstruction, the political systems of the southern states were used to reinstate as much of the old system as possible through "Jim Crow" segregation and disfranchisement of the freed slaves and their descendants. In the end, the revulsion of the majority of Americans against that system was a major factor in overturning the rights of the states to maintain their own social systems. As Abraham Lincoln repeatedly suggested, all Americans have had to pay dearly for the "original sin" of black slavery, and so it has been.

The Middle States, on the other hand, were already well on their way toward a redefinition of their commonwealths as marketplaces; hence the Federalist approach suited them. They, and especially the new states in the West settled by Middle Staters, were the first to embrace the Federalist model. Over time, more states moved away from clear-cut moral visions of their commonwealths, making that model even more attractive.

On the other hand, on those few occasions when it was tried, the federal constitution proved a very poor bulwark for commonwealth goals. The United States is simply too large and too diverse. Its worse failure was in connection with the prohibition of the consumption of alcoholic beverages, a moral goal written into the Constitution through the Eighteenth Amendment that had the effect of encouraging alcoholic consumption while at the same time promoting organized crime. Though it was repealed within half a generation, those negative aspects of its legacy are still with us. Federal inability to foster commonwealth does not lessen the importance of the commonwealth dimension in the states; if anything, the task of the states becomes even more important precisely because that task cannot be performed by the federal government. The latter has its own vital task in maintaining the marketplace.

How Is Liberty Best Fostered?

Thus the American political system and its constitutional tradition provide for the two great orientations of American political culture—marketplace and commonwealth—and the liberty associated with each through the maintenance of a compound republic—what we now call a federal system. The marketplace is the clue here. Federal liberty is best fostered through ordered rules of the game. These include fixed elections, separation of powers, guaranteed rights of access, due process, and federalism. Here it is not necessary to elaborate on these ordered rules of the game; the idea behind them should be clear. Fixed elections are necessary to ensure that the governors will always be responsible to and dependent upon the governed for their offices. Guaranteed rights of access ensure that the marketplace is kept open to all legitimate participants. Due process is necessary to maintain the people's standing in the marketplace and to adjudicate their claims upon each other and on the marketplace as a whole. Separation of powers is designed to reduce the concentration of power in any one individual or institution. Bicameralism is designed to provide the possibility of second thoughts in political decision making, to foster prudence, and to control enthusiasms.

Federal liberty is necessary to prevent the disasters of anarchy and the diseases of natural liberty. Federal liberty is possible without lapsing into totalitarian tyranny only when it is constitutionalized so that ordered rules are established by agreement among the participants in accordance with prudence and reason. As we all know, the founders believed that liberty could survive only if proper republican institutions were established to both contain and foster it. Federalism offers the means for combining the marketplace and the commonwealth, allowing for fostering both individual and communal liberties in appropriate ways.

Summarizing the Argument

The United States as a whole is built upon two contrasting conceptions of the political order, both of which can be traced back to the earliest settlement of the country. In the first, the political order is conceived as a marketplace in which the primary public relationships are the product of bargaining among individuals and groups acting out of self-interest. In the second, the political order is conceived to be a commonwealth—a state in which the whole people have an undivided interest—in which the citizens cooperate in an effort to create and maintain the best government in order to implement certain shared moral principles. These two conceptions have exercised an influence on government and politics throughout American history, sometimes in conflict and sometimes complementing each other. They are particularly important in defining the relation between power and justice, the two poles of politics that between them encompass the basic political concerns of all civil societies—namely, "who gets what, when, and how" (power) and who should do so in order to develop a good society (justice).

The major continuing task of every civil society is to shape the relation between these two faces of politics in a manner that best fits its situation. Indeed, its character as a civil society is in large measure determined by the relation between power and justice that shapes its political order. Consequently, a particular civil society's conceptions of the uses of power and the nature of justice are vital.

The Constitution and the Blessings of Liberty 173

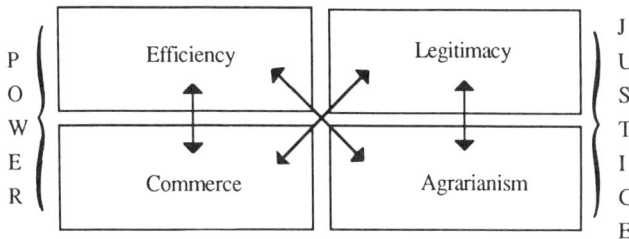

Figure 8.1 The matrix of value concepts in American culture.

We may conceptualize power and justice as two poles connected by a four-cell matrix as shown in figure 8.1. The top two cells of the matrix represent universal political demands; that is to say, in every polity there is a close relationship between efficiency and power and legitimacy and justice, in the sense that power is designed to be exercised according to the polity's accepted conception of efficiency and used to advance what that polity considers the legitimate ends of government. Thus Americans seek the efficient use of power in the pursuit of liberty, equality, and happiness. In the United States, efficiency means government that is energetic and efficacious with the least waste or the minimum expenditure of resources, while legitimacy is determined by the American understanding of liberty, equality, and happiness.

The lower two cells reflect the definitions of efficiency and legitimacy of any given polity. In the United States, efficiency is measured in predominantly commercial terms, as befits a great commercial republic. Commerce in this sense embodies the exchange of goods, services, and ideas. The federal republic has adhered closely to the original purpose of the United States Constitution to advance and protect commerce. Commerce is particularly valued because it is an efficient means of organizing, harnessing, and diffusing power through the marketplace in light of American values. Americans characteristically rely upon various kinds of marketplaces (political and economic and the marketplace of ideas) to protect and foster liberty as well as to protect property and promote enterprise.

Americans have changed their conventional definition of what is efficient in government as the organization of their commercial enterprises has changed. In the eighteenth century, efficiency meant first and foremost efficiency of competition among small-scale, relatively equal political entities within a political-economic framework that provided protection for the marketplace through active imposition of ordered rules of the game. All this reflected the political economy of the time, which rested upon many small enterprises. In the late nineteenth century it came to mean the hierarchical organization of enterprises in monopolies or oligopolies reflecting an economic system of large corporations built by great entrepreneurs. Government reformers, in turn, sought to build a power center to replace the existing noncentralized system in the name of efficiency.

During the first half of the twentieth century those corporations became complex bureaucracies governed by executive teams specializing in management and finance, and American definitions of governmental efficiency changed in the direction of bureaucratized power pyramids. More recently there is a change toward the decentralized conglomeration of synergistic organizations and work groups controlled on the basis of measures of their output. This has led to a new interest in decentralization in the name of more efficient government. In every case, both efficiency and commerce ar primarily related to the concerns of power and of its organization and management.

Legitimacy, on the other hand, is given meaning in the United States by the particularly American complex of values and aspirations associated with liberty, equality, and happiness, a kind of Whiggism that I have elsewhere termed "agrarianism."[9] This Whig or agrarian ideal envisions the United States as a commonwealth of self-governing freeholders, each with a tangible stake in his community and hence in American society as a whole, raised to new heights of human decency through the general diffusion of knowledge, religion, and morality. This ideal provides for the protection of individual liberties, the maintenance or fostering of equality, and the achievement of no small measure of happiness.

American Whiggish agrarianism stems from both the Puritan and the Jeffersonian roots of American life and has also undergone adaptations to the changing circumstances of American history from the days of the seventeenth-century Puritan village to late eighteenth-century Jeffersonian ward republic to the nineteenth-century commonwealth of homesteads to the twentieth-century suburb or exurb of freestanding homes. As the embodiment of the nation's social and political mystique (a future-oriented myth), it is the major source and test of legitimacy in the United States. Both legitimacy and agrarianism are related to the problem of attaining justice and are expressions of the continuing effort to create a more just society in the United States.

Each of the four cells in the matrix is modified by every other one. Thus, in every form it has taken, American agrarianism has had a strong commercial aspect, beginning with the Americans' desire to make a profit from the use of the land even while valuing closeness to it for moral reasons. Unlike feudal or peasant agrarianism, it has represented the effort to create a moral commonwealth of religiously inspired freeholders actively engaged in commerce in its various manifestations. By the same token, the values of agrarianism modify commercial efficiency at crucial junctures so that maximizing profits is not the only measure of efficiency in American life, even as those values themselves are tailored at some points to meet the demands of efficiency. The politically defined limits of commerce in America are set by the demands of agrarian legitimacy. Periodically the commercial aspects of American society have run wild, only to be pulled back in line sooner or later on the grounds that they have been set free illegitimately. For example, most monopolies are considered illegitimate even if they are efficient from a commercial point of view. This commonsense illegitimacy is defined in terms of liberty, equality, and happiness.

The Situation Today

In the twentieth century, particularly since the end of World War II, there has been a shift away from the earlier synthesis between marketplace and commonwealth in two ways. On one hand, the states have increasingly been denied their historic constitutional powers to support any particular moral order other than that of the marketplace within their boundaries, by decision of the United States Supreme Court. The Court has consistently interpreted the federal constitution in such a way as to extend the marketplace into the commonwealths. Thus the powers of government, particularly the state governments, have been denied in matters connected with transcendent moral issues—the relation between religion and state, obscenity and pornography, abortion, Sunday closings, and required days of rest, to name a few of the major issues.

In the case of segregation, this was a necessary and appropriate exercise of the Court's responsibility under the Constitution. In certain other cases, constitutionally more dubious (e.g., pornography), the Court's decisions reflected changed public opinion about the proper role of government in society, away from the idea that government should support a shared moral consensus and toward a greater emphasis on individualism and the right to privacy. In still other cases, the Court imposed its new understanding of the Constitution against the wishes of the states and of the people (e.g., abortion, school prayer), but even in these cases the people have been sufficiently divided to prevent reestablishing state powers in any specific area in which the moral issue predominated.

On the other hand, at least from the New Deal onward, the federal government undertook to establish a new morality of equality for the nation as a whole. It was supported in its efforts by the United States Supreme Court and, sooner or later, by the people. In terms of liberty, it can be said that the trend for the past fifty years has been to limit traditional individual liberties, especially in connection with property rights and freedom of association, on behalf of equality, while expanding individual liberties in matters of privacy and due process.

All of this has tended to emphasize the marketplace at the expense of the commonwealth, in the sense that federal interventions in areas that have taken on moral dimensions on closer look are designed to improve rights of access of all to the various marketplaces of American life or to protect their rights once in the marketplace. It seems to be a morality based upon raising the ordered rules of the game from morally sanctioned means to moral ends.

Most of the issues in question rest upon conceptions of morality that transcend the ordered rules of the game and may even require their partial suspension to achieve some higher end. That is what the Court has rejected. One need not reject the substance of the Court's decisions to recognize their effect on the body politic. They have contributed mightily to creating a new and very different moral climate in the United States, one in which the older expectations of commonwealth and community are now treated as oppressive examples of government intervention into private lives and interference with individual liberties. Thus the balance between marketplace and commonwealth upon which American federal democracy rested and through which the liberties of Americans were preserved, fostered, and contained has been dealt a severe blow. It remains to be seen whether the United States can survive that blow and remain the same kind of country it has been or, better yet, the country envisioned by its founders.

PART THREE

CONTINUITY

9

CONTRASTING MODELS OF REVOLUTIONARY LEADERSHIP

No dimension of the revolutions of the modern world has been more crucial to their outcome than leadership. Think of Cromwell, Washington, Napoleon, and Lenin; of Samuel Adams, Robespierre, and Trotsky. The mere mention of the names clarifies the question. In an age of revolutions, in which every revolution at least pretends to democratic ends, it is the leadership of each that has made the difference.

In March 1783 George Washington assembled the officers of his army at Newburgh, New York, for an act that most clearly expressed the standard for American revolutionary leadership. At one time every American schoolchild knew the story and at least the gist of Washington's words. The Continental Army, fresh from its victory over the British and in the aftermath of the peace treaty signed between the newly recognized United States of America and Great Britain, was instructed to disband without the soldiers and officers receiving the pay due them. Feeling was running high in certain circles in the army that the Confederation Congress was unable to govern and that the only way to save the country was for the army to take power and install Washington as the head of a new government—to transform Washington into a Cromwell. Washington, rejecting all such thoughts, used his farewell to his officers to drive the point home, beginning so dramatically by pulling out his spectacles to read his farewell address with the comment, "Gentlemen, you will permit me to put on my spectacles, for I have not only grown gray but almost blind in the service of my country," thereby bringing tears to the eyes of his compatriots and winning the day before he read a word of his text.[1] The myth alone has inspired generations of Americans to respect their democratic institutions even when they seem to be functioning less than adequately.

In every aspect of his career George Washington set a new and special example of revolutionary leadership. His leadership was assured through his commanding moral posture rather than through any particular brilliance. His principal talent was in holding together semivoluntary coalitions, military and political. Every office he held was gained through legitimate means, either election or appointment. Although he was personally ambitious, his ambitions were all directed to achieving position within a constitutional framework. Radical in his opposition to British encroachments on American liberties and in his advocacy of American independence, he was conservative in his emphasis on maintaining constitutional processes and institutional continuity as far as possible. Perhaps the best single word to describe his leadership is "sober." In this respect he is the exemplar of Martin Diamond's definition of the American Revolution as a "revolution of sober expectations."[2]

Unfortunately, Washington's standard for revolutionary leadership has not been widely emulated outside the United States, just as the American Revolution has been emulated far less than the French Revolution by other modern revolutionary movements. The standard for revolutionary leadership for most of the world has been set by Robespierre and Napoleon, not by Washington and his compatriots. Robespierre reflects the impatience of the ideologist fanatically committed to his cause with any restraints that might prevent him from achieving total social and political revolution. Napoleon is the model opportunist of great ambition and talent who emerges out of the wreckage of revolution to inherit power by brilliantly combining a certain lip service to revolutionary ideals with implementation of those aspects of the original revolutionary program that advance his popularity and legitimacy while aborting all the others. What Robespierre and Napoleon were to France, Lenin and Stalin were to Russia. And the Russian Revolution is only the most prominent example of the repetition of the French revolutionary pattern. In this contrast the American Revolution gains even greater luster.

The Problem: Revolution and Great Ambition

Political ambition, like other kinds of ambition, is a basic human appetite. John Adams went so far as to suggest that ambition was *the* basic human appetite, which may have reflected more upon him than upon humanity but is not entirely wide of the mark.[3] Like other human appetites, ambition is not evenly distributed among the population, but enough people with substantial political ambition are naturally drawn to political careers to make the problem of controlling it a major aspect of constitutional government. Indeed, the other founders of the United States were as aware of this problem as was Adams and devoted much of their concern for constitutional design to dealing with it. *The Federalist* emphasizes that the American Constitution is designed so that ambition will counteract ambition, that being a basic reason for introducing checks and balances into the political system.[4]

Revolutions by their very nature stimulate ambition and offer new opportunities for its exercise, especially, but not exclusively, for people new to the political arena. Moreover, revolutions are particularly attractive to those very few who have extraordinary political ambition. Such people are likely to exist in every generation, and if they cannot capitalize upon a revolution not of their own creation, they seek to generate one for their own purposes. Abraham Lincoln was acutely aware of this problem and provided one of the most felicitous discussions of it in his well-known address before the Young Men's Lyceum of Springfield:

> That our government should have been maintained in its original form from its establishment until now [1838], is not much to be wondered at. It had many props to support it through that period, which now are decayed, and crumbled away. Through that period, it was felt by all, to be an undecided experiment; now, it is understood to be a successful one. Then, all that sought celebrity and fame, and distinction, expected to find them in the success of that experiment. Their *all* was staked upon it:—their destiny was *inseparably* linked with it. Their ambition aspired to display before an admiring world, a practical demonstration of the truth of a proposition, which had hitherto been considered, at best no better than problematical; namely, *the capability of a people to govern themselves*. If they succeeded, they were to be immortalized; their names were to be transferred to counties and

cities, and rivers and mountains; and to be revered and sung, and toasted through all time. If they failed, they were to be called knaves and fools, and fanatics for a fleeting hour; then to sink and be forgotten. They succeeded. The experiment is successful; and thousands have won their deathless names in making it so. But the game is caught; and I believe it is true, that with the catching, end the pleasures of the chase. This field of glory is harvested, and the crop is already appropriated. But new reapers will arise, and *they*, too, will seek a field. It is to deny, what the history of the world tells us is true, to suppose that men of ambition and talents will not continue to spring up amongst us. And, when they do, they will as naturally seek the gratification of their ruling passion, as others have *so* done before them. The question, then, is, can that gratification be found in supporting and maintaining an edifice that has been erected by others? Most certainly it cannot. Many great and good men sufficiently qualified for any task they should undertake, may ever be found, whose ambition would aspire to nothing beyond a seat in Congress, a gubernatorial or a presidential chair; *but such belong not to the family of the lion, or the tribe of the eagle* [.] What! think you these places would satisfy an Alexander, a Caesar, or a Napoleon? Never! Towering genius disdains a beaten path. It seeks regions hitherto unexplored. It sees *no distinction* in adding story to story, upon the monuments of fame, erected to the memory of others. It *denies* that it is glory enough to serve under any chief. It *scorns* to tread in the footsteps of *any* predecessor, however illustrious. It thirsts and burns for distinction; and, if possible, it will have it, whether at the expense of emancipating slaves, or enslaving freemen. Is it unreasonable then to expect, that some man possessed of the loftiest genius, coupled with ambition sufficient to push it to its utmost stretch, will at some time, spring up among us? And when such a one does, it will require the people to be united with each other, attached to the government and laws, and generally intelligent, to successfully frustrate his designs.

Distinction will be his paramount object; and although he would as willingly, perhaps more so, acquire it by doing good as harm; yet, that opportunity being past, and nothing left to be done in the way of building up, he would set boldly to the task of pulling down.[5]

Lincoln properly suggests that the principal leaders in revolutionary times will not be people of ordinary political ambition but are likely to be of the family of the lion and the tribe of the eagle, who are potentially very dangerous to the body politic—certainly to republican institutions. Most civil societies that have undergone revolutions have been unable to control this product of revolution. Of the four great revolutions of the modern epoch, only one, the American, was able to do so.

The English Revolution (civil war), despite the great tradition of the liberties of Englishmen and the extensive institutionalization of that tradition over the previous 450 years or more, produced Oliver Cromwell, who seized power in the name of the revolution and became a despot bound only by his sense of God's expectations and his inclination to benevolence. Neither was sufficient to prevent public dissatisfaction with his rule and the ultimate restoration of the monarchy. However lacking in character the Stuarts were, the institution of the monarchy was preferable for Englishmen, even most of those of the Puritan persuasion, to a despotism, however benevolent, that seemed to be heading toward a new dynasty.

I have already suggested that the French and Russian revolutions failed even more miserably from this perspective. The traditions of English liberty rather quickly brought down Cromwell's regime and in relatively short order transformed the monarchy as well. The French Revolution produced its Robespierre as quickly as the English civil war produced Cromwell. But since Robespierre lacked all sense of restraint, neither bowing to God nor possessing a spirit of benevolence, his excesses were exacerbated just as quickly, and his downfall was more rapid and painful. His fate did not dampen the ambitions of his successors, since the situation was structurally oriented to encourage similar excesses. Only their lack of talent prevented them from achieving similar dominance until Napoleon, who was both more talented and less principled than Robespierre, came along. Although he captured the imagination of France and has held the affections of his countrymen to this day, any objective observer would have to rank him as an utter betrayer of the revolution, even though he capitalized on revolutionary ideals to bleed France on a hundred battlefields and to assert his own absolute power as ruler of that hapless country.

Napoleon's ambition knew no bounds and was further fed by his assessment that, as an upstart, he needed one success after another to stay in power. As a result he overreached himself and fell, not only bringing back the Bourbons, but starting a tradition of French military defeat that has persisted ever since. (Since the early days of his ascendancy, France has not won a war against an equal power, except on the backs of its allies.) Moreover, the struggle between those who desired Napoleonic leadership and those who feared it kept France in turmoil for the next 150 years until Charles de Gaulle, the first French leader to follow the Washingtonian model, albeit with a French style, brought the French Revolution to a successful conclusion by securing the involvement of the full political spectrum in writing the Constitution of the Fifth Republic. Under his leadership a regime was inaugurated that had the consent of virtually all the French people for the first time since 1789.

The Russian Revolution brought an even worse result, since Russia had even fewer institutional and cultural restraints on the excesses of leaders than did France. When the Bolsheviks seized power in an absolutist state their leader, V. I. Lenin, simply used the existing absolutist tradition to become the Russian Revolution's Robespierre without suffering the same consequences. Lenin consolidated the power of his party and regime, leaving both intact to be inherited by Joseph Stalin after a relatively mild power struggle among possible successors.

Lenin destroyed any possibility of democratic republicanism and the introduction of civil liberties through his ruthless pursuit of revolutionary goals. Stalin reinforced the results and went beyond Lenin for reasons more personal than ideological. Between the two of them they generated the greatest bloodbath of the twentieth century and possibly of all time, utterly aborting the ideals they presumably sought to advance and imposing upon the peoples of the Soviet Union a despotism more comprehensive and penetrating in its scope than any known before, one that continues to this day in the USSR's totalitarian police state.

In each of these cases, the goals of the revolutionaries were admirable enough (if in some cases too utopian to stand a chance of success). They were perverted by the leaders spawned by the revolutions themselves. To state that is not sufficient, however, to explain why these revolutions spawned such leadership and the American Revolution did not. However important, leadership is but one factor in revolutionary situations. Two other factors of equal weight are the character of popular participation and the institutionalization of the results. Every revolution could and should be assessed in terms of the action of the public that made or joined it, in the character of its revolutionary leadership, and in the way its goals were subsequently institutionalized.

It is in the nature of revolutions that there will be popular involvement. That is what distinguishes them from rebellions, coups d'etat, or palace uprisings. So it is not the existence of popular participation, but its character and quality that constitutes the crucial question.

The characteristic manifestations of popular participation in the American Revolution were the town meetings and the committees of correspondence, the state militias and the Continental Line: in other words, *self-organized* means of popular expression. Contrast that with the principal image of the French Revolution, the Parisian mob storming the Bastille or cheering on the reign of terror; or the Russian Revolution with its "masses" storming the Winter Palace and other institutions of the regime. In both cases the reality matched the image. Mobs and masses were important, and the successful leaders were those demagogues who could capture them or manipulators who learned how to turn them out. Only the English civil war, with its Puritan congregations and New Model Army, presents an image similar to that of the American Revolution.

This is not to say there were no mobs in the American Revolution. There were some. The best known were relatively lighthearted, like the highly organized "mob" that dumped the tea into Boston Harbor. Others—those that attacked the Tories—were far more vicious. But such mobs as emerged were small and local; their role was very minor in the overall scheme of things and had no real political significance. Certainly they did not influence the decisions of the governing bodies, local, provincial or state, or continental.[6]

So too, it may be added, were there occasional mobs during the English civil war, of the same relative unimportance. Cromwell seized power with an army behind him. Before that the king was deposed, tried, and executed by Parliament.

Thus the American Revolution had a precedent for organized popular action, but the Americans carried it to new heights in scope and spread. This in turn ensured that all revolutionary leaders were, from the first, representative of organized bodies of citizens and were empowered to act through legal and orderly processes of election or appointment. Leaders did not rise to power through usurpation because they could not. There never was a stage of anarchy in the American Revolution; power was transferred in an orderly fashion; often the same bodies previously authorized to govern under the British simply disbanded within that framework and reconstituted themselves within the new one on the basis of local and statewide political compacts. Delegates to the Continental Congresses were elected by those in similar bodies, and the congresses were never rump forums.

The American revolutionaries went to great lengths to develop or sharpen a theory of popular sovereignty through political compact to ensure the legitimacy of their actions.[7] But even more than theory, they maintained regular and proper procedures throughout the Revolution. Indeed, due process became a principal means of legitimization that was carried over into postrevolutionary American constitutionalism to maintain standards of right action by governments and legitimate channels for political and social change.

Stated in so few words, no doubt the picture seems prettier than it was in reality. There were, after all, Tories who were driven out of the country. Still, the American Revolution is the only one in which no one was executed for his political stance. While there might have been excesses in one locality or another, the overall picture presented here is the most accurate one.

The initial institutionalization of popular participation continued throughout the revolutionary period, from its prerevolutionary stages beginning in 1763 through the writing and ratification of the 1787 Constitution and the organization of the new federal government in 1789. It occurred in every arena, from the most local to the national, and moved forward as the Revolution progressed and then had to be consolidated. Moreover, there were consistent and continuous relationships between the institutions of each arena that interacted with one another to empower each other to act. To an extraordinary degree what formally became the American political system after completion of the adoption of the Articles of Confederation in March 1781 was a political system from the first, from 1763 onward. Elsewhere I have discussed and documented some of the patterns of interaction leading up to the Declaration of Independence.[8] Historians of the period have done the same in far greater depth with regard to the adoption of the Articles of Confederation and the Constitution of 1787. In the past few years there has been a spate of excellent studies on the interplay between local and state bodies with regard to the formation of the individual states and the adoption of their revolutionary era constitutions.[9] In sum, American revolutionary leaders had to function not only within the context of ordered popular control, but within an institutionalized framework that protected the Revolution and did not allow counterrevolutionary leaders even to appear.

Contrast this with the other three great revolutions. The English civil war, which did quite well in popular participation and produced good leadership in the first stages of the conflict with the king and for the war itself, failed in its efforts at institutionalization almost from the first. Although the existing institutions, both governmental and religious, prevented any serious manifestations of anarchy, they were unable to work out either the additional institutional apparatus or the interinstitutional relationships necessary to create a new overarching framework. This led to the collapse of the revolutionary movement within half a generation of the outbreak of civil war and to the restoration of the old Stuart regime. Without proper institutionalization in the countrywide arena, national leadership became a matter of usurpation, however fine its motive, and ultimately a betrayal of the revolution.

The French Revolution began with a variety of efforts to institutionalize the popular uprising, but all failed until Napoleon usurped power and imposed an institutional structure on the country. In the interim, France went through a period of virtual anarchy for nearly ten years. There is a school of American historiography that is fond of referring to the middle years of the 1780s as years of anarchy in the United States, but in fact even the occasional rebellion of debtors was localized and short and did not lead to a breakdown of the institutions of government anywhere—a great contrast to the French situation, where successive governmental experiments had virtually no staying power during the country's period of anarchy. While institutions were formally established, the struggle for their control was so violent on every level that their existence became almost meaningless.

Napoleon, like Cromwell before him and Stalin after, usurped power from within, after being chosen for a revolutionary office in a legitimate way; but it was usurpation all the same, carried further than by either Cromwell or Stalin in the sense that Napoleon finally abolished the revolutionary regime and established an empire in its place. The Napoleonic regime also was brief; in the end the old regime was restored and the revolution substantially aborted until a lesser revolution took place half a generation later. Napoleon's great legacy to France was the internal institutional structure he imposed on the country in both the governmental and the religious spheres. Apparently the French were so shaken by anarchy that they preferred to preserve Napoleon's hierarchical structure rather than try any further efforts to diffuse power broadly among the citizenry.

The Russian Revolution was even more substantially dominated by a period of anarchy than was the French Revolution, albeit for a shorter time. The Russian revolutionaries had no state or local institutions to build upon or that they could even capture and turn to their own ends. In effect, they had to build the country from the bottom up, which they claimed to do through the various levels of soviets serving the different arenas within the Russian empire. But the extent of the Bolshevik revolution was such that these soviets themselves were ultimately repressed and replaced by Bolshevik institutions bearing the same name but without the popular base.

The Russian case is almost the reverse of the English; popular participation was anarchic, and institutionalization came at the end of the revolution in the most heavy-handed manner. The prior anarchy enabled a small but very determined elite, capable of being far more ruthless than Napoleon, not only to impose on the country their own will and a regime of their design, but essentially to exterminate or expel all possible threats to that regime. In Russia, the ancien régime did not come back; instead there was usurpation from within, with Stalin seizing power from his revolutionary colleagues. The result was not a reactionary but reformable regime, as in England, or a slower process of consolidation of the revolution's gains, as in France, but a totalitarian police state.

The English could gain from a situation in which there was proper popular participation but insufficient institutionalization even though it took a little longer to do so and the revolution itself failed. The French could survive in a situation in which there was neither proper popular participation nor proper institutionalization; it simply took them longer to gain the results of the revolution. The worst result was in Russia, where there was a lack of proper popular participation but rapid institutionalization by a small elite to achieve the formal goals of the revolution, yet in such a way as to produce an utterly contrary actual result.

The Varieties of American Revolutionary Leadership and Their Common Denominator

The major figures of the American Revolution can be classified into four categories: the revolutionaries, exemplified by Samuel Adams and Patrick Henry; the statesmen, exemplified by Benjamin Franklin and Thomas Jefferson; the constitutional architects, exemplified by John Adams and James Madison; and the father of his country, George Washington—in a class by himself. While each category reflected the application of somewhat different talents to different tasks, what is most interesting for our purposes is the common denominator that kept them all within the American style of revolutionary leadership. Let us look at each in turn.

Revolutionaries

Revolutions are made by people, but people are made willing to initiate or join a revolution by a very select group of individuals capable of finding reasons why a revolution is necessary and then taking the action necessary to foment it. Two of the most prominent such figures in the American Revolution were Samuel Adams and Patrick Henry.

Samuel Adams (1722–1803), who lived to be eighty-one, was a professional politician throughout the revolutionary generation. He was the chief organizer of the opposition to the Stamp Act in Massachusetts and managed the Boston Tea Party. He is generally characterized as a "born revolutionary." He was a delegate to the Continental Congress throughout the active period of the war and signed the Declaration of Independence. At the same time he helped frame the Massachusetts Constitution and was the author of its bill of rights. Although he opposed the federal Constitution, he did not retire from state politics, being elected lieutenant governor in 1789 and becoming governor in 1794, an office he held for three years.

The contrast between Samuel Adams as a revolutionary and revolutionary ideologist and similar figures from the other major modern revolutions is striking in every respect. He was convinced of the rightness of his cause and the need to promote it with all the political and propaganda skills at his disposal. Adams did so because he viewed the people as capable of knowing their own interests, not as chained by habit and custom so that they had to be forcibly led to the right path even against their will, as was the view of most other revolutionaries. A clever user of mass action, he rejected mobs and carefully staged even his "mob" scenes so that those involved would maintain their control. He utterly rejected the notion of concentrating all power in the hands of the revolutionary elites, vigorously supporting checks and balances, federalism, and constitutionally protected rights. Adams's thought linked that of the Old Whigs or Commonwealthmen with Massachusetts Puritanism and the ideas of the Enlightenment. He and his fellow revolutionaries were as much bound by the political compact, indeed by the moral obligations of covenant, as anybody else, no matter how just their cause.[10]

Patrick Henry (1736–99) was somewhat more incongruous as a revolutionary. Although he, like Adams, came from a modest background, early in his career he became a wealthy trial lawyer. He too was revolutionized by the Stamp Act and soon came to be considered the most dangerous demagogue in Virginia. Like Adams, he was uncompromising toward the British. He became the first governor of the Commonwealth of Virginia and served from 1776 to 1779. Subsequently he led the opposition to Virginia's ratification of the federal Constitution, for the same reasons as Adams, namely that it concentrated too much power in the hands of a distant government. Nevertheless, he also supported checks and balances, federalism, and individual rights as elements in his political thought. Unlike Adams, Henry was not enamored of the details of politics, nor did he enjoy the routines of office. After 1794 he rejected a number of high offices offered to him, but in the year of his death he returned to the state legislature, this time as a Federalist, to support the new federal government against the Virginia Resolves. In his case too the combination is clear: a revolutionary in the American context meant one who stimulated popular action and then took on his responsibilities within the institutionalized framework of popular government.[11]

What is characteristic of both Adams and Henry is that both men not only encouraged popular action leading to revolution but made the transition to become major officeholders, in both cases governors of their commonwealths, during the revolutionary period and after the result was already institutionalized. They were very different from the kind of "professional revolutionaries" encountered in the other modern revolutions (or in the American in the person of Thomas Paine), whose talent was fomenting revolutions. Although both opposed the federal

Constitution of 1787, they did so not because they were opposed to the institutionalization of the results of the Revolution, but because they were convinced that a different mode of institutionalization was more faithful to the revolutionary goals they espoused. Both men died peacefully after illustrious careers, honored by their fellows.

What was the fate of the revolutionaries who sparked the other great revolutions? The list of those who met violent deaths in the throes of revolution is not only long but comprehensive. Who among them died in bed? Indeed, who among them even made the transition to power for other than a brief revolutionary moment before being led off to the guillotine or the firing squad?

Statesmen

Benjamin Franklin (1706–90) is the archetypal statesman of the American Revolution in myth and in reality. He played a prominent role in both the domestic and the foreign affairs of the fledgling republic and in the governance of his adopted Commonwealth of Pennsylvania. He was also the most famous American in the world at that time. As America's premier revolutionary diplomat, he too reflected a very different model than was to be found in other revolutions. In most of the other revolutions, professional diplomats with great personal ambition but no particular loyalty to any particular regime were co-opted by the revolutionary leadership to fulfill the tasks that Franklin took upon himself. As ideologists, the revolutionary elites were not prepared to trust anyone other than those entirely without ideas or convictions, mouthpieces who would serve any master. Franklin was anything but that.

Franklin's watchword was prudence, well tuned to a revolution of sober expectations. One of his major domestic roles was to see to it that the Revolution's expectations remained sober. There too his skills were principally diplomatic, whether in the Continental Congress and the Constitutional Convention, in the drafting of Pennsylvania's first constitution, or in daily political affairs.

Franklin was another long-lived revolutionary. Already prominent and in his sixties at the beginning of the revolutionary generation, he spent the first third of that generation in London representing Pennsylvania and other colonies, and there he became convinced that revolution was inevitable. So he returned home to serve in the Continental Congress and as a member of the committee that drafted the Declaration of Independence, where he played his usual bridging role. He was sent back to Europe for the duration of the war and the peace negotiations, where he used his considerable diplomatic skills to become the architect of the crucial alliance with France. He returned in time to serve as a member of the Constitutional Convention of 1787, helping to negotiate the acceptance of its compromises. He died in 1790 at the age of eighty-four, at once distinguished and beloved.[12]

If Franklin fairly reeked of prudence, Thomas Jefferson (1743–1826) presented himself as a radical. He was perhaps the most extremely ideological figure among the top leadership of the American Revolution, the only one to suggest semiutopian programs for restructuring society. The very use of the term sounds out of place in comparison with other revolutions—that too tells us something about the state of the American experience. Nevertheless, the two men had much in common besides their commitment to the cause of American liberty and the fact that they lived to almost the same age and died in pleasant surroundings after illustrious careers. Franklin was the prudent man who was a radical in the pursuit of liberty. Jefferson was the radical who was prudent in the pursuit of a stable republic. In today's terms, somewhat anachronistically, we can refer to both as "liberals." Both were Deists whose early training was within the framework of Calvinism or Reformed Protestantism—Franklin was a descendent of Massachusetts Puritans and Jefferson a descendant of Scots from Ulster. To use another anachronism, both were intellectuals in public affairs.

Jefferson entered political life in 1769, while the revolutionary generation was still in its formative stage, and stayed active politically until the end of his presidency forty years later. He rose to national prominence in 1774 on the very eve of the Revolution and was sent to the Continental Congress the next year, where, as we all know, he was the principal author of the Declaration of Independence. He returned to Virginia almost immediately thereafter to participate in the restructuring of his native commonwealth along republican lines, serving in the state legislature and then as governor from 1779 to 1781. He left the governorship only because of his wife's illness and death.

Jefferson returned to the Confederation Congress two years later and played a major role in shaping the legislative landmarks of the confederation era, from the plan for decimal coinage through the Northwest Ordinance of 1784. He spent the five years from 1784 to 1789 representing the United States in France and hence missed the Constitutional Convention. This experience gave him a firsthand view of prerevolutionary France and the beginnings of the French Revolution.

Jefferson came back to the United States to serve as the first secretary of state in Washington's cabinet, then resigned when Washington opted for Hamiltonian policies. In cooperation with James Madison, he founded the Democratic Republican party, today, as the Democratic party, the longest-lived popular political party in the world. He became his party's candidate for the presidency against John Adams in 1796. Although he lost to Adams, under the original terms of the federal Constitution he became vice-president. Since he was in the opposition, he spent little time in Washington, working instead to organize the party for the 1800 elections that brought him to the presidency, in which he served two terms, retiring in 1809 to Monticello. He remained there as an elder statesman until his death on July 4, 1826, the fiftieth anniversary of the Declaration of Independence.[13]

Significantly, Jefferson was highly disposed to support the French Revolution, not only in its earlier stages but through the 1790s. Indeed, he was accused by the Federalists of being a Jacobin, and he did have strong sympathies in that direction, at least intellectually and from a distance. Like Franklin, he liked France, even if he was appalled by the poverty in French cities and the reactionary ways of the ancien régime. As an intellectual, he was attracted to French culture. His sympathies for the French Revolution, however, were manifested in most un-Jacobin ways. Thus his opposition to the Federalist administration of John Adams with regard to the undeclared sea war with France was expressed through the Virginia Resolves, which claimed that states could prevent the enforcement of federal laws they deemed unconstitutional, a position that went against the Jacobin spirit in every respect. Moreover, he was a most un-Jacobin president; the biggest "usurpation" he undertook was the Louisiana Purchase, for which he himself wanted to obtain a constitutional amendment. Fortunately his sagacity won the day, and he decided that it was too good a bargain to pass up, so he exercised the executive powers of his office to complete the purchase.

There was indeed a moment when the Federalists assumed that his election to the presidency meant a Jacobin takeover. Jefferson's victory was labeled by his supporters "the revolution of 1800." Discussion was rife in the country suggesting that the transfer of administration from the Federalist party to the Democratic Republicans would bring a Jacobin-style revolution in its train. Jefferson made deliberate efforts to disabuse people of any such notions, just as Washington had earlier rejected suggestions that he lead a military coup. In his first inaugural address he summarized his position, stating, "We are all Federalists, we are all Republicans." Thus Jefferson, supposedly the archrevolutionary, first inaugurated the party system, which institutionalized ways to achieve change without revolution, and then presided over the transition of federal administrations from party to party with no disruption of the processes of government—two of the crucial inventions of modern democracy.

As was noted above, none of the other three revolutions came close to succeeding in either regard. The English civil war offered a dynastic transition that failed because of the inappropriateness of Cromwell's son and heir, Richard, and the overall rejection of the Cromwellian dictatorship. The French Revolution went from one bloody change of regime to another. It is to Napoleon's credit that once he seized power, he stopped the purges; but still, seizing power is not orderly succession, nor was the counterrevolution of the Bourbons who came after him, or the subsequent revolutions of 1830 and 1848, or the Paris Commune of 1870. It was not until the establishment of the Third Republic that peaceful transition from government to government became a reality in France, and even de Gaulle staged a kind of palace revolution 170 years later to finally bring the French Revolution to completion (or so it seems at this point). Transition in the Soviet regime started bloody, led to dictatorship, continued bloody, and now seems to be institutionalized in a less bloody but utterly undemocratic way.

Jefferson's own sense of his greatest accomplishments is reflected in the epitaph he chose for himself: "Author of the Declaration of Independence, of the Statute of Virginia for Religious Freedom, and Father of the University of Virginia." He was indeed a revolutionary, but a sober one, in the American mold, who gloried in the proclamation of human liberty and equality, the constitutionalization of individual rights, and the founding of a public university.

Constitutional Architects

For the two exemplary leaders in this category, I have chosen John Adams, the author of the Massachusetts Constitution—the model for state constitutional design—and James Madison, the principal author and expositor of the United States Constitution. John Adams (1735–1826) lived to be ninety-one, dying in bed on the same day as Jefferson, the fiftieth anniversary of the Declaration of Independence, equally venerated. He entered politics during the struggle over the Stamp Act and remained active until the end of his presidential term in 1801. He was a member of the Continental Congress from 1774 to 1778 and was one of the architects of the intersectional compromise that brought George Washington to the command of the Continental Army. With Jefferson and Franklin, he served on the committee to draft the Declaration of Independence and led the debate on its adoption.

Adams served in three capacities as an American diplomat: as commissioner to France, as a member of the commission that negotiated the peace treaty with Great Britain, and as the first envoy to that country. In 1779 to 1780 he was the principal author of the Massachusetts Constitution, his most enduring constitutional work. He was the country's first vice-president, serving under George Washington for both terms and then being elevated to the presidency in his own right. He served only one term, being defeated by Jefferson and the Democratic Republicans. Though he was strongly anti-Jacobin, his prudent behavior as president kept the United States from declaring war on France as most of his Federalist colleagues wished. He managed to confine hostilities to an undeclared sea war until differences between the two countries could be negotiated away.[14]

Adams's great constitutional monument, the Massachusetts Constitution, combines within it the principal dimensions of American constitutionalism—the constitution as political covenant and compact, a constitutionalized declaration of rights, and a frame of government resting upon checks and balances and separation of powers, all within a solidly republican framework. That it remains the constitution of that commonwealth over two hundred years later, with only the most minimal changes, is a reflection of its enduring value.[15]

James Madison (1751–1836) can be said to have been the first political scientist to have served the American people and, in a certain sense, the founder of American political science. He lived to be eighty-five. Graduating from

Princeton on the eve of the Revolution, his first major political role was participation in the drafting of the Virginia constitution in 1776. He served in the Confederation Congress from 1780 to 1783, where he advocated strengthening the powers of the federal government. He was the author of the Virginia Plan presented to the federal Constitutional Convention in 1787, and his leadership in the convention led to his being acknowledged as the "father of the Constitution." Once the convention ended, he helped lead the battle for ratification and was the principal author of *The Federalist*. However, he accepted the popular demand for the inclusion of a bill of rights in the federal Constitution as the price of ratification and submitted the principal draft for it when the First Congress convened.

Madison served in Congress from 1789 through 1797. With Jefferson, he founded the Democratic Republican party that won the "revolution of 1800," thereby introducing the principle of orderly change in control of the federal government. He was secretary of state during both terms of Jefferson's presidency and with Albert Gallatin, secretary of the treasury, was part of the triumvirate that headed the executive branch in those years.

Madison succeeded to the presidency after Jefferson and served two terms. Like Adams, he was not a particularly successful president, being better at designing constitutions than at operating them. Also like Adams, he was a true federalist, concerned with a properly governed nation and properly governed states and with a proper relationship between them. Thus, despite his strong nationalist tendencies, he could join with Jefferson in authoring the Virginia and Kentucky Resolves to interpose state law against federal legislation on constitutional grounds.

Unlike Samuel Adams and Patrick Henry, who saw the states as the organic polities and the confederation as a perpetual league of quite limited powers, John Adams and James Madison saw the system as an integral whole having a number of working parts—federal and state, executive, legislative, and judicial. In that sense Madison was the first to formulate the idea of the United States as a political system, complex and intricate, but a single whole nonetheless. Subsequent students of Madison's thought who are less attuned to the theory of federalism than he have assumed that he was either a frustrated centralizer or else inconsistent, since he sometimes supported strengthening the powers of the federal

Models of Revolutionary Leadership

government and sometimes those of the states. What they have failed to grasp is that he wanted to do both, as appropriate.[16]

It was Madison's intricate institutional design, as modified by other prudent revolutionaries of the Constitutional Convention, that provided a basis for consolidating the gains of the American Revolution and ensuring what has been, with one exception (the Civil War), an orderly yet dynamic government of a continental nation for nearly two hundred years. It is significant that we can point to no figures similar to Adams and Madison in any of the other three revolutions. None had constitutional architects, since none were ever constitutionalized in the same way, if at all.

Father of His Country

If James Madison was the father of the Constitution, George Washington (1732–99) was clearly the father of his country. Although his life was shorter than that of the others discussed here, he too died peacefully in bed—in fact, soon after he had accepted a commission as lieutenant general (then the senior rank) in the United States Army to prepare it for the incipient struggle with France. Washington's great skill was to be the exemplary leader who by moral example and prudent action could both lift the spirits of those he was leading and guide them to right action. He knew how to make the most of scarce resources and hence did not build any aspect of the Revolution on exploitation of the public he was serving. His compatriots and subsequent historians have agreed that his outstanding talent was the force, even majesty, of his personality. That, coupled with his moral commitment to a republican revolution, made him what he was.

After an early military career, Washington entered politics as part of his responsibilities as a country squire. He served in Virginia's House of Burgesses from 1759 to 1774, throughout the whole period of the buildup toward revolution. There he was one of the first to resist the British policy designed to impose England's authority on the colonies and thus became an early leader of the revolutionary party. Sent as a delegate to the Continental Congress in 1774, he hoped and subtly campaigned for command of the revolutionary armies after the battle of Lexington, and he was chosen commander-in-chief of the Continental forces on June 15, 1775.

From the time he assumed command on July 3 of that year until he relinquished it in December 1783, he was the preeminent soldier of the American Revolution. Often criticized for lack of military aggressiveness, he understood the nature of the campaign he was obliged to wage, given his scarce resources and the strength of his British opponents. He waged that campaign brilliantly, wearing down the British until French reinforcements helped him defeat them in the decisive battle of Yorktown. Washington comes down to us as a grand commander, when in fact he fought a semiguerrilla war, maintaining organized formations but after the first year rarely engaging the British in head-on combat. Between Monmouth in June 1778 and Yorktown in September 1781, he did not fight a single full-scale battle. Rather, he directed strategy for campaigns in other fields that were increasingly of a guerrilla character. Given the military tactics of the time, his thrusting and parrying were inventive and extraordinarily successful departures from the accepted modes.

It was natural for Washington to be chosen to preside at the federal Constitutional Convention. There the same personal qualities and skills that enabled him to lead the revolutionary army so successfully served him in good stead and made him the crucial figure in bringing together the different individuals with their positions so that a document emerged that was both acceptable and inspired. As in his role as commander, it was not the brilliance of his ideas but his sense of timing, his ability to conciliate people of strong views, and his sheer presence that made the difference.[17]

Unanimously elected first president of the United States, Washington proceeded to preside over the translation of the United States Constitution into a working government. As Leonard D. White has shown in his study *The Federalist*, in some respects this was his most brilliant achievement.[18] He gave meaning to the concept of chief magistrate as head of the executive branch of government, establishing in the process precedents that have endured to this day in a wide range of fields.

What is extraordinary about Washington is the degree to which he set the tone for the new United States of America in so many fields, from religious freedom to foreign affairs, from civil-military relations to the presidential management of the cabinet. Not the least of his contributions was teaching us and his successors what generals and presidents should not do as well as what they should. In essence, he embodied and helped shape the political culture of the United States as well as its institutions. That is what puts him in a class by himself. Canonized by the generations immediately after his own, he was then treated to a major debunking when later historians discovered that he was indeed human. Now that we have survived his humanization and indeed benefited from it, his true greatness is becoming more apparent on every level. He was indeed of the family of the lion and the tribe of the eagle.

The other great revolutions had figures of the same family and tribe but whose behavior and contributions were very different. Perhaps the most inspiring of them was Cromwell, who had many of the positive characteristics of Washington but neither his moderation nor his self-restraint. In the French Revolution, Robespierre was more like Samuel Adams gone mad, and Napoleon was Washington in reverse. In certain technical respects they had parallel careers. Both rose through the army; both presided over efforts to institutionalize the revolution, and both played major roles in the administrative organization of a new government. But those comparisons serve only to point up the differences between the two men rather than their similarities. Washington was the quintessential republican, conciliating, working always within the public framework of shared powers and authority, great because he could get men to work together, not because he could impose his will by gaining control of the top of the pyramid. Napoleon was the quintessential modern dictator, inspiring to his followers and his people, but in a coercive way and only from the top.

What is one to say about the Russian Revolution? There the tasks of Washington were shared by Lenin, Trotsky, and Stalin. The first, ruthless in his ideological commitment, functioned in ways diametrically opposed to the American. The second was a commander of armies like Washington but remained an outsider otherwise. And the third consolidated like Washington but was his very antithesis in moral qualities and personal self-abnegation.

What is common to all the Americans (and many others who could have been mentioned) is that they played several roles. Though their classification as models here has not been arbitrary, it is not as though Jefferson were not a constitutional architect, John Adams not a revolutionary, Madison not a statesman, and so forth. Indeed, what is characteristic of them all is that all served in both the executive and the legislative branches of government of their respective states or the

United States or both, and in no case did they ever confuse the responsibilities of one branch with those of the other. In general it can be said that neither did they confuse the responsibilities of the state and federal governments, though there the issue is less clear-cut. In some respects this is the best indicator of the special quality of American revolutionary leaders—their sense of what was appropriate in the institutional context as well as what was necessary to achieve the revolutionary goal.

The Problem Resolved: A Different Model of Revolutionary Leadership

I have already suggested that it is the combination of proper modes of popular involvement, political institutionalization, and leaders committed to prudence that produced the different model of leadership characteristic of the American Revolution. Eric Hoffer summed up the matter: "Precisely a society that can get along without leaders is the one that's producing leaders." It is fitting to sum up by retelling Hoffer's story of his experience during the Great Depression with a work gang in the San Bernardino Mountains.[19]

> During the Depression, a construction company had to build a road in the San Bernardino Mountains, and the man who was in charge, instead of calling up . . . an employment agency . . . sent out two trucks to skid row . . . anybody who could climb up on that truck was hired, even if you had only one leg . . . they . . . drove us out to the San Bernardino Mountains, and . . . dumped us on the side of the hill. The company had only one man on the job, and he didn't even open his mouth. We found there bundles of equipment and supplies and then we started to sort ourselves out.
>
> . . . it's the most glorious experience I ever had. We had so many carpenters, so many blacksmiths, so many cooks, so many foremen, so many men who could drive a bulldozer, handle a jackhammer. . . . We put up the tents, put up the cook's shack, the toilet, the shower bath, cooked supper.
>
> Next morning, we went out and started to build a road. If we had to write the Constitution, there would have been somebody there who knew all the "whereases" and the "wherefores." And we could . . . have built America.

> We were just a shovelful of slime scooped off the pavement of skid row, yet we could have built America on the side of the hill in the San Bernardino Mountains. Now you show me people anywhere in the world with such diffuse competence. It's fantastic. In other words, when I talk about Americans being a skilled people, I don't mean only technical skills, I mean social and political skills.
>
> The vigor of a society should be gauged by its ability to get along without outstanding leaders. When I said that at the University of Stanford, all the young intellectuals . . . ran after me . . . and said, "Mr. Hoffer, the vigor of society should be gauged by its ability to produce great leaders." And then I stood there and I said, "Brother, this is just what happened. Precisely a society that can get along without leaders is the one that's producing leaders."

Hoffer may have exaggerated somewhat, especially since he spoke only of the first dimension: popular involvement. The founding fathers understood that with it there had to be political institutionalization as well. They devoted themselves as much to that end as to making the Revolution in the first place.

One final note: it remained for Abraham Lincoln to sense and consider the one problem that transcends both the character of popular involvement and the nature of the political institutions. Let us return to his address before the Young Men's Lyceum:

> In the great journal of things happening under the sun, we, the American People, . . . find ourselves in the peaceful possession, of the fairest portion of the earth, as regards extent of territory, fertility of soil, and salubrity of climate. We find ourselves under the government of a system of political institutions, conducing more essentially to the ends of civil and religious liberty, than any of which the history of former times tells us. We, when mounting the stage of existence, found ourselves the legal inheritors of these fundamental blessings. We toiled not in the acquirement or establishment of them—they are a legacy bequeathed us, by a *once* hardy, brave, and patriotic, but *now* lamented and departed race of ancestors. Theirs was the task (and nobly they performed it) to possess themselves, and through themselves, us, of this goodly land; and to uprear upon its hills and its

valleys, a political edifice of liberty and equal rights; 'tis ours only, to transmit these, the former, unprofaned by the foot of an invader; the latter, undecayed by the lapse of time, and untorn by usurpation—to the latest generation that fate shall permit the world to know. This task of gratitude to our fathers, justice to ourselves, duty to posterity, and love for our species in general, all imperatively require us faithfully to perform.

Lincoln continues by raising the question:

At what point then is the approach of danger to be expected? I answer, if it ever reach us, it must spring up amongst us. It cannot come from abroad. If destruction be our lot, we must ourselves be its author and finisher. As a nation of freemen, we must live through all time, or die by suicide.

Lincoln suggests that internal disorder is the only possible way to bring down the American polity, because sooner or later internal disorder will bring down

the strongest bulwark of any Government, and particularly of those constituted like ours, may effectually be broken down and destroyed—I mean the *attachment* of the People. . . . At such a time and under such circumstances, men of sufficient talent and ambition will not be wanting to seize the opportunity, strike the blow, and overturn that fair fabric, which for the last half century, has been the fondest hope, of the lovers of freedom, throughout the world.

Lincoln in his address focused on the question of the mob's taking the law into its own hands—in other words, improper popular involvement. His response to that was to endorse the maintenance of the political institutions bequeathed the Americans by the founders:

Let every American, every lover of liberty, every well wisher to his posterity, swear by the blood of the Revolution, never to violate in the least particular, the laws of the country; and never to tolerate their violation by others. As the patriots of seventy-six did to the support of the Declaration of Independence, so to the support of the Constitutions and Laws, let every American pledge his life, his property, and his sacred honor—let every man remember that to violate the law, is to trample on the blood of his father, and to tear the character of his own, and his children's liberty. Let reverence for the laws, be breathed by every American mother, to the lisping babe that prattles on her lap—let it be taught in schools, in seminaries, and in colleges;—let it be written in Primers, spelling books, and Almanacs;—let it be preached from the pulpit, proclaimed in legislative halls, and enforced in courts of justice. And, in short, let it become the *political religion* of the nation.

Lincoln knew that proper popular involvement and institutionalization are not enough, for they will not necessarily control those who belong to the family of the lion or the tribe of the eagle. His answer is perhaps less than fully satisfying, returning as he does to a reliance on a proper political religion. We are left to rely upon that, to which we can add the fostering of a proper political culture of the kind that animated George Washington and his compatriots.

THE CONSTITUTION, THE UNION, AND THE LIBERTIES OF THE PEOPLE

Introduction

In February 1861 Abraham Lincoln, the president-elect of the United States, traveled from his home in Springfield, Illinois, to Washington, D.C., for his inauguration as chief magistrate. When he left Springfield on February 11, he faced a nation already divided. The seven states of the Deep South had seceded, beginning with South Carolina in December 1860 and followed by Georgia, Florida, Alabama, Mississippi, Louisiana, and Texas in January and early February. Just the week before, their representatives had assembled in Montgomery, Alabama, to form the Confederate States of America, and their constitutional convention was still in session.

Lincoln knew he was a minority president, elected by a solid majority in the northern states but almost without support south of the Mason-Dixon Line and the Ohio River. The first president since Andrew Jackson to be involved in a serious four-way race for the office, he had received little more than 40 percent of the total votes cast. Indeed, that the United States had a president at all was due only to the existence of the electoral college system, which enabled the country to produce a chief magistrate even in such adverse circumstances.

Lincoln's trip from Springfield to Washington occupied the better part of a month and was deliberately planned to bring him in contact with the states, sections, and people that composed the core of the Union. Presidential campaigns in Lincoln's day did not involve a candidate's formally going out to seek the votes of his fellow citizens. The candidate remained at home, ostensibly too modest to compete for votes, while his supporters did what they could on his behalf. Thus the whistle-stop campaign technique, which was to become famous by the turn of the century and to shape the image of presidential politics until the 1950s, when the airplane replaced railroad travel, was in the future. Still, the railroads had become a factor in American life, and the president-elect could utilize the network of iron that bound together the various segments of the country to conduct a different kind of whistle-stop tour—to present himself to the American people, North and South, East and West, ask for their support, and indicate to them that he was not an oafish radical but a man of reason and good sense who would do what he could and, indeed, what he must to preserve the Union.

The president-elect's whistle-stop tour took him on a zigzag course from what was then still the relatively raw "West" of Illinois, not even a generation removed from the frontier, down to the very edge of the South in Cincinnati, up through the heart of the Middle States to that part of New York State settled by New England Yankees, down along the East Coast through what was already emerging as the urban heartland of the country, and then into Washington. In the course of the three-week trip, he delivered nineteen speeches, of which seven were major addresses, and fifty-two whistle-stop remarks. Almost all were recorded for posterity, either in his own hand or by reporters following the entourage.[1] The result was as full a statement of Abraham Lincoln's idea of constitutional liberty and union in the United States as he has left us. Following his words, it is possible to recognize how he also used the opportunity to refine his thoughts on the character of the American polity and to develop the ones he would return to again and again over the next four years. Beyond that, it is to a very substantial extent a summation of Lincoln's political teaching, his legacy to the people of the United States and the world. As always, the mature Lincoln was very careful in his expression, choosing his words and his emphasis, setting forth his argument with great discretion and without exaggeration, even for effect.

What follows is a selection of those words that express Lincoln's political testament, his understanding of the American constitutional tradition, with a brief examination of their content. To emphasize the process of refinement Lincoln's ideas underwent, the material is analyzed in the order in which it was delivered rather than thematically. That order also reflects the different audiences Lincoln addressed. All together, the materials build to a climax in Philadelphia, where Lincoln spoke at Independence Hall and addressed his remarks to the entire American people. They culminate in the first inaugural address where the various themes are reworked in summary form.

Roots, Mobility, and Technology in American Society

Lincoln set the stage for his traveling seminar in American political ideas in his farewell address to his neighbors (February 11, 1861), where, by describing his own relationship to Springfield, he provides us with a description of those aspects of American society that relate to roots and mobility.

> My friends—No one, not in my situation, can appreciate my feeling of sadness at this parting. To this place, and the kindness of these people, I owe every thing. Here I have lived a quarter of a century, and have passed from a young to an old man. Here my children have been born, and one is buried. I now leave not knowing when, or whether ever, I may return, with a task before me greater than that which rested upon Washington. Without the assistance of that Divine Being, who ever attended him, I cannot succeed. With that assistance I cannot fail. Trusting in Him, who can go with me, and remain with you and be every where for good, let us confidently hope that all will yet be well. To His care commending you, as I hope in your prayers you will commend me, I bid you an affectionate farewell.[2]

The address is one of those single-paragraph gems not uncommon in nineteenth-century America, when men otherwise not considered orators managed to combine decent sentiment with a felicity of expression in a few short sentences. The Gettysburg Address is undoubtedly the finest of that genre. Robert E. Lee's farewell to his troops at Appomattox Courthouse on April 10, 1865, contains several of the same phrases as Lincoln's farewell to Springfield.

Like so many Americans, Lincoln was a migrant. As a child he moved with his family from his place of birth in Kentucky to Indiana and then again to Illinois, and as an adult he made at least two additional moves within Illinois before settling in Springfield. Springfield became his adopted city, and he considered it home almost from the moment he arrived. In this regard he is typical of so many Americans whose "home" is the place where they choose to live as adults. That his children did not continue to live in Springfield makes his case all the more typical. In American fashion, which recognizes the right of every man to choose his home, Lincoln is also associated with Springfield, where he made his mark as a citizen, far more so than with his actual birthplace. In paying tribute to Springfield as the place where his children were born, Lincoln transposes the notion of home as the "land where our fathers died" so often expressed by patriots.

The seriousness and depth of Lincoln's piety are apparent in these few words. In suggesting that the issue is really whether Americans are on God's side rather than the reverse, he strikes the note he is to maintain throughout the Civil War, which rejects a certain kind of vulgar patriotism frequently found in such circumstances.

Lincoln's reference to "a task . . . greater than that which rested upon Washington" should be read in light of his well-known address to the Springfield Young Men's Lyceum in 1838, where he discusses the political problem of human greatness and the great ambition it provokes. There he suggests that only political foundings or their equivalent can provide a sufficient field for expressing great political ambition in ways that are not dangerous to the regime. Lincoln himself had a full measure of great ambition, and his reference here suggests that he perceived the future task of maintaining the Union as equivalent to the task of its founding.

Indiana: Posing the Question

Lincoln begins his discourse on the state of the United States at Lafayette, Indiana (February 11), with a reference to the impact of technology on community and society and how it has transformed communications within his own lifetime. In doing so, he strikes a theme that is common to Americans of all generations.

> Fellow Citizens: —We have seen great changes within the recollection of some of us who are the older. When I first came to the west, some 44 or 45 years ago, at sundown you had completed a journey of some 30 miles which you had commenced at sunrise, and thought you had done well. Now only

> six hours have elapsed since I left my home in Illinois where I was surrounded by a large concourse of my fellow citizens, almost all of whom I could recognize, and I find myself far from home surrounded by the thousands I now see before me, who are strangers to me. Still we are bound together, I trust in Christianity, civilization and patriotism, and are attached to our country and our whole country. While some of us may differ in political opinions, still we are all united in one feeling for the Union. We all believe in the maintainance of the Union, of every star and every stripe on the glorious flag, and permit me to express the sentiment that upon the union of the States, there shall be between us no difference.³

Lincoln carefully distinguishes between the ties of community—personal recognition—and those of society where people are bound by cultural artifact ("Christianity, civilization and patriotism"). It is, of course, particularly important to Lincoln's consistent argument going back at least a decade that the Union must stay together, if only because the geography of the country does not permit its successful division. Here he reinforces that argument by emphasizing the way technological change enhances unity.

Lincoln strikes the keynote of his theme in his reply to Governor Oliver P. Morton's welcome to him when he arrives in Indianapolis, the capital of Indiana (February 11).

> You have been pleased to address yourselves to me chiefly in belief of this glorious Union in which we live, in all of which you have my hearty sympathy, and, as far as may be within my power, . . . my hearty consideration. . . . To the salvation of this Union there needs but one single thing—the hearts of a people like yours. When the people rise in masses in behalf of the Union and the liberties of their country, truly may it be said, "The gates of hell shall not prevail against them." . . .
>
> I wish you to remember now and forever that . . . if the union of these States, and the liberties of this people, shall be lost, it is but little to any one man of fifty-two years of age, but a great deal to the thirty millions of people who inhabit these United States, and to their posterity in all coming time. It

> is your business to rise up and preserve the Union and liberty, for yourselves, and not for me. I desire they shall be constitutionally preserved.
>
> I, as already intimated, am but an accidental instrument, temporary, and to serve but for a limited time, but I appeal to you again to constantly bear in mind that with you, and not with politicians, not with Presidents, not with officeseekers, but with you, is the question, "Shall the Union and shall the liberties of this country be preserved to the latest generation?"[4]

The question he poses, "Shall the Union and shall the liberties of this country be preserved to the latest generation?" remains the enduring political question of the American polity, combining as it does the two central concerns of the United States as a civil society. Notice, too, how he defines his own role as that of a mere, even an "accidental" instrument.

Lincoln gets down to the details of his theme in his first major speech by stating his theories of statehood and federalism.

> Do the lovers of the Union contend that they will resist coercion or invasion of any State, understanding that any or all of these would be coercing or invading a State? If they do, then it occurs to me that the means for the preservation of the Union they so greatly love, in their own estimation, is of a very thin and airy character. If sick, they would consider the little pill of the homeopathist as already too large for them to swallow. In their view, the Union, as a family relation, would not be anything like a regular marriage at all, but only as a sort of free-love arrangement,—(laughter)—to be maintained on what that sect call passionate attraction. (Continued laughter.) But, my friends, enough of this.
>
> What is the particular sacredness of a State? I speak not of the position which is given to a State in and by the Constitution of the United States, for that all of us agree to—we abide by; but the position assumed, that a State can carry with it out of the Union that which it holds in sacredness by virtue of its connection with the Union. I am speaking of that assumed right of a State, as a primary principle, that the Constitution should rule all that is less than itself, and ruin all that is bigger than itself. But I ask, wherein does consist that right? If a State, in one instance, and a county in another, should be equal in extent of territory, and equal in the number of people, wherein is

that State any better than the county? Can a change of name change the right? By what principle of original right is it that one-fiftieth or one-ninetieth of a great nation, by calling themselves a State, have the right to break up and ruin that nation as a matter of original principle? . . . Where is the mysterious, original right, from principle, for a certain district of country with inhabitants, by merely being called a State to play tyrant over all its own citizens, and deny the authority of everything greater than itself.[5]

It is here that he first uses the analogy of the Union as "a regular marriage" as distinct from a "free-love arrangement." The understanding of states' rights that he enunciates here is to be repeated throughout the remainder of his political career. Lincoln's theory of federalism, like that which prevailed among the founding fathers, conceives of the United States as a single nation in a single country and at least implies that *all* governments are simply instrumentalities of the people and have no sacred character of their own. He even suggests that territorial democracy as an instrumentality makes no distinction in the value of governments other than that of size, implying that the larger—and, consequently, the more comprehensive—the arena, the more consideration is due it because it aggregates the will of more people. He goes so far as to suggest openly that size in this sense should be the *only* criterion for measuring importance in a democracy. Notice Lincoln's effort to distinguish between constitutional rights and what he terms primary principles.

Ohio: Confronting the South and the Copperheads

Ohio, then as now one of the most diverse states in the Union in the character of its population, offered Lincoln his first opportunity to address all the elements composing the Republic—natives and immigrants, Northerners and Southerners, Democrats and Republicans, Unionists and Secessionists. Moreover, as a state bordering the South, it offered him a platform to reach out to that section as well. He took full advantage of the opportunity. In his first remarks in Ohio, in reply to the chairman of the reception committee that met him in Cincinnati, he sets the tone by referring to the "citizens of Cincinnati, Ohio, and Kentucky."

Lincoln gave three major addresses in Cincinnati (February 12). The first was addressed explicitly to the citizens of Ohio and Kentucky and implicitly to all Americans. The second was addressed explicitly to the people of Kentucky and implicitly to all Southerners, while the third was addressed explicitly to the Germans who had settled in Cincinnati and implicitly to all "ethnics" and all those who had immigrated to American shores.

In his first speech, Lincoln took advantage of the opportunity presented by the fact that the mayor of Cincinnati who welcomed him was a Democrat to discuss the respect due the presidency no matter who was incumbent in the office and, by the extension, to the free institutions of the United States whose preservation was the great question of the day.

> I am reminded by the address of your worthy Mayor, that this reception is given not by any one political party, and even if I had not been so reminded by His Honor . . . I could not look upon this vast assemblage without being made aware that all parties were united in this reception. This is . . . as it should ever be when any citizen of the United States is constitutionally elected President of the United States. Allow me to say that I think what has occurred here to-day could not have occurred in any other country on the face of the globe, without the influence of the free institutions which we have unceasingly enjoyed for three-quarters of a century. There is no country where the people can turn out and enjoy this day precisely as they please, save under the benign influence of the free institutions of our land.[6]

In the course of his talk, Lincoln invoked the generation of the founding fathers, referring explicitly to three Southerners who were preeminently Americans and strong unionists: George Washington, the father of his country; Thomas Jefferson, the first man to be elected president from an opposition party and the accepted author of the states' rights doctrine; and James Madison, the father of the United States Constitution and the Virginia Resolutions.

> I have spoken . . . in Cincinnati . . . a year previous to the late Presidential election. On that occasion, in a playful manner, but with sincere words, I addressed much of what I said, to the Kentuckians. I gave my opinion that we, as Republicans, would ultimately beat them as Democrats . . . I also told them how I expected they would be treated, after they should have been

> beaten. . . . "We mean to treat you, as near as we possibly can, as Washington, Jefferson and Madison treated you. We mean to leave you alone, and in no way to interfere with your institutions; to abide by all and every compromise of the Constitution, and, in a word, coming back to the original proposition, to treat you, so far as degenerated men (if we have degenerated) may, according to the examples of those noble fathers—Washington, Jefferson and Madison. We mean to remember that you are as good as we; that there is no difference between us, other than the difference of circumstances. We mean to recognize, and bear in mind always, that you have as good hearts in your bosoms as other people, or as we claim to have, and treat you accordingly."
>
> Fellow citizens of Kentucky—friends—brethren, may I call you—in my new position, I see no occasion, and feel no inclination, to retract a word of this. If it shall not be made good, be assured, the fault shall not be mine.[7]

By making a pun on the word *degenerated*, Lincoln implicitly raises the question whether his generation was inferior to the generation of the founders. Lincoln's choice of figures is in itself important, since it reflects recognition of both the popular heroes of the founding and his own sense of who were the key figures in the founding of the United States—the father of his country, the author of the Declaration of Independence, and the father of the Constitution.

In the opening of his speech, Lincoln makes a point of the uniqueness of the United States as a land where free institutions and respect for those institutions prevail. In essence, the rest of the speech is devoted to a discussion of the need to preserve those institutions and the country that sustains them intact. Explicit in that discussion—as in so many other of his addresses—is Lincoln's sense of the coming and going of generations, each of which is called to its own particular task yet is also limited by the mortality of its members.

> In a few short years, I and every other individual man who is now living will pass away. I hope that our national difficulties will also pass away, and I hope we shall see in the streets of Cincinnati—good old Cincinnati—for centuries to come, once every four years her people give such a reception as this to the Constitutionally elected President of the whole United States. I hope you shall all join in that reception, and that you shall also welcome

your brethren far across the river to participate in it. We will welcome them in every State of the Union, no matter where they are from.[8]

In this respect Lincoln has a biblical view of time and its progression, just as he has a biblical view of humanity and its acts.

> trusting that the good sense of the American people, on all sides of all rivers in America, under the Providence of God, who has never deserted us, that we shall again be brethren, forgetting all parties—ignoring all parties. My friends I now bid you farewell.[9]

Making his appeal to the South via an appeal to Kentuckians, Lincoln makes reference to his "native state," though we know that his sentiments regarding home lay elsewhere. The essence of his speech is a call to Southerners to accept the results of the presidential election even though these results will lead to the inauguration of a Republican, anathema to them, suggesting how the institutions of the United States allow them to do so without running a great risk for their future.

> I do not deny the possibility that the people may err in an election; but if they do, the true [remedy] is in the next election, and not in the treachery of the person elected.[10]

Two principal political teachings are to be found in this address. The first concerns the obligations of statesmen to use words honestly, carefully, and well.

> During the present winter, it has been greatly pressed upon me by many patriotic citizens, Kentuckians among others, that I could in my position, by a word, restore peace to the country. But what word? I have many words already before the public; and my position was given me on the faith of those words. Is the desired word to be confirmatory of these; or must it be contradictory to them? If the former, it is useless repetition; if the latter, it is dishonorable and treacherous.
>
> Again, it is urged as if the word must be spoken before the fourth of March. Why? Is the speaking the word a "sine qua non" to the inauguration? Is there a Bell-man, A Breckinridge-man, or a Douglas-man, who would tolerate his own candidate to make such terms, had he been elected? Who amongst you would not die by the proposition, that your candidate, being

elected, should be inaugurated, solely on the conditions of the Constitution, and laws, or not at all. What Kentuckian, worthy of his birth place, would not do this? Gentlemen, I too, am a Kentuckian.

Nor is this a matter of mere personal honor. No man can be elected President without some opponents, as well as supporters; and if when elected, he cannot be installed, till he first appeases his enemies, by breaking his pledges, and (sic) betraying his friends, this government, and all popular government, is already at an end. Demands for such surrender, once recognized, and yielded to, are without limit, as to nature, extent, or repetition. They break the only bond of faith between public, and public servant; and they distinctly set the minority over the majority. Such demands acquiesced in, would not merely be the ruin of a man, or a party; but as a precedent they would ruin the government itself.[11]

The second deals with the responsibility of statesmen in a democracy to keep faith with their supporters as part of the principle of majority rule.

During the winter just closed, I have been greatly urged, by many patriotic men, to lend the influence of my position to some compromise, by which I was, to some extent, to shift the ground upon which I had been elected. This I steadily refused. I so refused, not from any party wantonness, nor from any indifference to the troubles of the country. I thought such refusal was demanded by the view that if, when a Chief Magistrate is Constitutionally elected, he cannot be inaugurated till he betrays those who elected him, by breaking his pledges, and surrendering to those who tried and failed to defeat him at the polls, this government and all popular government is already at an end. Demands for such surrender, once recognized, are without limit, as to nature, extent and repetition. They break the only bond of faith between public and public servant; and they distinctly set the minority over the majority.[12]

Lincoln's third speech addresses the third great constituency in the United States (natives of the North, natives of the South, and immigrants who have to choose between the two). Apparently, the welcoming speech by the chairman of the committee representing the German industrial associations was rigorous and theoretical in the manner of German philosophy. Lincoln responds accordingly,

The Constitution, the Union, and Liberties

but in the manner of an American, pragmatically avoiding commitment where he feels that is the statesmanlike thing to do.

> Mr. Chairman: I thank you and those whom you represent, for the compliment you have paid me, by tendering me this address. In so far as there is an allusion to our present national difficulties, which expresses, as you have said, the views of the gentlemen present, I shall have to beg pardon for not entering fully upon the questions, which the address you have now read, suggests.
>
> I deem it my duty—a duty which I owe to my constituents—to you, gentlemen, that I should wait until the last moment, for a development of the present national difficulties, before I express myself decidedly what course I shall pursue. I hope, then, not to be false to anything that you have to expect of me.[13]

Lincoln takes the opportunity provided by the speech to set forth his ideas on economic and social democracy. As is always the case with Lincoln, very few words say much.

> I agree with you, Mr. Chairman, that the working men are the basis of all governments, for the plain reason that they are the most numerous, and as you added that those were the sentiments of the gentlemen present, representing not only the working class, but the citizens of other callings than those of the mechanic, I am happy to concur with you in these sentiments, not only of the native born citizens, but also of the Germans and foreigners from other countries.
>
> Mr. Chairman, I hold that while man exists, it is his duty to improve not only his own condition, but to assist in ameliorating mankind; and therefore, without entering upon the details of the question, I will simply say, that I am for those means which will give the greatest good to the greatest number. . . .
>
> In regard to the Germans and foreigners, I esteem them no better than other people, nor any worse. (Cries of "good.") It is not my nature, when I see a people borne down by the weight of their shackles—the oppression of tyranny—to make their life more bitter by heaping upon them greater

> burdens; but rather would I do all in my power to raise the yoke, than to add anything that would tend to crush them.
>
> Inasmuch as our country is extensive and new, and the countries of Europe are densely populated, if there are any abroad who desire to make this the land of their adoption, it is not in my heart to throw aught in their way, to prevent them from coming to the United States.[14]

The lack of sentimentality about either workers or immigrants is notable, yet implicit in his words is a sense of America's mission in this world.

In Columbus, Lincoln addressed the Ohio legislature (February 13), the first of four legislatures he was to address in the course of his journey. That speech was followed by one to the public from the steps of the state capitol. Before the legislature, Lincoln is concerned with "that God who has never forsaken this people" (the phrase, taken directly from the Bible, is used twice in the speech) and with how he as a leader must best serve both. Outside, he directs his remarks to the people themselves, suggesting what civic virtue is required of them.

In speaking to the legislature, Lincoln somewhat extends the remarks he made in Cincinnati regarding the relationship between his generation and that of the founding fathers, suggesting that whatever the relative qualities of the two generations, the tasks of the present one may be even greater than those of the former.

> I cannot but know what you all know, that, without a name, perhaps without a reason why I should have a name, there has fallen upon me a task such as did not rest even upon the Father of his country, and so feeling I cannot but turn and look for the support without which it will be impossible for me to perform that great task. I turn, then, and look to the American people and to that God who has never forsaken them.[15]

The sum and substance of the speech, however, is suited to the forum. He is speaking to political leaders, and he speaks to them as one political leader to others, dwelling on the reasons for his silence on the specifics of his plans to deal with secession.

> Allusion has been made to the interest felt in relation to the policy of the new administration. In this I have received from some a degree of credit for

having kept silence, and from others some deprecation. I still think that I was right. In the varying and repeatedly shifting scenes of the present, and without a precedent which could enable me to judge by the past, it has seemed fitting that before speaking upon the difficulties of the country, I should have gained a view of the whole field, to be sure, after all, being at liberty to modify and change the course of policy, as future events may make a change necessary.[16]

In doing so, he suggests some important lessons of statesmanship.

At Steubenville (February 14), Lincoln phrases more sharply the question he posed to the Kentuckians, namely, What are the rights of the Southerners under the Constitution? and relates that question to the larger question of majority rule. Here he more clearly links "the people," "the Divine Power," and "the Constitution" as the triadic source of authority in the American political life and explains how that authority operates through majority rule.

> Mr. Chairman and Fellow-Citizens:—The subject of the short address which has been made to me, though not an unfamiliar one, involves so many points, that in the short time allotted to me, I shall not be able to make a full and proper response. Though the people have made me by electing me, the instrument to carry out the wishes expressed in the address, I greatly fear that I shall not be the repository of the ability to do so. Indeed I know I shall not, more than in purpose, unless sustained by the great body of the people, and by the Divine Power, without whose aid we can do nothing. We everywhere express devotion to the Constitution. I believe there is no difference in this respect, whether on this or on the other side of this majestic stream. I understand that on the other side, among our dissatisfied brethren, they are satisfied with the Constitution of the United States, if they can have their rights under the Constitution. The question is, as to what the Constitution means—"What are their rights under the Constitution?" That is all. To decide that, who shall be the judge? Can you think of any other, than the voice of the people? If the majority does not control, the minority must— would that be right? Would that be just or generous? Assuredly not! Though the majority may be wrong, and I will not undertake to say that they were not wrong in electing me, yet we must adhere to the principle that the

majority shall rule. By your Constitution you have another chance in four years. No great harm can be done by us in that time—in that time there can be nobody hurt. If anything goes wrong, however, and you find you have made a mistake, elect a better man next time. . . .

These points involve the discussion of many questions which I have not time to consider. I merely give them to you for your reflection. I almost regret that I alluded to it at all.[17]

The New Urban-Industrial Frontier of Pennsylvania and Ohio: Broadening the Discourse

From rural central Ohio, whose cities were primarily devoted to agribusiness and its commerce, Lincoln moved on to the westernmost manifestations of the urban-industrial frontier—the borderlands of western Pennsylvania and eastern Ohio. There he broadened his discourse to focus on issues appropriate to what was then the newest American frontier. At Pittsburgh he was extremely well received by an obviously sympathetic public.

In a major address (February 15) whose major elements were prepared in advance, Lincoln further developed his reasons for speaking in general terms rather than about specifics, a policy he was to follow throughout his presidency, speaking about specifics only when the time for action was at hand.

> And here, fellow citizens, I may remark that in every short address I have made to the people, and in every crowd through which I have passed of late, some allusion has been made to the present distracted condition of the country. It is naturally expected that I should say something upon this subject, but to touch upon it at all would involve an elaborate discussion of a great many questions and circumstances, would require more time than I can at present command, and would perhaps unnecessarily commit me upon matters which have not yet fully developed themselves. . . .
>
> My intention is to give this subject all the consideration which I possibly can before I speak fully and definitely in regard to it—so that, when I do speak, I may be as nearly right as possible. And when I do speak, fellow-citizens, I hope to say nothing in opposition to the spirit of the Constitution,

contrary to the integrity of the Union, or which will in any way prove inimical to the liberties of the people or to the peace of the whole country.[18]

In stating his canons of judgment as to when to speak and what to say, he refers to the three points of departure of his political thought "the spirit of the Constitution . . . the integrity of the Union . . . the liberties of the people."

Lincoln's choice of Pittsburgh as a place to interrupt the Ohio leg of his journey becomes apparent in the body of the speech, which focuses on a discussion of the tariff. Thus, in western Pennsylvania he broadens his discourse on the American polity. Up until now he has very deliberately focused on the general interest that holds (or should hold) all Americans together. In doing so, Lincoln acknowledged the existence of special interests but deliberately downplayed them. Here he indicates in his very first remarks that he will dwell upon "what is properly styled [the] peculiar interest" of the "citizens of Pennsylvania."

> Fellow citizens, as this is the first opportunity which I have had to address a Pennsylvania assemblage, it seems a fitting time to indulge in a few remarks upon the important question of a tariff—a subject of great magnitude, and one which is attended with many difficulties, owing to the great variety of interests which it involves. So long as direct taxation for the support of government is not resorted to, a tariff is necessary. The tariff is to the government what a meal is to the family; but, while this is admitted, it still becomes necessary to modify and change its operations according to new interests and new circumstances. So far there is little difference of opinion among politicians, but the question as to how far imposts may be adjusted for the protection of home industry, gives rise to various views and objections. I must confess that I do not understand this subject in all its multiform bearings, but I promise you that I will give it my closest attention, and endeavor to comprehend it more fully.[19]

Lincoln's decision as to the appropriateness of this topic obviously had been made some time before, and his remarks had been prepared in manuscript, although he deviated from the prepared text as he actually spoke.[20] Even so, he avoids premature commitments. Pleading ignorance, he promises his audience, which in the heart of the new iron manufacturing district of America is very much concerned about the tariff, that he intends to educate himself on the matter.

> I have long thought that if there be any article of necessity which can be produced at home with as little or nearly the same labor as abroad, it would be better to protect that article. Labor is the true standard of value. If a bar of iron, got out of the mines of England, and a bar of iron taken from the mines of Pennsylvania, be produced at the same cost, it follows that if the English bar be shipped from Manchester to Pittsburg, and the American bar from Pittsburg to Manchester, the cost of carriage is appreciably lost. (Laughter.) If we had no iron here, then we should encourage its shipment from foreign countries; but not when we can make it as cheaply in our own country. This brings us back to our first proposition, that if any article can be produced at home with nearly the same cost as abroad, the carriage is lost labor.
>
> The treasury of the nation is in such a low condition at present that this subject now demands the attention of Congress, and will demand the immediate consideration of the new Administration. The tariff bill now before Congress may or may not pass at the present session. I confess I do not understand the precise provisions of this bill, and I do not know whether it can be passed by the present Congress or not. It may or may not become the law of the land—but if it does, that will be an end of the matter until a modification can be effected, should it be deemed necessary. If it does not pass (and the latest advices I have are to the effect that it is still pending) the next Congress will have to give it their earliest attention.[21]

In the meantime, he gives a classic exposition of the role of party platforms in American politics and the degree to which they reflect compromises and are therefore subject to subsequent interpretation.

> The Chicago platform contains a plank upon this subject, which I think should be regarded as law for the incoming administration. In fact, this question, as well as all other subjects embodied in that platform, should not be varied from what we gave the people to understand would be our policy when we obtained their votes.

> I must confess that there are shades of difference in construing even this plank of the platform. But I am not now intending to discuss these differences, but merely to give you some general ideas upon this subject.[22]

Note how Lincoln defines the tariff—as a revenue-raising device, not as a means of protecting industry. The latter appears to be a secondary consequence. Moreover, he at least hints at the desirability of levying direct taxes. Indeed, a year later he presided over the introduction of the first federal income tax.

Lincoln's remarks regarding labor and wealth, sectionalism, and the role of Congress as the place in which various sectional interests are to be represented are worth further notice.

> According to my political education, I am inclined to believe that the people in the various sections of the country should have their own views carried out through their representatives in Congress, and if the consideration of the Tariff bill should be postponed until the next session of the National Legislature, no subject should engage your representatives more closely than that of a tariff. And if I have any recommendation to make, it will be that every man who is called upon to serve the people in a representative capacity, should study this whole subject thoroughly, as I intend to do myself, looking to all the varied interests of our common country, so that when the time for action arrives adequate protection can be extended to the coal and iron of Pennsylvania, the corn of Illinois, and the "reapers of Chicago." Permit me to express the hope that this important subject may receive such consideration at the hands of your representatives, that the interests of no part of the country may be overlooked, but that all sections may share in common the benefits of a just and equitable tariff.[23]

Lincoln suggests that those interests are manifested for practical political purposes on a geographic or sectional basis. Recognizing this as legitimate, Lincoln nevertheless suggests that his task (as president) is to weigh special interests in light of the general interest in all cases. Lincoln's prepared text adds a more carefully reasoned exposition of his theory of interest, class, and section within a polity and the role of Congress in adjusting them. A week later, in Harrisburg, he specifically mentioned the care with which he chose his words on that occasion.[24]

Lincoln's discussion of executive-legislative relations in his prepared text has him endorsing the predominant nineteenth-century view. Legislation is the province of the Congress, with the president influencing the process only indirectly or through his veto power.

Reaching Cleveland, Lincoln entered greater New England for the first time—the regions settled by westward-moving New England Yankees, the strongest partisans of Abolition. There he began by reiterating his central theme "respect to [sic] the Union, the constitution and the laws . . . the cause of liberty" (February 15). Turning to the issue of federal enforcement of the fugitive slave laws, in an Abolitionist stronghold, he indicated that as president he would feel obliged to continue enforcing these laws, despite his personal feelings on the matter.

> What is happening now will not hurt those who are farther away from here. Have they not all their rights now as they ever have had? Do they not have their fugitive slaves returned now as ever? Have they not the same Constitution that they have lived under for seventy odd years? Have they not a position as citizens of this common country, and have we any power to change that position? (Cries of "No.") What then is the matter with them? Why all this excitement? Why all these complaints? As I said before, this crisis is all artifical. It has no foundation in facts. It was not argued up, as the saying is, and cannot, therefore, be argued down. Let it alone and it will go down of itself.[25]

Lincoln was not wrong in his assessment of the "artificiality" (as he defined it) of the crisis. No doubt he understood that this would not necessarily prevent it from getting out of hand. Here his attempt to persuade the public on both sides of the line led him to exaggerate the likelihood that it would "go down of itself."

New York: Popularizing the Theme

Upon entering New York, a by-now-tired Lincoln seemed to revive. At Westfield, he engaged in political banter directed toward the young lady who had written to suggest he grow a beard. At Dunkirk he made a strong symbolic gesture toward the American flag (February 16).

Standing as I do, with my hand upon this staff, and under the folds of the American flag, I ASK YOU TO STAND BY ME SO LONG AS I STAND BY IT.[26]

In Buffalo (February 16) he renewed the themes he had struck in Ohio, sharpening his assessment of the United States as "this favored land" and its inhabitants as "this great and intelligent people" and adding a reference to the future growth of the country (appropriately, after his viewing the expanding industrial frontier). His speech, read in full, provides a summary statement of the themes he had developed in the Middle West as well as the flavor of the trip.

> Mr. Mayor, and Fellow-Citizens of Buffalo and the State of New York:—I am here to thank you briefly for this grand reception given to me, not personally, but as the representative of our great and beloved country. (Cheers.) Your worthy Mayor has been pleased to mention in his address to me, the fortunate and agreeable journey wich I have had from home, on my rather circuitous route to the Federal Capital. I am very happy that he was enabled in truth to congratulate myself and companions [company] on that fact. It is true we have had nothing, thus far, to mar the pleasure of the trip. We have not been met alone by those who assisted in giving the election to me—I say not alone—but by the whole population of the country through which we have passed. This is as it should be.
>
> Had the election fallen to any other of the distinguished candidates instead of myself, under the peculiar circumstances, to say the least, it would have been proper for all citizens to have greeted him as you now greet me. It is evidence of the devotion of the whole people to the Constitution, the Union, and the perpetuity of the liberties of this country. (Cheers.) I am unwilling, on any occasion, that I should be so meanly thought of, as to have it supposed for a moment that I regard these demonstrations as tendered to me personally. They should be tendered to no individual man. They are tendered to the country, to the institutions of the country, and to the perpetuity of the [liberties of the] country for which these institutions were made and created.
>
> Your worthy Mayor has thought fit to express the hope that I may be able to relieve the country from its present—or I should say, its threatened difficulties. I am sure I bring a heart true to the work. (Tremendous

applause.) For the ability to perform it, I must trust in that Supreme Being who has never forsaken this favored land, through the instrumentality of this great and intelligent people. Without that assistance I shall surely fail. With it I cannot fail.

When we speak of threatened difficulties to the country, it is natural that there should be expected from me something with regard to particular measures. Upon more mature reflection, however, others will agree with me that when it is considered that these difficulties are without precedent, and have never been acted upon by any individual situated as I am, it is most proper I should wait, see the developments, and get all the light I can, so that when I do speak authoritatively I may be as near right as possible. (Cheers.) When I shall speak authoritatively, I hope to say nothing inconsistent with the Constitution, the Union, the rights of all the States, of each State, and of each section of the country, and not to disappoint the reasonable expectations of those who have confided to me their votes.

In this connection allow me to say that you, as a portion of the great American people, need only to maintain your composure. Stand up to your sober convictions of right, to your obligations to the Constitution, act in accordance with those sober convictions, and the clouds which now arise in the horizon will be dispelled, and we shall have a bright and glorious future; and when this generation has passed away, tens of thousands will inhabit this country where only thousands inhabit (it) now.

I do not propose to address you at length—I have no voice for it. Allow me again to thank you for this magnificent reception, and bid you farewell.[27]

Lincoln then whistle-stopped rapidly through the Mohawk valley—the state's heartland where moralistic Yankees and individualistic Middle Staters mixed—stopping next at Albany (February 18).

Albany meant another round of speeches—a reply to the city's mayor, a reply to Governor Morgan of New York, and an address to the New York legislature. By this time Lincoln's trip eastward was taking on something of a processional air, and his remarks were restricted accordingly. His references are almost entirely to the state pride of New Yorkers, whose state had grown so much since the founding of the Republic, but the implications of his remarks need not be lost upon us. In his reply to the governor, Lincoln adds a word or two about the role of political parties in a democracy and the relations among them.

> Almost all men in this country, and in any country where freedom of thought is tolerated, attach themselves to political parties. It is but ordinary charity to attribute this to the fact that in so attaching himself to the party which his judgment prefers, the citizen believes he thereby promotes the best interests of the whole country; and when an election is passed, it is altogether befitting a free people, that until the next election, they should be as one people.[28]

Remarks to the crowd at Poughkeepsie (February 19) were more extensive than those he made to the legislature in Albany, perhaps because the crowds in the Empire State were friendlier than the political leadership, as events were soon to prove. His words at Poughkeepsie are notable primarily because he reduces to a string of pregnant sentences framed in platform rhetoric the more elaborate and less emotionally stated principles that he had developed in Ohio. The crowd's response shows that he did indeed catch them with his rhetoric.

> It is with your aid, as the people, that I think we shall be able to preserve—not the country, for the country will preserve itself, (cheers), but the institutions of the country—(great cheering); those institutions which have made us free, intelligent and happy—the most free, the most intelligent and the happiest people on the globe.[29]

In Poughkeepsie, Lincoln drew a distinction between the country and its institutions. Recognizing that countries survive almost no matter what, he emphasizes that survival is not enough, that it is the proper maintenance of proper institutions that gives a country its tone and its reason for existence. In the American case, excellent institutions have been responsible for America's special place among the countries of the world.

Contemporary students of politics and society should be especially interested in the question of size as a political factor, as demonstrated by the difference of Lincoln's audiences in New York City and the rest of the country. The former, whose population was nearing one million, was already too big to allow Lincoln to speak to the people as a whole, undivided.

> In fact, I do not propose making a speech this afternoon. I could not be heard by any but a very small fraction of you at best.[30]

Instead, he had to politely decline to address the crowd and to speak to a self-segregated elite.

Lincoln arrived in New York City on February 19 and spoke briefly from the balcony at the Astor House. At a reception tendered him at the Astor House on that day, Lincoln for the first time addressed what we would call today the eastern establishment separately from the people as a whole. In doing so, he repeated the essence of the message he had left with the Ohio legislature.

> It was not intimated to me that I was brought into the room where Daniel Webster and Henry Clay had made speeches, and where one in my position might be expected to do something like those men, or do something unworthy of myself or my audience. I therefore will beg you to make very great allowance for the circumstances under which I have been by surprise brought before you. Now, I have been in the habit of thinking and speaking for some time upon political questions that have for some years past agitated the country, and if I were disposed to do so, and we could take up some one of the issues as the lawyers call them, and I were called upon to make an argument about it to the best of my ability, I could do that without much preparation. But that is not what you desire to be done here tonight. I have been occupying a position, since the Presidential election, of silence, of avoiding public speaking, of avoiding public writing. I have been doing so because I thought, upon full consideration, that was the proper course for me to take . . . I have not kept silent . . . from any party wantonness, or from any indifference to the anxiety that pervades the minds of men about the aspect of the political affairs of this country. I have kept silence for the reason that I supposed it was peculiarly proper that I should do so until the time came when, according to the customs of the country, I should speak officially. (Voice, partially interrogative, partially sarcastic, "Custom of the country?") I heard some gentlemen say, "According to the custom of the country;" I alluded to the custom of the President-elect at the time of taking his oath of office. That is what I meant by the custom of the country. I do suppose that while the political drama being enacted in this country at this time

> is rapidly shifting in its scenes, forbidding an anticipation with any degree of certainty today what we shall see tomorrow, that it was peculiarly fitting that I should see it all up to the last minute before I should take ground, that I might be disposed by the shifting of the scenes afterwards again to shift.[31]

Again the tone is of one leader speaking to others, amplified by the fact that, as befitted New York City, the Astor House crowd consisted of leadership from diverse fields, not simply from politics. In front of a perhaps hostile audience, Lincoln reiterated his three pillars:

> I said several times upon this journey, and I now repeat it to you, that when the time does come I shall then take the ground that I think is right—(interruption by cries of "Good," "good," and applause)—the ground I think is right for the North, for the South, for the East, for the West, for the whole country—(cries of "Good," "Hurrah for Lincoln," and great applause). And in doing so I hope to feel no necessity pressing upon me to say anything in conflict with the Constitution, in conflict with the continued Union of these States—(applause)—in conflict with the perpetuation of the liberties of these people—(cheers)—or anything in conflict with anything whatever that I have ever given you reason to expect from me.[32]

Replying to Mayor Fernando Wood the next day, Lincoln once again takes on the caution of a Christian confronting the lions.

> Mr. Mayor—It is with feelings of deep gratitude that I make my acknowledgment for this reception which has been given me in the great commercial city of New York. I cannot but remember that this is done by a people who do not by a majority agree with me in political sentiments. It is the more grateful [to me] because in this reception I see that, in regard to the great principles of our government, the people are very nearly or quite unanimous.[33]

Wood, who would later prove to be a Copperhead of the first order, had already made clear his opposition to Lincoln and the Republicans the previous November. In front of men whose stated position was to allow the South to leave peaceably rather than engage in civil war, Lincoln pointedly makes clear his own more resolute position.

> There is nothing that can ever bring me willingly to consent to the destruction of this Union, under which not only the commercial city of New York, but the whole country has acquired its greatness, unless it were to be that thing for which the Union itself was made. I understand a ship to be made for the carrying and preservation of the cargo, and so long as the ship can be saved, with the cargo, it should never be abandoned. This Union should likewise never be abandoned unless it fails and the probability of its preservation shall cease to exist without throwing the passengers and cargo overboard. So long, then, as it is possible that the prosperity and the liberties of the people can be preserved in the Union, it shall be my purpose at all times to preserve it.34

Referring to the close links between the prosperity of New York City, long since the first in the land in economic life, and the continued maintenance of the Union, Lincoln's analogy is attuned to the commercial interests and outlook of New York City.

New Jersey: Building toward the Climax

Aside from bantering whistle-stop remarks, Lincoln's major thrust in New Jersey involved separate speeches to the Senate and General Assembly at Trenton, each of which carried his thought a step further. Lincoln was in an especially flattering mood in New Jersey, flattering people, politicians, and the state itself. The thrust of his remarks was to draw analogies between the Revolutionary War, so much of which was fought in New Jersey, and the present crisis, emphasizing the importance of preserving the independent nation that the revolutionists created.

> I cannot but remember the place that New Jersey holds in our early history. In the early Revolutionary struggle, few of the States among the old Thirteen had more of the battlefields of the country within their limits than old New Jersey. May I be pardoned if, upon this occasion, I mention that away back in my childhood, the earliest days of my being able to read, I got hold of a small book, such a one as few of the younger members have ever seen, "Weem's Life of Washington." I remember all the accounts there given of the battlefields and struggles for the liberties of the country, and

> none fixed themselves upon my imagination so deeply as the struggle here at Trenton, New Jersey. The crossing of the river; the contest with the Hessians; the great hardships endured at that time, all fixed themselves on my memory more than any single revolutionary event; and you all know, for you have all been boys, how these early impressions last longer than any others. I recollect thinking then, boy even though I was, that there must have been something more than common that those men struggled for. I am exceedingly anxious that that thing which they struggled for; that something even more than National Independence; that something that held out a great promise to all the people of the world to all time to come; I am exceedingly anxious that this Union, the Constitution, and the liberties of the people shall be perpetuated in accordance with the original idea for which that struggle was made, and I shall be most happy indeed if I shall be an humble instrument in the hands of the Almighty, and of this, his almost chosen people, for perpetuating the object of that great struggle.[35]

Lincoln not only returned to his theme—the Union, the Constitution, and the liberties of the people—but also added a new and pregnant phrase in his description of the Americans, calling them "the almost chosen people." His analogy to the Jews is both pious (in the sense that he does not claim for the Americans an honor and a burden God has bestowed upon another people) and ironic. He implies that the imperfections of the American people keep them from being fully chosen; they are only almost.

Addressing the New Jersey General Assembly, for the first time Lincoln makes it clear that he will fight if the South will not return in peace.

> I shall do all that may be in my power to promote a peaceful settlement of all our difficulties. The man does not live who is more devoted to peace than I am. (Cheers.) None who would do more to preserve it. But it may be necessary to put the foot down firmly. (Here the audience broke out into cheers so loud and long that for some moments it was impossible to hear Mr. Lincoln's voice. He continued:) And if I do my duty, and do right, you will sustain me, will you not? (Loud cheers, and cries of "Yes," "Yes," "We will.") Received, as I am, by the members of a Legislature the majority of whom do not agree with me in political sentiments, I trust that I may have

their assistance in piloting the ship of State through this voyage, surrounded by perils as it is; for, if it should suffer attack now, there will be no pilot ever needed for another voyage.[36]

The response from a legislative body dominated by Democrats is all that Lincoln could have wished for.

Pennsylvania, Philadelphia, and the Declaration of Independence

The climax of Lincoln's trip was his sojourn in Pennsylvania, which included his climatic address at Independence Hall in Philadelphia on Washington's Birthday. Throughout his adult life, Lincoln had insisted that all his political principles flowed from the Declaration of Independence.[37] Now, on his way to the seat of the national government to assume the highest office in the land at a time when the Union itself seemed to be falling apart, he was in the very city and at the very place where the Declaration was written and adopted. He made full use of the moment.

Lincoln struck the note for his visit in his reply to the greetings of Mayor Alexander Henry of Philadelphia. First reiterating the themes he had shaped on the way east, he concluded his brief remarks by indicating the extent of his devotion to the Declaration of Independence and the Constitution, utilizing biblical language and phraseology to do so ("May my right hand forget its cunning and my tongue cleave to the roof of my mouth," Psalms 137:5–6).

> Mr. Mayor and Fellow-Citizens of Philadelphia—I appear before you to make no lengthy speech. I appear before you to thank you for the reception. The reception you have given me tonight is not to me, the man, the individual, but to the man who temporarily represents, or should represent, the majesty of the nation. (Applause.) It is true, as your worthy Mayor has said, that there is great anxiety amongst the citizens of the United States at this time. I say I deem it a happy circumstance that the dissatisfied portion of our fellow citizens do not point us to anything in which they are being injured, or about to be injured, from which I have felt all the while justified in concluding that the crisis, the panic, the anxiety of the country at this time is

artificial. If there be those who differ with me upon this subject, they have not pointed out the substantial difficulty that exists. (Tremendous cheering.)

I do not mean to say that this artificial panic has not done harm. That it has done much harm I do not deny. The hope that has been expressed by your worthy Mayor, that I may be able to restore peace and harmony and prosperity to the country, is most worthy in him; and most happy indeed shall I be if I shall be able to fulfill and verify that hope. (Cheers.)

I promise you in all sincerity, that I bring to the work a sincere heart. Whether I will bring a head equal to that heart, will be for future time to determine. It were useless for me to speak of the details of the plans now. I shall speak officially on next Monday week, if ever. If I should not speak, then it were useless for me to do so now. (If I do speak, then it is useless for me to do so now.) When I do speak, as your worthy Mayor has expressed the hope, I will take such grounds as I shall deem best calculated to restore peace, harmony and prosperity to the country, and tend to the perpetuity of the nation, and the liberty of these States and all these people.

Your worthy Mayor has expressed the wish, in which I join with him, that if it were convenient for me to remain with you in your city long enough to consult, (your merchants and manufacturers;) or, as it were, to listen to those breathings rising within the consecrated walls where the Constitution of the United States, and, I will add, the Declaration of American Independence was originally framed, I would do so.

I assure you and your Mayor that I had hoped on this occasion, and upon all occasions during my life, that I shall do nothing inconsistent with the teachings of those holy and most sacred walls.

I have never asked anything that does not breathe from those walls. All my political warfare has been in favor of the teachings coming forth from that sacred hall. May my right hand forget its cunning and my tongue cleave to the roof of my mouth, if ever I prove false to those teachings.[38]

On Washington's Birthday, 1861, Lincoln spoke from Declaration Hall to the people of Philadelphia and through them, to the nation. His words must be read in their entirety.

Mr. Cuyler:—I am filled with deep emotion at finding myself standing here in the place where were collected together the wisdom, the patriotism, the devotion to principle, from which sprang the institutions under which we live. You have kindly suggested to me that in my hands is the task of restoring peace to our distracted country. I can say in return, sir, that all the political sentiments I entertain have been drawn, so far as I have been able to draw them, from the sentiments which originated, and were given to the world from this hall in which we stand. I have never had a feeling politically that did not spring from the sentiments embodied in the Declaration of Independence. (Great cheering.) I have often pondered over the dangers which were incurred by the men who assembled here and adopted that Declaration of Independence—I have pondered over the toils that were endured by the officers and soldiers of the army, who achieved that Independence. (Applause.) I have often inquired of myself what great principle or idea it was that kept this Confederacy so long together. It was not the mere matter of the separation of the colonies from the mother land; but something in that Declaration giving liberty, not alone to the people of this country, but hope to the world for all future time. (Great applause.) It was that which gave promise that in due time the weights should be lifted from the shoulders of all men, and that all should have an equal chance. (Cheers.) This is the sentiment embodied in that Declaration of Independence.

Now, my friends, can this country be saved upon that basis? If it can, I will consider myself one of the happiest men in the world if I can help to save it. If it can't be saved upon that principle, it will be truly awful. But, if this country cannot be saved without giving up that principle—I was about to say I would rather be assassinated on this spot than to surrender it. (Applause.)

Now, in my view of the present aspect of affairs, there is no need of bloodshed and war. There is no necessity for it. I am not in favor of such a course, and I may say in advance, there will be no blood shed unless it be forced upon the Government. The Government will not use force unless force is used against it. (Prolonged applause and cries of "That's the proper sentiment.")

> My friends, this is a wholly unprepared speech. I did not expect to be called upon to say a word when I came here—I supposed I was merely to do something towards raising a flag. I may, therefore, have said something indiscreet (cries of "no, no"), but I have said nothing but what I am willing to live by, and in the pleasure of Almighty God, die by.[39]

In acknowledging his commitment to the principles of the Declaration, he raises the tone of his entire trip to the highest plane. No longer is his theme simply the survival of the Constitution and the liberties of the American people in the face of an immediate crisis; it is the Declaration and the country that created it as the hope of the world for all people for all time.

Lincoln would arrive in Washington by the end of the month ultimately committed to saving the Union in order to preserve the reality of that great truth. All the compromises he would make in the first two years of the war, all the abuse he would receive for making those compromises, all the claims he would subsequently set forth to justify those compromises must be read in light of the commitment he made publicly at the place that for him was the most sacred in the whole world. So moved was Lincoln by that place that he, who had been so careful to prepare his most significant remarks well before delivering them at each point on his journey, did not prepare, did not dare to prepare to speak at Independence Hall; yet his closing words reflect the oathlike character of his extemporaneous talk and how he felt bound by them as by an oath. One seeks an analogy for Lincoln at Independence Hall on Washington's Birthday, 1861. It can only be found in the biblical descriptions of leaders covenanting with their people to gain legitimate entitlement to their high office.

We may well ponder whether Lincoln would have made so revealing a speech had he prepared himself beforehand, given his reluctance to be too revealing during the course of the journey. His second speech, at the flag-raising ceremony at Independence Hall, certainly reflects the restoration of careful caution that had marked his utterances up until the time he was overwhelmed by personal emotions at that place.

> Fellow Citizens:—I am invited and called before you to participate in raising above Independence Hall the flag of our country, with an additional star upon it.[40] (Cheers.) I propose now, in advance of performing this very

pleasant and complimentary duty, to say a few words. I propose to say that when that flag was originally raised here it had but thirteen stars. I wish to call your attention to the fact, that, under the blessing of God, each additional star added to that flag has given additional prosperity and happiness to this country until it has advanced to its present condition; and its welfare in the future, as well as in the past, is in your hands. (Cheers.) Cultivating the spirit that animated our fathers, who gave renown and celebrity to this Hall, cherishing that fraternal feeling which has so long characterized us as a nation, excluding passion, ill-temper and precipitate action on all occasions, I think we may promise ourselves that not only the new star placed upon that flag shall be permitted to remain there to our permanent prosperity for years to come, but additional ones shall from time to time be placed there, until we shall number as was anticipated by the great historian, five hundred millions of happy and prosperous people. (Great applause.) With these few remarks, I proceed to the very agreeable duty assigned me.[41]

Several specific points should be noted in reading Lincoln's words. He begins by reiterating the importance of institutions in shaping men, even in shaping wisdom, patriotism, and devotion to principle, at least the first and last of which are often assumed to be inherent in men independent of their institutions. Lincoln suggests that they are not—that even wisdom is dependent upon humans' developing within an appropriate institutional framework.

Lincoln emphasizes that all his *political sentiments* are from the Declaration. This is at once a broad and a narrow claim. His religious principles, for example—to which he refers in the final paragraph of his first speech and in his second—necessarily have another source. Moreover, Lincoln strongly suggests that the former must flow from the latter.

From Philadelphia, Lincoln journeyed to his last stop, the Pennsylvania state capital at Harrisburg. At his one brief pause along the way, in Lancaster, he reiterated his threefold theme in a manner that combined political banter and seriousness of purpose. In Harrisburg itself he made two speeches, one a reply to the lengthy greetings of Governor Andrew J. Curtin, who was to become, barely two months later, one of his strongest supporters in mobilizing the Union for war, and the second to the state legislature. In his reply to Governor Curtin, he took the occasion to allude to the principles of peace upon which Pennsylvania as a

Quaker commonwealth was founded, adopting them as his own, while at the same time implying his willingness to utilize the military forces symbolized by the militia that greeted him to preserve the Union.[42]

Lincoln's speeches in Pennsylvania and, most particularly, his speech to the state legislature are markedly different from those made in Ohio and New York, because Pennsylvania had supported him strongly in the presidential election. Thus he could speak there as if among friends. Consequently he took the opportunity to clarify his remarks regarding civil war, indicating explicitly that he is prepared to fight a war to save the Union, though he hopes to avoid it.

Lincoln's references to his speech of that same morning in Philadelphia help us to understand that speech all the better, and his commentary on the ceremonies that accompanied it is characteristic of the man's conception of himself as an instrument rather than an engineer.

> I for the first time appear at the Capitol of the great Commonwealth of Pennsylvania, upon the birthday of the Father of his Country. In connection with that beloved anniversary connected with the history of this country, I have already gone through one exceedingly interesting scene this morning in the ceremonies at Philadelphia. Under the kind conduct of gentlemen there, I was for the first time allowed the privilege of standing in old Independence Hall (enthusiastic cheering), to have a few words addressed to me there and opening up to me an opportunity of expressing with much regret that I had not more time to express something of my own feelings excited by the occasion—somewhat to harmonize and give shape to the feelings that had been really the feelings of my whole life.
>
> Besides this, our friends there had provided a magnificent flag of the country. They had arranged it so that I was given the honor of raising it to the head of its staff (applause); and when it went up, I was pleased that it went to its place by the strength of my own feeble arm. When, according to the arrangement, the cord was pulled and it flaunted gloriously to the wind without an accident, in the light (bright) glowing sunshine of the morning, I could not help hoping that there was in the entire success of that beautiful ceremony, at least something of an omen of what is to come. (Loud applause.) Nor could I help, feeling then as I often have felt, that in the whole of that proceeding I was a very humble instrument. I had not provided the

flag; I had not made the arrangement for elevating it to its place; I had applied but a very small portion of even my feeble strength in raising it. In the whole transaction, I was in the hands of the people who had arranged it, and if I can have the same generous cooperation of the people of this nation, I think the flag of our country may yet be kept flaunting gloriously.[43]

From Springfield, capital of Illinois, to Harrisburg, capital of Pennsylvania, Lincoln reiterated his self-perception as merely the instrument of something greater than himself—the American people, the Almighty, the larger thrust of human efforts to achieve liberty—rather than a social engineer or a manipulator of others.

Washington and the First Inaugural

The culmination of Lincoln's journey was set down on successive pieces of paper on the last three days of February 1861. On February 26, Lincoln formally accepted the presidency in writing as provided in the Constitution.

With deep gratitude to my countrymen for this mark of their confidence; with a distrust of my own ability to perform the required duty under the most favorable circumstances, now rendered doubly difficult by existing national perils; yet with a firm reliance on the strength of our free government, and the ultimate loyalty of the people to the just principles upon which it is founded, and above all an unshaken faith in the Supreme Ruler of nations, I accept this trust. Be pleased to signify my acceptance to the respective Houses of Congress.[44]

Here Lincoln is more specific about the relationship between his political and religious sentiments.

On the twenty-seventh, Lincoln arrived in Washington and responded to the welcome brought by the mayor of that city, and on the twenty-eighth he appeared publicly in Washington for the first time to receive a serenade from the citizenry. Washington in 1861 was a southern city, overall. Thus, his reply to the mayor is directed specifically to Southerners as befits his first statement on slave territory.

Mr. Mayor—I thank you, and through you the municipal authorities of this city by whom you are accompanied for this welcome; and as it is the first

> time in my life, since the present phase of politics has presented itself in this country, that I have said anything publicly within a region of country where the institution of slavery exists, I will take this occasion to say, that I think very much of the ill feeling that has existed and still exists between the people of the section from whence I came and the people here, is owing to a misunderstanding between each other which unhappily prevails. I therefore avail myself of this opportunity to assure you, Mr. Mayor, and all the gentlemen present, that I have not now, and never have had, any other than as kindly feelings toward you as to the people of my own section. I have not now, and never have had, any disposition to treat you in any respect otherwise than as my own neighbors. I have not now any purpose to withhold from you any of the benefits of the Constitution, under any circumstances, that I would not feel myself constrained to withhold from my own neighbors; and I hope, in a word, when we shall become better acquainted—and I say it with great confidence—we shall like each other the more.[45]

He struck this theme in a more elaborate fashion in his response to the serenade.

Throughout his journey, Lincoln had promised to break his silence on substantive policy at the first opportunity. The first opportunity presented itself on March 4, when he gave his first inaugural address. That address is a fitting conclusion to his month of geographic and intellectual movement.

The address as a whole is a series of summary statements of the themes Lincoln struck on his journey and that he here either acknowledges or elaborates. It is a careful speech directed to the most immediate issue of the day—maintaining peace and union. Following the lines set forth on his journey, he took the most conservative stance possible, even agreeing to the enforcement of the fugitive slave laws (which he personally considered a moral abomination), although in a carefully worded way that did not commit the national government to new legislation on the subject.

The central theme of the speech is the maintenance of the indivisability of the union of states.

> I hold, that in contemplation of universal law, and of the Constitution, the Union of these States is perpetual. Perpetuity is implied, if not expressed, in the fundamental law of all national governments. It is safe to assert that no

> government proper, ever had a provision in its organic law for its own termination. Continue to execute all the express provisions of our national Constitution, and the Union will endure forever—it being impossible to destroy it, except by some action not provided for in the instrument itself.
>
> Again, if the United States be not a government proper, but an association of States in the nature of contract merely, can it, as a contract, be peaceably unmade, by less than all the parties who made it? One party to a contract may violate it—break it, so to speak; but does it not require all to lawfully rescind it?

Lincoln justifies the rights of the states to maintain their own domestic institutions not on the grounds of state sovereignty but because their position is essential to the national balance of power that maintains the American political fabric.

The newly inaugurated president continues with the discussion of his political theory of the Union. Tracing the Union back to preindependence days, he presents support for the perpetuity of the Union from both the nationalist and the federalist perspectives. In doing so, he lays the groundwork for maintaining both the authority and the services of the national government in the seceding states, both essential if government is to be preserved. (Lincoln's view of historical fact was to be made constitutional doctrine by the United States Supreme Court in 1936.) A month later the war would start, in a manner consistent with the policy Lincoln laid out in his inaugural address. It would continue on the same basis, and just as the authority of the federal government would ultimately be asserted, so too would the services provided by it to every part of the Union be restored to the seceding states as well.

> In legal contemplation, the Union is perpetual, confirmed by the history of the Union itself. The Union is much older than the Constitution. It was formed in fact, by the Articles of Association in 1774. It was matured and continued by the Declaration of Independence in 1776. It was further matured and the faith of all the then thirteen States expressly plighted and engaged that it should be perpetual, by the Articles of Confederation in 1778. And finally, in 1787, one of the declared objects for ordaining and establishing the Constitution, was *"to form a more perfect union."*

The Constitution, the Union, and Liberties 241

> But if destruction of the Union, by one, or by a part only, of the States, be lawfully possible, the Union is *less* perfect than before the Constitution, having lost the vital element of perpetuity.
>
> It follows from these views that no State, upon its own mere motion, can lawfully get out of the Union,—that *resolves* and *ordinances* to that effect are legally void; and that acts of violence, within any State or States, against the authority of the United States, are insurrectionary or revolutionary, according to circumstances.

From his theory of the Union, Lincoln moves on to his philosophy of popular government and the relationship between rule by majority and the constitutional protection of the right of minorities, elaborating upon the thoughts in his previous speeches with simplicity and clarity.

> If, by the mere force of numbers, a majority should deprive a minority of any clearly written constitutional right, it might, in a moral point of view, justify revolution—certainly would, if such right were a vital one. But such is not our case. All the vital rights of minorities, and of individuals, are so plainly assured to them, by affirmations and negations, guarranties and prohibitions, in the Constitution, that controversies never arise concerning them. But no organic law can ever be framed with a provision specifically applicable to every question which may occur in practical administration. No foresight can anticipate, nor any document of reasonable length contain express provisions for all possible questions. Shall fugitives from labor be surrendered by national or by State authority? The Constitution does not expressly say. *May* Congress prohibit slavery in the territories? The Constitution does not expressly say. *Must* Congress protect slavery in the territories? The Constitution does not expressly say.
>
> From questions of this class spring all our constitutional controversies, and we divide upon them into majorities and minorities. If the minority will not acquiesce, the majority must, or the government must cease. There is no other alternative; for continuing the government, is acquiescence on one side or the other. If a minority, in such case, will secede rather than acquiesce, they make a precedent which, in turn, will divide and ruin them; for a minority of their own will secede from them, whenever a majority refuses

to be controlled by such minority. For instance, why may not any portion of a new confederacy, a year or two hence, arbitrarily secede again, precisely as portions of the present Union now claim to secede from it. All who cherish disunion sentiments, are now being educated to the exact temper of doing this. Is there such perfect identity of interests among the States to compose a new Union, as to produce harmony only, and prevent renewed secession?

Plainly, the central idea of secession, is the essence of anarchy. A majority, held in restraint by constitutional checks, and limitations, and always changing easily, with deliberate changes of popular opinions and sentiments, is the only true sovereign of a free people. Whoever rejects it, does, of necessity, fly to anarchy or to despotism. Unanimity is impossible; the rule of a minority, as a permanent arrangement, is wholly inadmissible; so that, rejecting the majority principle, anarchy, or despotism in some form, is all that is left.

Further on, he considers the role and limits of judicial review in a democratic polity.

I do not forget the position assumed by some, that constitutional questions are to be decided by the Supreme Court; nor do I deny that such decisions must be binding in any case, upon the parties to a suit, as to the object of that suit, while they are also entitled to very high respect and consideration, in all parallel cases, by all other departments of the government. And while it is obviously possible that such decision may be erroneous in any given case, still the evil effect following it, being limited to that particular case, with the chance that it may be over-ruled, and never become a precedent for other cases, can better be borne than could the evils of a different practice. At the same time the candid citizen must confess that if the policy of the government, upon vital questions, affecting the whole people, is to be irrevocably fixed by decisions of the Supreme Court, the instant they are made, in ordinary litigation between parties, in personal actions, the people will have ceased to be their own rulers, having, to that extent, practically resigned their government into the hands of that eminent tribunal. Nor is there, in this view, any assault upon the court, or the judges. It is a duty,

The Constitution, the Union, and Liberties

> from which they may not shrink, to decide cases properly brought before them; and it is no fault of theirs, if others seek to turn their decisions to political purposes.

Lincoln turns, in his concluding argument, to North American political geography and how it affects the maintenance of the Union. Again the themes are familiar.

> Physically speaking, we cannot separate. We cannot remove our respective sections from each other, nor build an impassable wall between them. A husband and wife may be divorced, and go out of the presence, and beyond the reach of each other; but the different parts of our country cannot do this. They cannot but remain face to face; and intercourse, either amicable or hostile, must continue between them. Is it possible then to make that intercourse more advantageous, or more satisfactory, *after* separation than *before*? Can aliens make treaties easier than friends can make laws? Can treaties be more faithfully enforced between aliens, than laws can among friends? Suppose you go to war, you cannot fight always; and when, after much loss on both sides, and no gain on either, you cease fighting, the identical old questions, as to terms of intercourse, are again upon you.

Lincoln suggests deliberateness and avoidance of haste or precipitous action.

> This country, with its institutions, belongs to the people who inhabit it. Whenever they shall grow weary of the existing government, they can exercise their *constitutional* right of amending it, or their *revolutionary* right to dismember, or overthrow it.
>
> The chief Magistrate derives all his authority from the people, and they have conferred none upon him to fix terms for the separation of the States. The people themselves can do this also if they choose; but the executive, as such, has nothing to do with it. His duty is to administer the present government, as it came to his hands, and to transmit it, unimpaired by him, to his successor.
>
> Why should there not be a patient confidence in the ultimate justice of the people? Is there any better, or equal hope, in the world? In our present differences, is either party without faith of being in the right? If the Almighty

> Ruler of nations, with his eternal truth and justice, be on your side of the North, or on yours of the South, that truth, and that justice, will surely prevail, by the judgment of this great tribunal, the American people.
>
> By the frame of the government under which we live, this same people have wisely given their public servants but little power for mischief; and have, with equal wisdom, provided for the return of that little to their own hands at very short intervals.
>
> While the people retain their virtue, and vigilance, no administration, by any extreme of wickedness or folly, can very seriously injure the government, in the short space of four years.

The conclusion of the first draft of the address was sharp and even belligerent; Lincoln set the choice before the American people in no uncertain terms, utilizing a powerful biblical verse to make it clear.

> In *your* hands, my dissatisfied fellow countrymen, and not in *mine*, is the momentous issue of civil war. The government will not assail *you*, unless you *first* assail *it*. You can have no conflict, without being yourselves the aggressors. *You* have no oath registered in Heaven to destroy the government, while *I* shall have the most solemn one to "preserve, protect, and defend" it. *You* can forbear the *assault* upon it; *I* can *not* shrink from the *defense* of it. With *you*, and not with *me*, is the solemn question of "Shall it be peace, or a sword?"

In the final version, however, he sounds like the compassionate Lincoln we have enshrined in our country's national memory:

> I am loth to close. We are not enemies, but friends. We must not be enemies. Though passion may have strained, it must not break our bonds of affection. The mystic chords of memory, stretching from every battlefield, and patriot grave, to every living heart and hearthstone, all over this broad land, will yet swell the chorus of the Union, when again touched, as surely they will be, by the better angels of our nature.

11

COPING WITH CONSTITUTIONAL CRISES

Virtually every democratic polity has at some time in its history come to a point when normal constitutional processes have failed to accommodate some crisis and to achieve the political changes needed to meet or transcend that crisis, requiring extraconstitutional action to preserve constitutional democracy. In some polities this has been a one-time situation, in others it is a regular feature of political life—so much so that their very democratic character is questionable. In any case, it is an issue with serious implications for democratic government.

The United States, which Americans perceive to be one of the most stable, if not the most stable, of democratic polities, has had at least three and perhaps four such constitutional crises in its history. The first two were connected with its founding, namely the revolution against Britain and the adoption of the Constitution; the others with the country's "original sin"—the problem of slavery and black rights, a problem never fully accommodated within normal constitutional politics.

While celebrating their revolution, Americans are ambivalent about its revolutionary character; yet it was indeed a revolution. Whether from the American perspective, which saw the British Empire as a kind of federation of self-governing entities, or from the British perspective, which viewed the peripheral countries of the empire as responsible to the imperial center in London, change was effected by other than constitutional means.¹ That this is not the featured way of describing the American Revolution no doubt is because even at the time Americans sought to minimize the extraconstitutional measures taken and immediately moved to constitutionalize them within new or reconstituted political frameworks.

The American argument was that since political sovereignty rests with the people, the people of the various bodies politic within the imperial federation could resume the direct exercise of their sovereignty and reconstitute their governments along more suitable lines.² This is what happened in each of the states, and this is what the representatives of the states came together to do—to found the United States of America.³ The American theory of popular sovereignty was enshrined, at least symbolically, in many of the constitutional documents of the revolutionary period and remained a living doctrine in one form or another until the Civil War. Subsequently it was taken off the shelf only to establish new states within the American federation, but it remains a potentially powerful tool for dealing with the problem raised here.

The Articles of Confederation were the first national product of the American effort at constitutionalization. Their perceived weakness led to the second product, begun in 1786 with the abortive Annapolis Convention that launched the process of constitutional reform in the new United States of America, leading to the 1787 constitutional convention in Philadelphia and ultimately to the replacement of the Articles with a new federal constitution. To do so the convention had to act beyond the charge given it by the Confederation Congress, its parent body, and to cross the line between legitimate constitutional action into what was at the very least a gray zone and probably amounted to a usurpation of constitutional powers. The convention succeeded because its usurpation was accepted by national consensus every step along the way.⁴

The constitutional convention of 1787 continued the process begun in Annapolis. The convention drafted an entirely new constitution for the United States, completely ignoring the Articles of Confederation except for the allusion in the Preamble—that the new instrument was designed to form a *more perfect* union. They provided for ratification of the new constitution by state conventions, bypassing the sitting state legislatures, and specified that it would go into effect upon ratification by nine of the thirteen states instead of holding to the Articles' requirement for unanimity in matters of constitutional change. The results were so successful that all but the most serious students of American history ignore the illegality inherent in the process.

It is not quite clear whether that theory of popular sovereignty was put into play at the Annapolis Convention, but the Philadelphia Convention turned to it to legitimize its actions by requiring that the proposed constitution be adopted by popular conventions in the states. That was the metaconstitutional answer to the constitutional crisis of 1786–87.

Another version of the popular sovereignty approach, initiated by Stephen A. Douglas, was tried in the 1850s to avert the constitutional crisis over slavery. His idea was to solve the problem of slavery in the territories by allowing the settlers of each new territory to choose whether it would be slave or free. This set off a rush by both sides to establish a sufficient presence in each territory, even temporarily, to control the decision, thereby generating a miniature civil war in Kansas that exacerbated the national crisis.

Not only was Douglas's idea practically unworkable, but it ran against the essence of the American constitutional tradition, which held that while all governments are derived from the people, constitutional decisions shall never be made by transient majorities. Popular sovereignty in the American political tradition always involves a balance between popular initiatives and self-imposed institutional constraints. Douglas's theory relied on the former but made no provision for the latter, hence it had disastrous consequences.[5]

In the crisis over slavery, the southern states applied what they believed to be the same rationale for seceding that the American colonies had used in their revolt against Britain. In fact, it is not quite clear whether the southern theoreticians and statesmen relied on popular sovereignty or on something new—state sovereignty, which reified their states as primordial polities following the organic theories of John C. Calhoun. Calhoun, in a major break with earlier American political ideas, rejected the idea that the original civil society was based on a covenant or compact in favor of an organic theory of the polity. He held that true polities are those that develop organically so that a natural aristocracy of wealth and talent ("the best and the brightest") emerges to govern and has the means and leisure to do so, while those who are natural slaves assume (or are reduced to) their proper place in society.

According to Calhoun each state was such an organic society, hence its sovereignty was primary. The federal union was a secondary political order, formed by the states by compact for their benefit, which could not claim precedence over the interests of any state.

Calhoun's justification of rule by the planter class and the maintenance of slavery, which became standard southern doctrine, directly justified secession as a legitimate exercise of state sovereignty. It also was a perfect example of the organic theory and its center-periphery model. As such, it broke with the American constitutional tradition.[6] Lincoln's arguments, presented in chapter 10, were in direct and deliberate confrontation with that organic theory and its implications.

Be that as it may, the constitutional crisis of preserving the Union and emancipating the slaves was ultimately resolved by the most extraconstitutional of means—war. To successfully prosecute that war, President Abraham Lincoln had to expand the powers of the presidency to their limits and beyond, taking clearly extraconstitutional actions, a number of which were later held to be such by the United States Supreme Court after the war had been safely won. They included, among other things, suspension of habeas corpus, extension of martial law over loyal parts of the Union, administrative detention of suspected southern supporters, emancipation of the slaves in the rebellious states as a war measure, suppression of newspapers, and arranging for the secession of western Virginia from Virginia. (Ironically, the court that made those decisions was presided over by Chief Justice Salmon P. Chase, who had been one of the most vociferous advocates of extreme action when he was secretary of the treasury in Lincoln's cabinet.)

Much as he admired the founding fathers and the Declaration of Independence, which formed the cornerstone of his political thought as president, Lincoln could not fall back on their arguments of popular sovereignty to justify his actions. Instead he developed a doctrine of metaconstitutionalism, arguing for the primary right of the United States to exist and suggesting that the task of a statesman in his position was to recognize that the Constitution without the Union would not be a constitution. Hence the first task was preserving the Union in order to preserve the Constitution.[7]

This is a dangerous doctrine if carried too far. Lincoln's greatness lay not in his enunciation of the doctrine, but in the way he carried it out. He did not try to pretend that his actions were constitutional; rather, he played the role of the suffering servant of the people who took upon himself the burden of extraconstitutional and even unconstitutional actions and was prepared to submit himself to judgment and punishment once the Union and the Constitution were saved.[8] Thus his actions did not establish precedents. The most extreme ones were struck down by the Supreme Court, as mentioned above.

Most important, at no time were any of his actions glossed over with sophistries, as was the case with many constitutional changes wrought by similarly informal means in the twentieth century and simultaneously or retroactively justified through the most sophisticated of sophistries. The first of these was the assumption of extraordinary powers over the economy and internal security matters by the federal executive branch during World War I. The latter were similar to those Lincoln assumed in the Civil War, whereas the former, which included nationalization of the railroads, represented a new departure. These had relatively little long-range impact; most Americans were repelled by the experience. Indeed, state actions emulating the federal government led to the beginning of United States Supreme Court application of the Bill of Rights to the states in the *Gitlow v. New York* (1925), thereby precipitating a long-term constitutional revolution on behalf of greater individual rights.

In fact, Lincoln's extraconstitutional efforts to save the Union were preceded in 1803 by President Thomas Jefferson's extraconstitutional efforts to expand it through the Louisiana Purchase. As Henry Adams brilliantly portrays in his *History of the Administrations of Thomas Jefferson*, Jefferson used the powers inherent in the presidency to purchase the Louisiana Territory from France. Not only was that act constitutionally problematic in itself but, through the treaty of purchase, the United States promised that the settled parts of the Territory would be admitted to the Union as states equal to those already members of the federation, an exercise of power far in excess of any the presidency has ever claimed since.

To compound Jefferson's violation of the Constitution as he and his secretary of state, James Madison, had interpreted it only five years earlier in the Virginia and Kentucky resolutions, Jefferson, with Madison's support, then extended American rule over Louisiana as if it were a European-style colony, not part of a union of free people. Jefferson instituted absolute rule under presidential authority and secured an act of Congress providing for the governance of the settled part of the territory, renamed the Territory of Orleans (now the state of Louisiana) under presidential rule. Under it the governor, territorial officers, a territorial legislative council, and a judiciary, all were appointed by the president without even the formality of Senate confirmation. All held office either at the president's pleasure or for fixed terms, leaving their future in the hands of the chief magistrate.

Jefferson himself privately believed that his acts were unconstitutional and wanted to ask Congress to amend the Constitution to legitimize his acts. Madison and Albert Gallitin, the secretary of the treasury and third man of the Jeffersonian ruling triumvirate, persuaded him otherwise for strategic reasons, so as not to suggest to the French and Spanish that the treaty was not legitimate. This was to be avoided especially since the Spanish had a good case against the French who, on securing a retrocession of the territory by Spain, had promised the latter country that they would never transfer it to any foreign power.

The idea of a constitutional amendment died in Jefferson's cabinet, and the president proceeded to violate many of his own principles. He did so to extend the territory of the United States of America so as to, in his mind, secure American liberty for a thousand years by assuring a sufficient public domain to build a nation of yeoman farmers that would never be dominated by the commercial or industrial classes. The combination of a real opportunity and Jefferson's ideological commitment to a particular kind of civil society got the better of his constitutional scruples.

In the end, Jefferson's dictatorial presidential rule turned out to be a flitting phase as Congress and the administration undertook to organize a more acceptable form of territorial government. In 1812, nine years after the Purchase, Louisiana was admitted to the Union as a state, while the rest of the original Louisiana territory was absorbed into the Union in the manner of the Old Northwest and Old Southwest, with each segment achieving statehood in due course.

The difference between Lincoln's extraconstitutional acts and Jefferson's lay in Lincoln's acknowledgment of their tragic necessity in contrast to Jefferson's effort to publicly ignore the fact that they were extraconstitutional and to allow his supporters to build elaborate justifications for them. In this respect, Jefferson acted like a later president, Franklin Delano Roosevelt, who did the same in connection with the New Deal. Perhaps this kind of inconsistency is a characteristic of Jeffersonian politics, just as Federalist and Whig politics may be more likely to accept inconsistency openly as one of the paradoxes of life and not seek to justify inconsistencies constitutionally.

Later generations of Jeffersonians were to repudiate the Jeffersonian violation of the constitutional compact, well after the fact. That repudiation reached its apogee in Chief Justice Roger Taney's opinion in the Dred Scott case in 1857. Henry Adams, on the other hand, argues that, with that violation, the Constitution was forever changed from a compact which provided for a federal government of limited, delegated powers to the constitution of a nation. While the extreme state's rights argument would not be finally rejected as a possibility until Lincoln saved the Union sixty years later, the Louisiana Purchase changed the argument which divided the country's two major parties to a sectional one. Whoever would be in control of the general government henceforth would accept a broader view of its powers and he who sat in the presidency would be more likely to accept a broader view yet.

It was in this spirit that the New Deal reinterpreted the commerce clause of the United States Constitution to allow federal government intervention in all aspects of the country's economic life and the extensive federal regulation that flowed from it. It was here that sophisticated sophistry came into its own. Rather than doing what was needed to save the country from the ravages of the Great Depression and explaining that these were extraordinary measures that should not set precedents, supporters of the New Deal sought to constitutionally justify its acts or to denigrate the Constitution as outmoded. Lincoln, in contrast, called the baby by its name and shouldered the responsibility.

Lincoln's constitutional humility and the Chase court's constitutional rigor stand in striking contrast to the way the fourth crisis was handled—the civil rights revolution of the 1960s. At first it too was approached through constitutional means, with the United States Supreme Court leading the way. As the public response of both proponents and opponents of desegregation and integration began to get out of hand, however, the institutions seemed to have panicked from a constitutional point of view. It is true that extraordinary measures were called for, but in developing and applying those measures no effort was made to draw a line between what was normally constitutional and what was an extraordinary response to perhaps the greatest crisis to strike the American body politic since the Civil War.

Moreover, because no such separation was made, other notions came into play.[9] Thus the Voting Rights Act, which was necessary to correct the previous injustice of denying blacks the right to vote in the southern states, was in the name of equality extended to various northern and western states where there had never been a problem, but in which minorities simply had lower turnout rates, thereby extending federal intervention unnecessarily. Without going into further detail, it is possible to suggest that the fourth crisis was managed through extraconstitutional stretching of the Constitution, thereby establishing dangerous precedents for more normal times in the future, precedents that within a decade were to be invoked for massive federal intervention into the domains of the states through use of all the same sophistries.

Finally, most federal constitutional change in the United States is achieved through constitutional interpretation, principally but not exclusively by the federal Supreme Court. Given the flexible approach to constitutionalism characteristic of American political culture and the ambiguity deliberately built into the document itself, it is possible to go very far in legitimately introducing constitutional change through interpretation. That is a much studied and discussed subject that falls outside our purview, although at times the interpretations rendered seem no less extraconstitutional usurpations than the extraordinary actions considered here.

The American experience is paradigmatic. We see four approaches to the problem of extraconstitutional activity to deal with crises requiring fundamental political change: revolution, a constitutional coup freely ratified by the people, extraconstitutional activity by a leader who took the burden of unconstitutionality upon himself, and stretching the constitution itself in unconstitutional ways. What is common to all of them is the effort to minimize departure from the constitutional documents or traditions even while taking whatever action is necessary and simultaneously endorsing constitutional norms. In all four cases the American people have ignored or downplayed the constitutional problems involved so as to reemphasize the continuity of constitutionalism, emphasizing the myth at the expense of the exact truth.

Table 11.1 Paradigms of Domestic Extraconstitutional Change

Paradigm	Selected Examples
Revolution	American Revolution (1775–83)
Popularly ratified constitutional coup	Constitution of 1787 (1786–89)
Extraconstitutional action by great leader	American Civil War (1861–65)
Extraconstitutional stretching of the constitution	American Civil Rights Revolution (1964–68)
Temporary Military intervention	Latin America (repeatedly)
Organic adjustment	Britain (late seventeenth century)
Crown intervention	Spain (1977–78)

Implications

The experience of other countries suggests that there are other paradigms for achieving fundamental constitutional and political change in democratic republics through extraconstitutional means, several with variations.[10] All told, there are seven, summarized in table 11.1. To use a biological analogy, every so often there must be a mutation that cannot be accommodated by normal evolution. But the organism functions to keep that mutation well within bounds. If it fails, a serious constitutional breakdown will occur that is not so easily repaired.

The constitutional theories behind these paradigms for the management of extraconstitutional change fall into two categories. The first encourages recourse to primordial popular sovereignty, and the second relies on a guardian of the polity (nation or state). Under the first, the prevailing constitutional theory recognizes that sovereignty is vested in the people, who have the right to resume their direct exercise of it and to redelegate governing powers as they see fit. Under the second, an especially charismatic leader or an especially endowed institution possesses a residual power of trusteeship that can be exercised when the need arises. It hardly need be said that the United States relies primarily on the principle of popular sovereignty, although even it has experienced and benefited from guardians of the polity. In most other countries, the situation is reversed.

Other distinctions that seem to make a difference are whether the polity involved serves a new society—one settled in the modern epoch as a result of migration to a new frontier—or an old one with a deeply established web of human relationships, including political ones, that had to undergo modernization in place. The very character of the commitment to democratic republicanism tends to be different in each case. Equally different are the approaches to extra-constitutional action to achieve fundamental political change.

One of the principal differences between new and old societies is the importance to them of their constitutions. In new societies, constitutions often play a major role in giving identity to the society itself. The United States is the fullest expression of that effect. In old societies, the body politic has a long-established sense of identity so that constitutions often carry no more weight than as artifacts of particular regimes.

Conclusion

In our proper and admirable concern for the American tradition of constitutional government and the American role in the nurturing and spread of constitutional democracy in the world, we should not overlook the perennial and universal problem of what happens when normal constitutional behavior is not enough. As much as the development of constitutional standards, norms, instruments, and behavior is critical to constitutional government, so too is the ability to deal with those exceptional situations. Here too the American experience has provided some of the basic and most successful paradigms, and it can also teach us something about the pitfalls of improper response. It is well worth the effort to explore that dimension of constitutional government as well as the more conventional ones.

APPENDIX A

THE ARTICLES OF CONFEDERATION

Congress resolved on June 11, 1776, that a committee should be appointed to draw up articles of confederation between the soon-to-be-independent states. A plan proposed by John Dickinson of Pennsylvania formed the basis of the articles as proposed to Congress and, after some debate and a few changes, adopted November 15, 1777. Representatives of the states signed the Articles of Confederation during 1778 and 1779; Maryland alone refused to ratify them until Congress arrived at some satisfactory solution of the western lands question. The Articles were finally ratified and in force on March 1, 1781. The debates on the Articles, Jefferson's notes on the debates, and the official letter of Congress accompanying the Articles, can be found in Elliot's *Debates* (1861 ed.), 1:69 ff. The Articles of Confederation constituted the first effort by Americans to solve the problem of federal union and should be studied in comparison with the Albany Plan of Union and the 1787 Constitution. On the Articles of Confederation see Richard Frothingham, *Rise of the Republic of the United States*, chap. 12; George Bancroft, History Author's last rev. vol. 5, chap. 14; Andrew C. McLaughlin, *Confederation and Constitution*, chap. 3; and George T. Curtis, *Constitutional History of the United States*, vol. 1.

The Articles are reproduced here from Richardson, ed., *Messages and Papers*, vol. 1 (Chelsea House), pp. 9 ff.

To ALL TO WHOM these Presents shall come, we the undersigned Delegates of the States affixed fixed to our Names send greeting. Whereas the Delegates of the United States of America in Congress assembled did on the fifteenth day of November in the Year of our Lord One Thousand Seven Hundred and Seventy seven, and in the Second Year of the Independence of America agree to certain articles of Confederation and perpetual Union between the States of Newhampshire, Massachusettes-bay, Rhodeisland and Providence Plantations, Connecticut, New York, New Jersey,

Pennsylvania, Delaware, Maryland, Virginia, North-Carolina, South-Carolina and Georgia in the Words following, viz. "Articles of Confederation and perpetual Union between the states of Newhampshire, Massachusetts-bay, Rhodeisland Providence Plantations, Connecticut, New-York, New-Jersey, Pennsylvania, Delaware, Maryland, Virginia, North-Carolina, South-Carolina and Georgia."

Article I. The Stile of this confederacy shall be "The United States of America."

Article II. Each state retains its sovereignty, freedom and independence, and every Power, Jurisdiction and right, which is not by this confederation expressly delegated to the United States, in Congress assembled.

Article III. The said states hereby severally enter into a firm league of friendship with each other, for their common defence, the security of their Liberties, and their mutual and general welfare, binding themselves to assist each other, against all force offered to, or attacks made upon them, or any of them, on account of religion, sovereignty, trade, or any other pretence whatever.

Article IV. The better to secure and perpetuate mutual friendship and intercourse among people of the different states in this union, the free inhabitants of each of these states, paupers, vagabonds and fugitives from Justice excepted shall be entitled to all privileges and immunities of free citizens in the several states; and the people of each state shall have free ingress and regress to and from any other state, and shall enjoy therein all the privileges of trade and commerce, subject to the same duties, impositions and restrictions as the inhabitants thereof respectively, provided that such restriction shall not extend so far as to prevent the removal of property imported into any state, to any other state of which the Owner is an inhabitant; provided also that no imposition, duties or restriction shall be laid by any state on the property of the united states, or either of them.

If any Person guilty of or charged with treason, felony, or other high misdemeanor in any state, shall flee from Justice, and be found in any of the united states, he shall upon demand of the Governor or executive power, of the state from which he fled, be delivered up and removed to the state having jurisdiction of his offence.

Full faith and credit shall be given in each of these states to the records, acts and judicial proceedings of the courts and magistrates of every state.

Article V. For the more convenient management of the general interests of the united states, delegates shall be annually appointed in such manner as the legislature of each state shall direct, to meet in Congress on the first Monday in November, in every year, with a power reserved to each state, to recall its delegates, or any of them, at any time within the year, and to send others in their stead, for the remainder of the Year.

No state shall be represented in Congress by less than two, nor by more than seven Members; and no person shall be capable of being a delegate for more than three years in any terms of six years; nor shall any person, being delegate, be capable of holding any office under the united states, for which he, or another for his benefit receives any salary, fees or emolument of any kind.

Each state shall maintain its own delegates in a meeting of the states, and while they act as members of the committee of the states.

In determining questions in the united states, in Congress assembled, each state shall have one vote.

Freedom of speech and debate in Congress shall not be impeached or questioned in any Court, or place out of Congress, and the members of congress shall be protected in their persons from arrests and imprisonments, during the time of their going to and from, and attendance on congress, except for treason, felony, or breach of the peace.

Article VI. No state without the Consent of the united states in congress assembled, shall send any embassy to, or receive and embassy from, or enter into any conference, agreement, or alliance or treaty with any King, prince or state; nor shall any person holding any office of profit or trust under the united states, of any of them, accept of any present, emolument, office or title of any kind whatever from any king, prince or foreign state; nor shall the united states in congress assembled, or any of them grant any title of nobility.

No two or more states shall enter into any treaty, confederation or alliance whatever between them, without the consent of the united states in congress assembled, specifying accurately the purposes for which the same is to be entered into, and how long it shall continue.

No state shall lay any imposts or duties, which may interfere with any stipulations in treaties, entered into by the united states in congress assembled, with any king, prince or state, in pursuance of any treaties already proposed by congress, to the courts of France and Spain.

No vessels of war shall be kept up in time of peace by any state, except such number only, as shall be deemed necessary by the united states in congress assembled, for the defence of such state, or its trade; nor shall any body of forces be kept up by any state, in time of peace, except such number only, as in the judgement of the united states, in congress assembled, shall be deemed requisite to garrison the forts necessary for the defence of such state; but every state shall always keep up a well regulated and disciplined militia, sufficiently armed and accoutred, and shall provide and constantly have ready for use, in public stores, a due number of field pieces and tents, and a proper quantity of arms, ammunition and camp equipage.

No state shall engage in any war without the consent of the united states in congress assembled, unless such state be actually invaded by enemies, or shall have received certain advice of a resolution being formed by some nation of Indians to invade such state, and the danger is so imminent as not to admit of a delay, till the united states in congress assembled can be consulted; nor shall any state grant commissions to any ships or vessels of war, nor letters of marque or reprisal, except it be after a declaration of war by the united states in congress assembled, and then only against the kingdom or state and the subjects thereof, against which war has been so declared, and under such regulations as shall be established by the united states in congress assembled, unless such state be infested by pirates, in which case vessels of war may be fitted out for that occasion, and kept so long as the danger shall continue, or until the united states in congress assembled shall determine otherwise.

Article VII. When land-forces are raised by any state for the common defence, all officers of or under the rank of colonel, shall be appointed by the legislature of each state respectively by whom such forces shall be raised, or in such manner as such state shall direct, and all vacancies be filled up by the state which first made the appointment.

Article VIII. All charges of war, and all other expences that shall be incurred for the common defence or general welfare, and allowed by the united states in congress assembled, shall be defrayed out of a common treasury, which shall be supplied by the several states, in proportion to the value of all land within each state, granted to or surveyed for any Person, as such land and the buildings and improvements thereon shall be estimated according to such mode as the united states in congress assembled, shall from time to time direct and appoint. The taxes for paying that proportion shall be laid and levied by the authority and direction of the legislatures of the several states within the time agreed upon by the united states in congress assembled.

Article IX. The united states in congress assembled, shall have the sole and exclusive right and power of determining on peace and war, except in the cases mentioned in the sixth article—of sending and receiving ambassadors—entering into treaties and alliances, provided that no treaty of commerce shall be made whereby the legislative power of the respective states shall be restrained from imposing such imposts and duties of foreigners, as their own people are subjected to, or from prohibiting the exploration or importation of any species of goods or commodities whatsoever—of establishing rules for deciding in all cases, what captures on land or water shall be legal, and what manner prizes taken by land or naval forces in the service of the united states shall be divided or appropriated.—of granting letters of marque and reprisal in times of peace—appointing courts for the trial of piracies and felonies committed on the high seas and establishing courts for receiving and determining finally appeals in all cases of captures, provided that no member of congress shall be appointed a judge of any of the said courts.

The united states in congress assembled shall also be the last resort on appeal in all disputes and differences now subsisting or that hereafter may rise between two or more states concerning boundary, jurisdiction or any other cause whatever; which authority shall always be exercised in the manner following. Whenever the legislative or executive authority or lawful agent of any state in controversy with another shall present a petition to congress, stating the matter in question and praying for a hearing, notice thereof shall be given by order of congress to the legislative or executive authority of the other state in controversy, and a day assigned for the appearance of the parties by their lawful agents, who shall then be directed to appoint by joint consent, commissioners or judges to constitute a court for hearing and determining the matter in question: but if they cannot agree, congress shall name three persons out of each of the united states, and from the list of such persons each party shall alternately strike out one, the petitioners beginning, until the number shall be reduced to thirteen; and from that number not less than seven, nor more than nine names as congress shall direct, shall in the presence of congress be drawn out by lot, and the persons whose names shall be so drawn or any five of them, shall be commissioners or judges, to hear and finally determine the controversy, so always as a major part of the judges who shall hear the cause shall agree in the determination: and if either party shall neglect to attend at the day appointed, without shewing reasons, which congress shall judge sufficient, or being present shall refuse to strike, the congress shall proceed to nominate three persons out of each state, and the secretary of congress shall strike in behalf of such party absent or refusing: and the judgement and sentence of the court to be appointed, in the manner before prescribed, shall be final and conclusive; and if any of the parties shall refuse to submit to the authority of such court, or to appear to defend their claim cause, or cause, the court shall nevertheless proceed to pronounce sentence, or judgement, which shall in like manner be final and decisive, the judgement or sentence and other proceedings being in either case transmitted to congress, and lodged among the acts of congress for the security of the parties concerned: provided that every commissioner, before he sits in judgement, shall take an oath to be administered by one of the judges of the supreme or superior court of the state, where the cause shall be tried, "well and truly to hear and determine the matter in question, according to the best of his judgment, without favour, affection or hope of reward:" provided also that no state shall be deprived of territory for the benefit of the united states.

All controversies concerning the private right of soil claimed under different grants of two or more states, whose jurisdictions as they may respect such lands, and the states which passed such grants are adjusted, the said grants or either of them being at the same time claimed to have originated antecedent to such settlement of jurisdiction, shall on the petition of either party to the congress of the united states, be finally determined as near as may be in the same manner as is before prescribed for deciding disputes respecting territorial jurisdiction between different states.

The united states in congress assembled shall also have the sole and exclusive right and power of regulating the alloy and value of coin struck by their own authority, or by that of the respective states—fixing the standard of weights and measures throughout the united states—regulating the trade and managing all affairs with the Indians, not members of any of the states, provided that the legislative right of any state within its own limits be not infringed or violated—establishing and regulating post-offices from one state to another, throughout all the united states, and exacting such postage on the papers passing thro' the same as may be requisite to defray the expences of the said office—appointing all officers of the land forces, in the service of the united states, excepting regimental officers—appointing all the officers of the naval forces, and commissioning all officers whatever in the service of the united states—making rules for the government and regulation of the said land and naval forces, and directing their operations.

The united states in congress assembled shall have authority to appoint a committee, to sit in the recess of congress, to be denominated "A Committee of the States," and to consist of one delegate from each state; and to appoint such other committees and civil officers as may be necessary for managing the general affairs of the united states under their direction—to appoint one of their number to preside, provided that no person be allowed to serve in the office of president more than one year in any term of three years; to ascertain the necessary sums of Money to be raised for the service of the united states, and to appropriate and apply the same for defraying the public expences—to borrow money, or emit bills on the credit of the united states, transmitting every half year to the respective states an account of the sums of money so borrowed or emitted,—to build and equip a navy—to agree upon the number of land forces, and to make requisitions from each state for its quota, in proportion to the number of white inhabitants in such state; which requisition shall be binding, and thereupon the legislature of each state shall appoint the regimental officers, raise the men and cloath, arm and equip them in a soldier like manner, at the expence of the united states, and the officers and men so cloathed, armed and equipped shall march to the place appointed, and within the time agreed on by the united states in congress assembled: But if the united states in congress assembled shall, on consideration of circumstances judge proper that any state should not raise men, or should raise a smaller number than its quota, and that any other state should raise a greater number of men than the quota thereof, such extra number shall be raised, officered, cloathed, armed and equipped in the same manner as the quota of such state, unless the legislature of such state shall judge that such extra number cannot be safely spared out of the same, in which case they shall raise officer, cloath, arm and equip as many of such extra number as they judge can be safely spared. And the officers and men so cloathed, armed and equipped, shall march to the place appointed, and within the time agreed on by the united states in congress assembled.

The united states in congress assembled shall never engage in war, nor grant letters of marque and reprisal in time of peace, nor enter into any treaties or alliances, nor coin money, nor regulate the value thereof, nor ascertain the sums and expences necessary for the defence and welfare of the united states, or any of them, nor emit bills, nor borrow money on the credit of the united states, nor appropriate money, nor agree upon the number of vessels of war, to be built or purchased, or the number of land or sea forces to be raised, nor appoint a commander in chief of the army or navy, unless nine states assent to the same: nor shall a question on any other point, except for adjourning from day to day be determined, unless by the votes of a majority of the united states in congress assembled.

The congress of the united states shall have power to adjourn to any time within the year, and to any place within the united states, so that no period of adjournment be for a longer duration than the space of six Months, and shall publish the Journal of their proceedings monthly, except such parts thereof relating to treaties, alliances or military operations as in their judgement require secresy; and the yeas and nays of the delegates of each state on any question shall be entered on the Journal, when it is desired by any delegate; and the delegates of a state, or any of them, at his or their request shall be furnished with a transcript of the said Journal, except such parts as are above excepted, to lay before the legislatures of the several states.

Article X. The committee of the states, or any nine if them, shall be authorised to execute, in the recess of congress, such of the powers of congress as the united states in congress assembled, by the consent of nine states, shall from time to time think expedient to vest them with; provided that no power be delegated to the said committee, for the exercise of which, by the articles of confederation, the voice of nine states in the congress of the united states assembled is requisite.

Article XI. Canada acceding to this confederation, and joining in the measures of the united states, shall be admitted into, and entitled to all the advantages of this union: but no other colony shall be admitted into the same, unless such admission be agreed to by nine states.

Article XII. All bills of credit emitted, monies borrowed and debts contracted by, or under the authority of congress, before the assembling of the united states, in pursuance of the present confederation, shall be deemed and considered as a charge against the united states, for payment and satisfaction whereof the said united states, and the public faith are hereby solemnly pledged.

Article XIII. Every state shall abide by the determinations of the united states in congress assembled, on all questions which by this confederation are submitted to them. And the Articles of this confederation shall be inviolably observed by every state, and the union shall be perpetual; nor shall any alteration at any time hereafter be made in any of them; unless such alteration be agreed to in a congress of the united states, and be afterwards confirmed by the legislatures of every state.

AND WHEREAS it hath pleased the Great Governor of the World to incline the hearts of the legislatures we respectively represent in congress, to approve of, and to authorize us to ratify the said articles of confederation and perpetual union. KNOW YE that we the under-signed delegates, by virtue of the power and authority to us given for that purpose, do by these presents, in the name and on behalf of our respective constituents, fully and entirely ratify and confirm each and every of the said articles of confederation and perpetual union, and all and singular the matters and things therein contained: And we do further solemnly plight and engage the faith of our respective constituents, that they shall abide by the determinations of the united states in congress assembled, on all questions, which by the said confederation are submitted to them. And that the articles thereof shall be inviolably observed by the states we respectively represent, and that the union shall be perpetual. In Witness whereof we have hereunto set our hands in Congress. Done at Philadelphia in the state of Pennsylvania the ninth Day of July in the Year of our Lord one Thousand seven Hundred and Seventy-eight, and in the third year of the independence of America.

APPENDIX B

THE NORTHWEST ORDINANCE OF 1787

SECTION 1. *Be it ordained by the United States in Congress assembled*, That the said Territory, for the purpose of temporary government, be one district, subject, however, to be divided into two districts, as future circumstances may, in the opinion of Congress, make it expedient.

SEC. 2. *Be it ordained by the authority aforesaid*, That the estates both of resident and nonresident proprietors in the said territory, dying intestate, shall descend to, and be distributed among, their children and the descendants of a deceased child in equal parts, the descendants of a deceased child or grandchild to take the share of their deceased parent in equal parts among them; and where there shall be no children or descendants, then in equal parts to the next of kin, in equal degree; and among collaterals, the children of a deceased brother or sister of the intestate shall have, in equal parts among them, their deceased parent's share; and there shall, in no case, be a distinction between kindred of the whole and half blood; saving in all cases to the widow of the intestate, her third part of the real estate for life, and one-third part of the personal estate; and this law relative to descents and dower shall remain in full force until altered by the legislature of the district. And until the governor and judges shall adopt laws as hereinafter mentioned, estates in the said territory may be devised or bequeathed by wills in writing, signed and sealed by him or her in whom the estate may be (being of full age), and attested by three witnesses; and real estates may be conveyed by lease and release, or bargain and sale, signed, sealed, and delivered by the person, being of full age, in whom these state may be, and attested by two witnesses, provided such wills be duly proved, and such conveyances be acknowledged, or the execution thereof duly proved, and be recorded within one year after proper magistrates, courts, and registers shall be appointed for that purpose; and personal property may be transferred by delivery, saving, however, to the French and Canadian inhabitants, and other settlers of the Kaskaskies, Saint Vincents, and the neighboring villages, who have heretofore professed themselves citizens of Virginia, their laws and customs now in force among them, relative to the descent and conveyance of property.

Sec. 3. *Be it ordained by the authority aforesaid,* That there shall be appointed, from time to time, by Congress, a governor, whose commission shall continue in force for the term of three years, unless sooner revoked by Congress; he shall reside in the district, and have a freehold estate therein, in one thousand acres of land, while in the exercise of his office.

Sec. 4. There shall be appointed from time to time, by Congress, a secretary, whose commission shall continue in force for four years, unless sooner revoked; he shall reside in the districts, and have a freehold estate therein, in five hundred acres of land, while in the exercise of his office. It shall be his duty to keep and preserve the acts and laws passed by the legislature, and the public records of the district, and the proceedings of the governor in his executive department, and transmit authentic copies of such acts and proceedings every six months to the Secretary of Congress. There shall also be appointed a court, to consist of three judges, any two of whom to form a court, who shall have a common-law jurisdiction and reside in the district, and have each therein a freehold estate, in five hundred acres of land, while in the exercise of their offices; and their commissions shall continue in force during good behavior.

Sec. 5. The governor and judges, or a majority of them, shall adopt and publish in the district such laws of the original states, criminal and civil, as may be necessary, and best suited to the circumstances of the district, and report them to Congress from time to time, which laws shall be in force in the district until the organization of the general assembly therein, unless disapproved of by Congress; but afterward the legislature shall have authority to alter them as they shall think fit.

Sec. 6. The governor, for the time being, shall be commander-in-chief of the militia, appoint and commission all officers in the same below the rank of general officers; all general officers shall be appointed and commissioned by Congress.

Sec. 7. Previous to the organization of the general assembly the governor shall appoint such magistrates, and other civil officers, in each county or township, as he shall find necessary for the preservation of the peace and good order in the same. After the general assembly shall be organized, the powers and duties of magistrates and other civil officers shall be regulated and defined by the said assembly; but all magistrates and other civil officers, not herein otherwise directed, shall, during the continuance of this temporary government, be appointed by the governor.

Sec. 8. For the prevention of crimes, and injuries, the laws to be adopted or made shall have force in all parts of the district, and for the execution of process, criminal and civil, the governor shall make proper divisions thereof; and he shall proceed, from time to time, as circumstances may require, to lay out the parts of the district in which the Indian titles shall have been extinguished, into counties and townships, subject, however, to such alterations as may thereafter be made by the legislature.

Sec. 9. So soon as there shall be five thousand free male inhabitants, of full age, in the district, upon giving proof thereof to the governor, they shall receive authority, with time and place, to elect representatives from their counties or townships, to represent them in the general assembly: *Provided,* That for every five hundred free male inhabitants there shall be one representative, and so on, progressively, with the number of free male inhabitants, shall the right of representation increase, until the number of representatives shall amount to twenty-five; after which the number and proportion of representatives shall be regulated by the legislature: *Provided*, That no person be eligible or qualified to act as a representative unless he shall have been a citizen of one of the United States three years, and be a resident in the district, or unless he shall have resided in the district three years; and, in either case, shall likewise hold in his own right, in fee-simple, two hundred acres of land within the same: *Provided also*, That a freehold in fifty acres of land in the district, having been a citizen of one of the states, and being resident in the district, or the like freehold and two years' residence in the district, shall be necessary to qualify a man as an elector of a representative.

Sec. 10. The representatives thus elected shall serve for the term of two years; and in case of the death of a representative, or removal from office, the governor shall issue a writ to the county or township, for which he was a member, to elect another in his stead, to serve for the residue of the term.

Sec. 11. The general assembly, or legislature, shall consist of the governor, legislative council, and a house of representatives. The legislative council shall consist of five members, to continue in office five years, unless sooner removed by Congress; any three of them to be a quorum; and the members of the council shall be nominated and appointed in the following manner, to wit: As soon as representatives shall be elected the governor shall appoint a time and place for them to meet together, and when met they shall nominate ten persons, resident in the district, and each possessed of a freehold in five hundred acres of land, and return their names to Congress, five of whom Congress shall appoint and commission to serve as aforesaid; and whenever a vacancy shall happen in the Council, by death or removal from office, the house of representatives shall nominate two persons, qualified as aforesaid, for each vacancy, and return their names to Congress, one of whom Congress shall appoint and commission for the residue of the term; and every five years, four months at least before the expiration of the time of service of the members of the council, the said house shall nominate ten persons, qualified as aforesaid, and return their names to Congress, five of whom Congress shall appoint and commission to serve as members of the council five years, unless sooner removed. And the governor, legislative council, and house of representatives shall have authority to make laws in all cases for the good government of the district, not repugnant to the principles and articles in this ordinance established and declared. And all bills, having passed by a majority in the house, and by a majority in the council, shall be referred to the governor for his assent; but no bill, or legislative act whatever, shall be of any force without his assent. The governor shall have power to convene, prorogue, and dissolve the general assembly when, in his opinion, it shall be expedient.

Sec. 12. The governor, judges, legislative council, secretary, and such other officers as Congress shall appoint in the district shall take an oath or affirmation of fidelity, and of office; the governor before the president of Congress, and all other officers before the governor. As soon as a legislature shall be formed in the district, the council and house assembled, in one room, shall have authority, by joint ballot, to elect a delegate to Congress, who shall have a seat in Congress, with a right of debating, but not of voting, during this temporary government.

Sec. 13. And for extending the fundamental principles of civil and religious liberty, which form the basis whereon these republics, their laws, and constitutions are erected; to fix and establish those principles as the basis of all laws, constitutions, and governments, which forever hereafter shall be formed in the said territory; to provide, also, for the establishment of states, and permanent government therein, and for their admission to a share in the Federal councils on an equal footing with the original states, at as early periods as may be consistent with the general interest:

SEC. 14. It is hereby ordained and declared, by the authority aforesaid, that the following articles shall be considered as articles of compact between the original states and the people and states in the said territory, and forever remain unalterable, unless by common consent, to wit:

Article I

No person, demeaning himself in a peaceable and orderly manner, shall ever be molested on account of his mode of worship, or religious sentiments, in the said territory.

Article II

The inhabitants of the said territory shall always be entitled to the benefits of the writs of habeas corpus and of the trial by jury, of a proportionate representation of the people in the legislature, and of judicial proceedings according to the course of the common law. All persons shall be bailable, unless for capital offenses, where the proof shall be evident, or the presumption great. All fines shall be moderate; and no cruel or unusual punishment shall be inflicted. No man shall be deprived of his liberty or property, but by the judgment of his peers, or the law of the land, and, should the public exigencies make it necessary, for the common preservation, to take any person's property, or to demand his particular services, full compensation shall be made for the same. And, in the just preservation of rights and property, it is understood and declared that no law ought ever to be made or have force in the said territory that shall, in any manner whatever, interfere with or affect private contracts, or engagements, bona fide, and without fraud previously formed.

Article III

Religion, morality, and knowledge being necessary to good government and the happiness of mankind, schools and the means of education shall forever be encouraged. The utmost good faith shall always be observed toward the Indians; their lands and property shall never be taken from them without their consent; and in their property, rights, and liberty they never shall be invaded or disturbed unless in just and lawful wars authorized by Congress; but laws founded in justice and humanity shall, from time to time, be made, for preventing wrongs being done to them and for preserving peace and friendship with them.

Article IV

The said territory, and the states which may be formed therein, shall forever remain a part of this confederacy of the United States of America, subject to the Articles of Confederation, and to such alterations therein as shall be constitutionally made; and to all the acts and ordinances of the United

States in Congress assembled, conformable thereto. The inhabitants and settlers in the said territory shall be subject to pay a part of the federal debts contracted, or to be contracted, and a proportional part of the expenses of government to be apportioned on them by Congress, according to the same common rule and measure by which apportionments thereof shall be made on the other states; and the taxes for paying their proportion shall be laid and levied by the authority and direction of the legislatures of the district, or districts, or new states, as in the original states, within the time agreed upon by the United States in Congress assembled. The legislatures of those districts, or new states, shall never interfere with the primary disposal of the soil by the United States in Congress assembled, nor with any regulations Congress may find necessary for securing the title in such soil to the bona fide purchasers. No tax shall be imposed on lands the property of the United States; and in no case shall nonresident proprietors be taxed higher than residents. The navigable waters leading into the Mississippi and Saint Lawrence, and the carrying places between the same, shall be common highways, and forever free, as well to the inhabitants of the said territory as to the citizens of the United States, and those of any other states that may be admitted into the confederacy, without any tax, impost, or duty therefor.

Article V

There shall be formed in the said territory not less than three nor more than five states; and the boundaries of the states, as soon as Virginia shall alter her act of cession and consent to the same, shall become fixed and established as follows, to wit: The western state, in the said territory, shall be bounded by the Mississippi, the Ohio, and the Wabash rivers; a direct line drawn from the Wabash and Post Vincents, due north, to the territorial line between the United States and Canada; and by the said territorial line to the Lake of the Woods and Mississippi. The middle state shall be bounded by the said direct line, the Wabash from Post Vincents to the Ohio, by the Ohio, by a direct line drawn due north from the mouth of the Great Miami to the said territorial line, and by the said territorial line. The eastern state shall be bounded by the last-mentioned direct line, the Ohio, Pennsylvania, and the said territorial line: *Provided, however*, and it is further understood and declared, that the boundaries of these three states shall be subject so far to be altered, that, if Congress shall hereafter find it expedient, they shall have authority to form one or two states in that part of the said territory which lies north of an east and west line drawn through the southerly bend or extreme of Lake Michigan. And whenever any of the said states shall have sixty thousand free inhabitants therein, such state shall be admitted by its delegates into the Congress of the United States, on an equal footing with the original states, in all respects whatever; and shall be at liberty to form a permanent constitution and state government: *Provided*, The constitution and government, so to be formed, shall be republican, and in conformity to the principles contained in these articles, and, so far as it can be consistent with the general interest of the confederacy, such admission shall be allowed at an earlier period, and when there may be a less number of free inhabitants in the state than sixty thousand.

Article VI

There shall be neither slavery nor involuntary servitude in the said territory, otherwise than in the punishment of crimes, whereof the party shall have been duly convicted: *Provided always*, That any person escaping into the same, from whom labor or service is lawfully claimed in any one of the original states, such fugitive may be lawfully reclaimed, and conveyed to the person claiming his or her labor or service as aforesaid.

Be it ordained by the authority aforesaid, That the resolutions of the 23d of April, 1784, relative to the subject of this ordinance, be, and the same are hereby, repealed, and declared null and void.

Done by the United States, in Congress assembled, the 13th day of July, in the year of our Lord 1787, and of their sovereignty and independence the twelfth.

NOTES

1 An Almost-Covenanted Polity

1 Cf. Daniel J. Elazar, *Exploring Federalism* (University: University of Alabama Press, 1987).
2 See Appendix A.
3 The best study describing these sources is Andrew McLaughlin, *The Foundations of American Constitutionalism* (New York, 1932).
4 There is a vast literature on the federal theology and its implications for the United States. Perry Miller's works are the starting point for reading in this field. See, in particular, his two volumes *The New England Mind* (Boston: Beacon Press, 1939 and 1953), and *Errand into the Wilderness* (Cambridge: Harvard University Press, 1956). Some of the most recent materials on the subject include Donald S. Lutz and Jack D. Warden, *A Covenanted People: The Religious Traditions and the Origins of American Constitutionalism* (Providence: John Carter Brown Library, 1987), and John Kincaid and Daniel J. Elazar, eds., *The Covenant Connection: Federal Theology and the Origins of Modern Politics* (Greenville: Carolina Academic Press, 1988).
5 William James, *A Pluralistic Universe* (Cambridge: Harvard University Press, 1977), 145; see also Henry Levinson, "William James and Federal Republican Principle," *Publius* 9, no. 4 (Fall 1979).
6 Edward Bellamy, *Looking Backward, or 200–1887* (1888).
7 Herbert Croly, *The Promise of American Life* (New York: E. P. Dutton, 1963).
8 See, for example, Ferdinand Kinsky, "Personalism and Federalism," and Alexandre Marc, "New and Old Federalism: Faithful to the Origins," in *Publius* 9, no. 4 (Fall 1979): 117–42.
9 The first to formulate and document this thesis was Carl Becker in *The Declaration of Independence* (New York: Vintage, 1958).

10 See, for example, Hector St. John Crevecoeur, *Letters from an American Farmer* (1769); Max Lerner, *America as a Civilization* (New York: Simon and Schuster, 1957); Alexis de Tocqueville, *Democracy in America* (New York: Harper & Row, 1966).
11 John Winthrop, "A Model of Christian Charity."
12 Seymour Martin Lipset, *The First New Nation* (New York: Basic Books, 1979).

2 **Pluralism, Federalism, and Liberty**

1 The commitment to pluralism is a commitment to multiple ways of human expression built into the universe itself, whose existence is therefore legitimate and even necessary for the world to function, as distinct from being an ephemeral phenomenon resulting from human deficiency, to be at best tolerated out of generosity or necessity until the day comes when some form of monism will prevail. This definition follows that of William James, the great American philosopher of pluralism, who gave intellectual form and substance to American reality. See his *A Pluralistic Universe* (Cambridge: Harvard University Press, 1977). James also made the connection between federalism and pluralism. See Henry S. Levinson, "William James and the Federal Republican Principle," *Publius* 9, no. 4 (Winter 1979): 65–86.
2 The history of Pennsylvania in the days of its preeminence is to be found in Frederick B. Tolles, *Meeting House and Counting House: The Quaker Merchants of Colonial Philadelphia, 1682–1763* (Chapel Hill: University of North Carolina Press, 1948); Carl and Jessica Bridenbaugh, *Rebels and Gentlemen: Philadelphia in the Age of Franklin* (New York: Reynal and Hitchcock, 1942); E. Digby Baltzell, *Philadelphia Gentlemen: The Making of an Upper Class* (Glencoe, Ill.: Free Press, 1958); Sam Bass Warner, *The Private City: Philadelphia, Three Periods of Its Growth* (Philadelphia: University of Pennsylvania Press, 1968): Russell J. Ferguson, *Early Western Pennsylvania Politics* (Pittsburgh: University of Pittsburgh Press, 1938); Howard M. Jenkins, ed., *Pennsylvania, Colonial and Federal: A History, 1608–1903* (Philadelphia: Pennsylvania Historical Publishing Association, 1903); John P. Selsam, *The Pennsylvania Constitution of 1776*: A Study in Revolutionary Democracy (Philadelphia: University of Pennsylvania Press, 1936). Henry Adams places Pennsylvania in proper national perspective in his *History of the United States during the Administrations of Thomas Jefferson* (New York: Library of America, 1986), especially chaps. 2 and 4.
3 Thomas J. Condon, *New York Beginnings: The Commercial Origins of New Netherland* (New York: New York University Press, 1968); Louis B. Wrights, *The Atlantic Frontier: Colonial American Civilization* (New York: Alfred A. Knopf, 1947).
4 Cf. Oscar Handlin, *Adventure in Freedom: Three Hundred Years of Jewish Life in America* (New York: McGraw-Hill, 1954).
5 Perry Miller, *The New England Mind: The Seventeenth Century* (Boston: Beacon Press, 1939); Perry Miller, *The New England Mind: From Colony to Province* (Boston: Beacon Press, 1953); idem, *Orthodoxy in Massachusetts, 1630–1650* (New York: Harper and Brothers, 1933); Edmund S. Morgan, *The Puritan Dilemma: The Story of John Winthrop* (Boston: Little, Brown, and Ithaca:

1958); idem, *Visible Saints: The History of a Puritan Idea* (New York: Great Seal Books, and Ithaca: Cornell University Press, 1961); Edmund S. Morgan, ed., *Puritan Political Ideas, 1558–1794* (Indianapolis: Bobbs-Merrill, 1965).

6. W. J. Cash, *The Mind of the South* (New York: Alfred A. Knopf, 1960); W. Lloyd Warner et al., Yankee City Series (New Haven: Yale University Press, 1942); L. C. Grey, "History of Agriculture in the Southern United States to 1860," in *Contributions to American Economic History*, ed. Carnegie Institute, 2 vols. (Washington, DC.: Carnegie Institute, 1933); T. J. Wertenbaker, *The Old South: The Founding of American Civilization* (New York, C. Scribner's Sons, 1942); James W. Silver, ed., *Mississippi: The Closed Society* (New York: Harcourt Brace Jovanovich, 1963).

7. W. Lloyd Warner et al., *Democracy in Jonesville* (New York: Harper, 1949); Gerhard Lenshi, *The Religious Factor* (Garden City, N.Y.: Doubleday, 1961); John T. Flanigan, *American Is West* (Minneapolis: University of Minnesota Press, 1945); Lewis Atherton, *Main Street on the Middle Border* (Bloomington: Indiana University Press, 1954).

8. Daniel J. Elazar, *Cities of the Prairie: The Metropolitan Frontier in American Politics* (New York: Basic Books, 1970), especially the Postscript, "The Civil Community at Midfrontier."

9. For a convenient overview of this trend see Murray Friedman, "Religion and Politics in an Age of Pluralism, 1945–1976: An Ethno-cultural View," *Publius* 10, no. 3 (Summer 1980): 45–76.

10. Elazar, *Cities of the Prairie*, Postscript, and Daniel J. Elazar et al., *Cities of the Prairie Revisited* (Lincoln: University of Nebraska Press, 1986).

11. The classic definition of federal liberty was provided by John Winthrop in his May 1645 speech to the Massachusetts General Court, reproduced in Edmund S. Morgan, ed., *Puritan Political Ideas, 1558–1774* (Indianapolis: Bobbs-Merrill, 1965), pp. 138–39.

12. American folklore emphasizes natural men, as in "The Ballad of John Henry" or the stories of Paul Bunyan, Davy Crockett, and Mike Fink. See Dixon Wecter, *The Hero in America* (Ann Arbor: University of Michigan Press, 1963).

13. A summary of this exchange was published as Martin Diamond, "On the Relationship of Federalism and Decentralization," in Daniel J. Elazar et al., *Cooperation and Conflict: Reading in American Federalism* (Itasca, Ill.: F. E. Peacock, 1969), pp. 72–81.

14. Harold J. Laski, "The Obsolescence of Federalism," *New Republic*, May 3, 1939, pp. 367–69.

15. Morton Grodzins, *The American System: A New View of Government in the United States*, ed. Daniel J. Elazar (Chicago: Rand McNally, 1966).

16. See Daniel J. Elazar, *Exploring Federalism* (University: University of Alabama Press, 1987).

17. Franz Neumann, "Federalism and Freedom: A Critique," in *Federalism, Mature and Emerging*, ed. Arthur W. Macmahon, Columbia University Bicentennial Conference Series (New York: Doubleday, 1955).

3 Land and Liberty in American Civil Society

1. See Daniel J. Elazar, "Are We a Nation of Cities?" in *A Nation of Cities*, ed. Robert Goldwin (Chicago: Rand McNally, 1968).

2   Perry Miller discusses this thoroughly in his many works on American Puritanism. See in particular *Errand into the Wilderness* (Cambridge: Harvard University Press, 1956).

3   A recent discussion of the role of land is found in Hayyim Simha Nahmani, *Human Rights in the Old Testament* (Tel Aviv: J. Chachik, 1964).

4   The concept of stewardship is delineated in the first two chapters of Genesis and again in Deuteronomy.

5   The distribution is outlined and described in Joshua, chapters 6–18.

6   Both the law of jubilee, which prevented the selling of family lands in perpetuity and the law of redemption, which set forth the patterns of redeeming family lands by repurchase, ransom, and marriage are stated in Leviticus, chapter 25.

7   See "Property, Land and Its Conveyance," in *Pictorial Biblical Encyclopedia*, ed. Gaalyahu Cornfield (New York: Macmillan, 1964).

8   Alan Pendleton Grimes discusses these lines of influence in *American Political Thought*, rev. ed. (New York: Holt, Rinehart, and Winston, 1960).

9   Page Smith discusses America's practical embodiment of the biblical vision in *As a City upon a Hill* (New York: Alfred A. Knopf, 1966). The first English settlers on American shores did indeed try collectivism as the means of working the land but quickly gave it up as a poor way to encourage production or attachment to the common enterprise. For a contemporary account of the collectivist experiment and its abandonment in the Plymouth colony, see William Bradford, *Bradford's History of Plymouth Plantation* (Boston: Wright and Potter, 1901).

10 Benjamin Horace Hibbard, *A History of Public Land Policies* (New York: Macmillan, 1924), p. 36. For the functioning of the system, see Thomas J. Wertenbaker, *The Puritan Oligarchy: The Founding of American Civilization* (New York: Grosset and Dunlap, 1947), and Robert E. Brown, *Middle Class Democracy: The Revolution in Massachusetts, 1691–1780* (Ithaca: Cornell University Press, 1955). The term "federal liberty" was defined by John Winthrop in his *History of New England* (Boston, 1649).

11 Alexis de Tocqueville has given us the classic description of town government in *Democracy in America* (1835), chap. 5.

12 Stewart Holbrook, *The Yankee Exodus* (New York: Macmillan, 1950). The persistence of the town system even in the face of suburbanization is well illustrated in William M. Dobriner, "The Natural History of a Reluctant Suburb," *Yale Review*: 399–412. (Spring 1960).

13 To the best of my knowledge, no adequate study of this phenomenon in Pennsylvania or the other Middle States exists. Daniel J. Boorstin's *The Americans: The Colonial Experience* (New York: Random House, 1958) provides some general information on the political and cultural aspects of settlement in that section. William Penn's *A Further Account of Pennsylvania* (London, 1685) offers a contemporary view of the purposes and structure of settlement in that colony by its founder. The best account of all is found in Henry Adams, *History of the United States during the Administrations of Thomas Jefferson* (New York: Library of America, 1986), chaps. 1, 2, and 4.

14 Thomas Jefferson describes the political meaning of this system in his *Notes on the State of Virginia* (1787), particularly in regard to the extension of voting rights.
15 I discuss this phenomenon in greater detail in my *Cities of the Prairie* (New York: Basic Books, 1970), chap. 4.
16 W. J. Cash offers the best overall study of this aspect of the South in *The Mind of the South* (New York: Alfred A. Knopf, 1941). See also John Dollard, *Class and Caste in a Southern Town* (New York: Doubleday, 1957). For a more sympathetic view of the southern system that confirms this analysis, see the works of the southern agrarians. A good discussion of the system in its earlier days can be found in Charles S. Sydnor, *Gentlemen Freeholders: Political Practices in Washington's Virginia* (Chapel Hill: University of North Carolina Press, 1952).
17 Cash, *Mind of the South*, discusses the post–Civil War variations on the plantation system in some detail.
18 Hibbard, *History of Public Land Policies*, pp. 36–37.
19 Merle Curti et al., *The Making of an American Community: A Case Study of Democracy in a Frontier County* (Stanford: Stanford University Press, 1959), demonstrates this in detail for one county in Wisconsin.
20 I have delineated this spread in *American Federalism: A View from the States* (New York: Thomas Y. Crowell, 1966), chaps. 4 and 5.
21 Ibid.
22 Hibbard, *History of Public Land Policies*, documents the policy struggles without drawing these implications. For a useful chronology of colonial and federal land use policies to 1962 see Bureau of Land Management, *Historical Highlights of Public Land Management* (Washington, D.C.: U.S. Department of the Interior, 1962).
23 Charles N. Glaab and A. Theodore Brown, *A History of Urban America* (New York: Macmillan, 1967).
24 Little is available in published form on the subtle (and not-so-subtle) reshaping of federal policies to accommodate regional and local differences. The files of the University of Chicago Federalism Workshop and my research notes for my study of urban politics in the Upper Mississippi Valley, all in the Archives of American and Comparative Federalism, Center for the Study of Federalism, Temple University, contain some data documenting this.
25 Mathias N. Orfield, *Federal Land Grants to the States with Special Reference to Minnesota* (Minneapolis: University of Minnesota Press, 1915), discusses colonial grants in some detail in part 1. The land division system used in the East is discussed in Hibbard, *History of Public Land Policies*, and Bureau of Land Management, *Historical Highlights of Public Land Management*.
26 Glaab and Brown, *History of Urban America*.
27 Samuel Lubell, *The Future of American Politics* (New York: Harper and Row, 1965).
28 The several studies of the suburban areas around Philadelphia bear this out. See in particular Oliver P. Williams, Harold Herman, Charles S. Liebman, and Thomas R. Dye, *Suburban Differences and Metropolitan Policies: A Philadelphia Story* (Philadelphia: University of Pennsylvania Press, 1965), and Charles E. Gilbert, *Governing the Suburbs* (Bloomington: Indiana University

Press, 1967). The Philadelphia situation is repeated around New York, Boston, and the small metropolitan centers along the East Coast. The comparative regional data on municipal annexations provide a useful statistical indicator of this phenomenon; see *The Municipal Year Book* (1963), p. 110.

29   It should be noted that the first rectangular survey was initiated in New England in 1713, and the technique was generally applied thereafter to areas still beyond the frontier of settlement in that section.

30   A number of specific studies focus on the continuing political impact of the rectangular survey; see, for example, Norman J. W. Thrower, *Original Survey and Land Subdivision* (Chicago: Rand McNally, 1966), and Thomas F. Hady and Clarence J. Hein, "Congressional Townships as Incorporated Municipalities," *Midwest Journal of Political Science* (November 1964).

31   Discussions of this can be found in Anselm Strauss, *Images of the American City* (New York: Holt, Rinehart and Winston, 1963).

32   Virtually every community study involving communities in the greater West documents this as a matter of course.

33   This trend is documented in the myriad city plans prepared by professional planners or planning consultants for communities in the greater West.

34   The political effects of the merging of the systems have not, to my knowledge, been explored except in historical footnotes.

35   This fundamental point about the nature of political decision making in the United States is discussed in Elazar, *American Federalism*, and Morton Grodzins, *The American System: A New View of Government in the United States*, ed. Daniel J. Elazar (Chicago: Rand McNally, 1966).

36   See Frederick Jackson Turner, *The Frontier in American History* (New York: Holt, 1921), and Ray Allen Billington, *America's Frontier Heritage* (New York: Holt, Rinehart and Winston, 1967), for the best discussions of classical American frontier theory and its implications. I elaborate on the theory proposed here in *Cities of the Prairie*, chap. 1. For an economic theory of American urbanization that parallels this thesis, see Wilbur R. Thompson, *A Preface to Urban Economics* (Baltimore: Johns Hopkins University Press, 1965), pp. 15–16.

37   Turner, *Frontier in American History*, and Billington, *America's Frontier Heritage*. See Billington's bibliography for additional works on the land frontier.

38   Lewis Mumford graphically discusses this in *The City in History* (New York: Harcourt, Brace and World, 1961) and in many of his other works. See also Editors of Fortune, *The Exploding Metropolis* (Garden City, N.Y.: Doubleday, 1958).

39   Lubell, *Future of American Politics*. See also Nathan Glazer and Daniel Patrick Moynihan, *Beyond the Melting Pot* (Cambridge: MIT Press, 1963).

40   The statistical details are taken from Elazar, "Are We a Nation of Cities?"

41   Henry Bamford Parkes discusses this agrarian impulse and its recandescence in *The American Experience* (New York: Alfred A. Knopf, 1947).

42 This point is made in many places in the new literature of American urbanism. See, for example, Robert C. Wood, *Suburbia* (Boston: Houghton-Mifflin, 1959), and Herbert J. Gans, *The Levittowners* (New York: Pantheon, 1967).

43 Strauss, *Images of the American City*, and Scott Greer, *The Emerging City* (New York: Free Press, 1962), discuss these images. See also Robert E. Spiller, *The Cycle of American Literature* (New York: Macmillan, 1955).

44 A partial list of exemplary cities that fit this description in all or most of its aspects would include:

Northeast	South	Midwest and West
Concord, N.H.	Richmond, Va.	Minneapolis, Minn.
Burlington, Vt.	Chapel Hill, N.C.	Saint Paul, Minn.
Hartford, Conn.	Columbia, S.C.	Duluth, Minn.
New Haven, Conn.	Nashville, Tenn.	Spokane, Wash.
Newport, R.I.	Chattanooga, Tenn.	Seattle, Wash.
Rochester, N.Y.	Charleston, W.Va.	Portland, Oreg.
Philadelphia, Pa.	Jacksonville, Fla.	Pasadena, Calif.
Washington, D.C.	Miami, Fla.	Denver, Colo.
Cleveland, Ohio	San Antonio, Tex.	Topeka, Kans.
Cincinnati, Ohio	Tulsa, Okla.	Kansas City, Mo.

45 John A. Kouwenhoven is the foremost contemporary interpreter of the vernacular tradition. See in particular his *Made in America* (Garden City, N.Y.: Doubleday, 1948). The comparative attendance figures are available annually in the *Britannica Book of the Year*.

46 See Jean Gottman, *Megalopolis: The Urbanized Northeastern Seaboard in the U.S.* (Cambridge: MIT Press, 1964).

47 John Dewey offers useful guidance as to what constitutes a public in *The Public and Its Problems* (Chicago: Swallow Press, 1954).

48 Vincent and Elinor Ostrom have provided the most comprehensive and path-breaking work on the subject. See, for example, Elinor Ostrom, "Size and Performance in a Federal System," *Publius* 6, no. 2 (Spring 1976): 33–75.

49 I forecast many of these trends in "Megalopolis and the New Sectionalism," *Public Interest* 11 (Spring 1986): 62–85.

50 See, for example, Norton Long, "The Three Citizenships," in "Serving the Public in a Metropolitan Society," *Publius* 6, no. 2 (Spring 1976): 13–33.

51 For an elaboration of the concept of civil community, see Daniel J. Elazar, *Building Cities in America* (Lanham, Md.: University Press of America and Center for the Study of Federalism, 1987).

4 The Declaration of Independence: The Founding Covenant of the American People

1. Carl Becker, *The Declaration of Independence* (New York: Vintage, 1958), p. 26, from *The Writings of Thomas Jefferson* (1869), 7:304.
2. Harry V. Jaffa, *Equality and Liberty: Theory and Practice in American Politics* (New York: Oxford University Press, 1965).
3. Daniel J. Elazar, "The Constitution, the Union, and the Liberties of the People," *Publius* 8, no. 3 (Summer 1978): 141–75.
4. Delbert R. Hillers, *Covenant: The History of a Biblical Idea* (Baltimore: Johns Hopkins University Press, 1969).

5 The Principles and Traditions Underlying American State Constitutions

I am indebted to John Kincaid for his work in delineating the directions for the study of state constitutional design.

1. Ronald M. Peters, *The Massachusetts Constitution of 1780: A Social Compact* (Amherst: University of Massachusetts Press, 1978).
2. Donald S. Lutz, "The Theory of Consent in the Early State Constitutions," *Publius* 9, no. 2 (Spring 1979): 11–42; idem, *Popular Consent and Popular Control: Whig Political Theory in the Early State Constitutions* (Baton Rouge: Louisiana State University Press, 1980).
3. Oscar Handlin and Mary Handlin, eds., *The Popular Sources of Political Authority: Documents on the Massachusetts Constitution of 1780* (Cambridge, Mass.: Belknap Press, 1966).
4. Daniel J. Elazar, ed., *Republicanism, Representation and Consent: Views of the Founding Era* (New Brunswick, N.J.: Transaction Books, 1979).
5. Martin Diamond, "Democracy and *The Federalist*: A Reconsideration of the Framers' Intent," *American Political Science Review* 53, 1 (March 1959): 52–68.
6. This was precisely the British view of representation rejected by the Americans in their struggle against taxation without representation.
7. Woodrow Wilson, "The Study of Administration," *Political Science Quarterly* 2, no. 1 (June 1887): 197–222. Vincent Ostrom, "Can Federalism Make a Difference?" *Publius* 3, no. 2 (Fall 1973): 197–237; and Daniel J. Elazar, "Federalism vs. Decentralization: The Drift from Authenticity," *Publius* 6, no. 4 (Fall 1976): 9–19.
8. In this respect the United States Constitution also differs from many other constitutions that are designed to be truly national in the sense of being plenary, supreme, and comprehensive in all respects.
9. Daniel J. Elazar, "State-Local Relations: Reviving Old Theory for New Practice," in *Partnership within the States: Local Self-Government in the Federal System*, ed. Stephanie Cole (Urbana, Ill., and Philadelphia: Institute of Government and Public Affairs and Center for the Study of Federalism, 1976).

10 Daniel J. Elazar, *American Federalism: A View from the States*, 2d ed. (New York: Thomas Y. Crowell, 1972); and Samuel C. Patterson, "The Political Cultures of the American States," in *Public Opinion and Public Policy*, ed. Norman R. Luttbeg (Homewood, Ill.: Dorsey Press, 1968), pp. 275–92.
11 Elazar, *American Federalism*.
12 Daniel J. Elazar, *Cities of the Prairie: The Metropolitan Frontier and American Politics* (New York: Basic Books, 1970).
13 Ibid.
14 Abraham Kaplan, *The Conduct of Inquiry* (San Francisco: Chandler, 1964).
15 Max Kadushin, *Organic Thinking* (New York: Jewish Theological Seminary of America, 1938).
16 Daniel J. Elazar and John Kincaid, "Covenant and Polity," *New Conversations* 4, no. 2 (Fall 1979): 4–8.

6 Confederation and Federal Liberty

1 Cf. Ivo D. Duchacek, "Consociations of Fatherlands: The Revival of Confederal Principles and Practices," in *Publius* 12, no. 4 (Fall 1982): 129–69, and Daniel J. Elazar, *Exploring Federalism* (University: University of Alabama Press, 1987).
2 John Winthrop, *History of New England (1630–1649)*, ed. John Savage (Boston, 1853), 2:279–82.
3 See Ralph Greenfield Adams, ed., *Selected Political Essays of James Wilson* (New York: Knopf, 1930), and Geoffrey Seed, *James Wilson, Scottish Intellectual and American Statesman* (Millwood, N.Y.: Icto Press, 1978).
4 It is important to note that the term "republican" did not come into general use in a positive sense until the winter of 1775–76, as the colonies moved toward independence through their new union, "the United States in Congress assembled." For a discussion of Whiggism and Republicanism in this period, see Donald S. Lutz, *Popular Consent and Popular Control* (Baton Rouge: University of Louisiana Press, 1980), 1–22.
5 Martin Diamond makes this point with great cogency in his writings on the United States Constitution. See, inter alia, "The Ends of Federalism," *Publius* 3, no. 2 (Fall 1973): 129–52.
6 Cf. Martin Diamond, "The Forgotten Doctrine of Ennumerated Powers," *Publius* 6, no. 4 (Fall 1976): 187–96.
7 Steven R. Boyd, "Antifederalists and the Acceptance of the Constitution: Pennsylvania, 1787–1792," *Publius* 9, no. 2 (Spring 1979): 123–38, is a case study of this process in one state.
8 Cf. Rosann Rothman, "Political Method in the Federal System: Albert Gallatin's Contribution," *Publius* 1, no. 2 (Winter 1972): 123–35. See also Daniel J. Elazar, *The American Partnership* (Chicago: University of Chicago Press, 1962).
9 Cf. Jack Rakove, "The Legacy of the Articles of Confederation," *Publius* 12, no. 4 (Fall 1982): 45–66.

7 Developing an American Theory of Federal Democracy

1. Martin Diamond, "*The Federalist*'s View of Federalism," in *Essays on Federalism*, ed. George S. Benson (Claremont, Calif.: Claremont Men's College, 1961); idem, "Democracy and the Federalist: A Reconsideration of the Framers' Intent," *American Political Science Review* (1959), pp. 64 ff.; idem, "On the Relationship of Federalism and Decentralization," in *Cooperation and Conflict: Readings in American Federalism*, ed. Daniel J. Elazar et al. (Itasca, Ill.: F. E. Peacock, 1969), pp. 78 ff.
2. W. W. Crosskey, *Politics and the Constitution*, 2 vols. (Chicago: University of Chicago Press, 1953).
3. See Daniel J. Elazar, *Exploring Federalism* (University: University of Alabama Press, 1987).
4. William Riker, *Federalism: Origin, Operation, Significance* (Boston: Little, Brown, 1964).
5. See, for example, their essays in Daniel J. Elazar, ed., *The Federal Polity* (New Brunswick, N.J.; Transaction Books, 1978). See also Vincent Ostrom, *The Political Theory of a Compound Republic*, rev. ed. (Lincoln: University of Nebraska Press, 1987).
6. Crosskey, *Politics and the Constitution*, e.g., vol. 1, chap. 4.
7. Cf. Daniel J. Elazar and John Kincaid, eds., *Covenant, Polity and Constitutionalism* (Lanham, Md.: University Press of America and Center for the Study of Federalism, 1980).
8. Donald Lutz, "From Covenant to Constitution in American Political Thought," *Publius* 10, no. 4 (Fall 1980): 101–35.
9. Charles Hyneman and Donald Lutz, eds., *American Political Writing during the Founding Era, 1760–1805*, 2 vols. (Indianapolis: Liberty Press, 1983).
10. Gottfried Dietze, *The Federalist: A Classic on Federalism and Free Government* (Baltimore: Johns Hopkins University Press, 1960); William B. Allen, "Federal Representation: The Design of the Thirty-fifth *Federalist Paper*," *Publius* 6, no. 3 (Summer 1976): 61–73.
11. Mason's views are clearly stated in the debates of the federal convention of 1787. See *Documents Illustrative of the Formation of the Union of the American States* (Washington, D.C.: Government Printing Office, 1927).
12. For example, *Federalist*, nos. 51 and 62. Vincent Ostrom has further systematized this concept in his *The Political Theory of a Compound Republic* (Lincoln: University of Nebraska Press, 1987).
13. This shorthand definition was first used by Israel's prime minister Menachem Begin in 1978; cf. Daniel J. Elazar, ed., *Self Rule/Shared Rule: Federal Solutions to the Middle East Conflict* (Ramat Gan: Turtledove, 1979).
14. For a fuller exposition of federal theory, see Daniel J. Elazar, *Exploring Federalism* (University: University of Alabama Press, 1987).
15. For an analytic description of the power structure of ancient Egypt, see Henri Frankfort et al, *Before Philosophy* (Baltimore: Penguin Books, 1949).
16. Ibid.

17 Cf. Martin Landau, "Federalism, Redundancy and System Reliability," in Daniel J. Elazar, ed., *The Federal Polity* (New Brunswick, N.J.: Transaction Books, 1978).
18 Cf. Delbert Hillers, *Covenant* (Baltimore: Johns Hopkins University Press, 1969).

8 The Constitution and the Blessings of Liberty

1 Donald S. Lutz, "The Purposes of American State Constitutions," *Publius* 12, no. 1 (Winter 1982): 27–44.
2 See chapter 2 above.
3 Cf. Dixon Wecter, *The Hero in America* (Ann Arbor: University of Michigan Press, 1963).
4 Tom Wolfe, *The Right Stuff* (New York: Bantam, 1983).
5 Martin Diamond, *A Revolution of Sober Expectations* (Washington, D.C.: American Enterprise Institute, 1976).
6 John Winthrop, *History of New England, 1630–1649*, ed. Sam Savage (Boston, 1853), 2: 279–82.
7 Wilson at the Pennsylvania ratifying convention as quoted in J. B. McMaster and F. B. Stone, *Pennsylvania and the Federal Constitution, 1787–1788* (New York: Da Capo, 1970).
8 Cf. *Publius* 12, no. 1 (Winter 1982), a special issue on state constitutional design, especially the introduction and part 1.
9 Cf. Daniel J. Elazar, *Cities of the Prairie* (New York: Basic Books, 1970), esp. chaps. 4, 5, and 6.

9 Contrasting Models of Revolutionary Leadership

1 The full story of Washington's gesture is told in John C. Fitzpatrick, ed. *The Writings of George Washington* (Washington, D.C.: Government Printing Office, 1931–44), 26:222–29.
2 Martin Diamond, *A Revolution of Sober Expectations* (Washington, D.C.: American Enterprise Institute, 1976).
3 See Peter Shaw, *The Character of John Adams* (Chapel Hill: University of North Carolina Press, 1976).
4 *The Federalist*, no. 51.
5 As cited in Abraham Lincoln, *Works* (New Brunswick, N.J.: Rutgers University Press, 1953), 1:108–15.
6 On American revolutionary mobs, see Moshe Hazani, "Samuel Adams and Saint-Just: Contrasting Examples of Professional Revolutionaries," in *Models of Revolutionary Leadership*, ed. Daniel J. Elazar and Ellis Katz (forthcoming).
7 Neil Riemer, *The Democratic Experiment: American Political Theory*, vol. 1 (Princeton: Van Nostrand, 1967); Clinton Rossiter, *Seed Time of the Republic: The Origin of the American Tradition of Political Liberty* (New York: Harcourt, Brace, 1953).
8 Daniel J. Elazar, "The States and the Congress Move toward Independence, 1775–1776," *Publius* 6, no. 1 (Winter 1976): 135–43 (see appendix A).

9   Willi Paul Adams, *The First American Constitutions: Republican Ideology and the Making of the State Constitutions in the Revolutionary Era* (Chapel Hill: University of North Carolina Press, 1980); Donald S. Lutz, *Popular Consent and Popular Control: Whig Political Theory in the Early State Constitutions* (Baton Rouge: Lousiana State University Press, 1980); Ronald M. Peters, Jr., *The Massachusetts Constitution of 1780: A Social Compact* (Amherst: University of Massachusetts Press, 1978).

10 Hazani, "Samuel Adams and Saint-Just."

11 Robert D. Meade, *Patrick Henry*, 2 vols. (Philadelphia: Lippincott, 1957–59).

12 Carl Becker, *Benjamin Franklin* (Ithaca, N.Y.: Cornell University Press, 1946); Paul W. Conner, *Poor Richards Politicks: Benjamin Franklin and His New American Order* (New York: Greenwood, 1980).

13 Dumas Malone, *Jefferson in His Times*, 6 vols. (Boston: Little, Brown, 1948–82); idem, *Thomas Jefferson as Political Leader* (New York: Greenwood, 1979).

14 Catherine D. Bowen, *John Adams and the American Revolution* (Boston: Little, Brown, 1950); Page Smith, *John Adams*, 2 vols. (Garden City, N.Y.: Doubleday, 1962).

15 Peters, *Massachusetts Constitution of 1780*.

16 Irving Brant, *James Madison*, 6 vols. (Indianapolis: Bobbs-Merrill, 1941–61); Marvin Meyers, *The Mind of the Founder* (Hanover and London: Brandeis University Press and University Press of New England, 1981).

17 Forrest Macdonald, *E Pluribus Unum: The Formation of the American Republic, 1776–1790* (New York: Houghton Mifflin 1965); James T. Flexner, *George Washington*, 3 vols. (Boston: Little, Brown, 1968–72).

18 Leonard D. White, *The Federalists: A Study in Administrative History* (New York: Greenwood, 1978); Douglass Southhall Freeman, *George Washington*, 7 vols. (New York: Scribner's, 1948–57).

19 Eric Hoffer in an interview with Eric Sevareid on CBS television (September 19, 1967).

10 The Constitution, the Union, and the Liberties of the People

1   The extract texts are reproduced in *The Complete Works of Abraham Lincoln* (New Brunswick, N.J.: Rutgers University Press), whose editors have included both the best versions and all known variants of Lincoln's various speeches. The quotations from those texts used in this article are taken from that source, hereafter cited as *Works*. For specific information on the sources of the texts used, see the footnotes accompanying those texts in the *Works*. I have edited and annotated the full text of Lincoln's words from February 11 through March 4, 1861, for publication in book form. Citations here refer to the original source of the text in question rather than to the *Works*.

2   In the Rutgers edition, this is the first of three versions and the one that was written out by Lincoln and his secretary John Nicolay on the train immediately after the event.

3   As published in the *Courier* (Lafayette, Indiana), February 12, 1861.

Notes to Pages 189–221   281

4 Text as compiled by editors of *Works* from extant versions.
5 *Indianapolis Daily Sentinal*, February 12, 1861.
6 *Cincinnati Daily Gazette*, February 13, 1861.
7 Ibid.
8 Ibid.
9 Ibid.
10 From original in Lincoln's hand, written in Springfield before February 11.
11 Ibid.
12 Ibid.
13 *Cincinnati Daily Commercial*, February 13, 1861.
14 Ibid.
15 *New York Herald*, February 14, 1861.
16 Ibid.
17 *American Union* (Steubenville, Ohio), February 20, 1861.
18 *Pittsburgh Dispatch*, Feburary 16, 1861.
19 Ibid.
20 The prepared text reads as follows:

   It is often said that the tariff is the specialty of Pennsylvania. Assuming that direct taxation is not to be adopted, the tariff question must be as durable as the government itself. It is a question of national house-keeping. It is to the government what replenishing the meal-tub is to the family. Ever-varying circumstances will require frequent modifications, as to amounts needed, and sources of supply. So far there is little difference of opinion among the people. It is as to whether, and how far, duties on imports, shall be adjusted to favor home production in the home market, that controversy begins. One party insists that such adjustment oppresses one class for the advantage of another; while the other party argues that with all its incidents, and in the long run, all classes are benefitted. In the Chicago Platform there is a plank upon this subject, which should be a general law, to the incoming administration. We should do neither more nor less than we gave the people reason to believe we would, when they gave us their votes. That plank is as I now read.

   [The 12th plank of the Chicago platform was here read.]

   As with all general propositions, doubtless there will be shades of difference in construing this. I have by no means, a thoroughly matured judgment upon this subject—especially as to details. Some general ideas are about all. I have long thought that to produce any necessary article at home, which can be made of as good quality, and with as little labor at home as abroad, would better be made at home, at least by the difference of the carrying from abroad. In such case, the carrying is demonstrably a dead loss of labor. For instance, labor being the true standard of value, is it not plain, that if equal labor get a bar of rail-road iron out of a mine in England, and another out of a mine in Pennsylvania, each can be laid down in a track at home, cheaper than they could exchange countries, at least by the cost of carriage. If there be a present cause why one can be both made and carried, cheaper, in *money* price, than the other can be made without carrying, that cause is an unnatural, and injurious one, and ought, gradually, if not rapidly, to be removed.

The condition of the Treasury at this time would seem to render an early revision of the tariff indispensable. The Morrill bill, now pending before Congress, may, or may not become a law. I am not posted as to its particular provisions; but if they are generally satisfactory, and the bill shall now pass, there will be an end for the present. If, however, it shall not pass, I suppose the whole subject will be one of the most pressing and important, for the next Congress. By the Constitution, the Executive may recommend measures which he may think proper; and he may veto those he thinks improper; and it is supposed he may add to these, certain indirect influences to affect the action of Congress. My political education strongly inclines me against a very free use of any of these means, by the Executive, to control the legislation of the country. As a rule, I think it better that Congress should originate, as well as perfect its measures, without external bias. I therefore would rather recommend to every gentleman who knows he is to be a member of the next Congress, to take an enlarged view, and post himself thoroughly so as to contribute his part to such an adjustment of the tariff, as shall produce a sufficient revenue, and in [sic] its other bearings so far as possible, be just and equal to all sections of the country and classes of the people.

21 *Pittsburgh Dispatch*, February 16, 1861.
22 Ibid.
23 Ibid.
24 To wit:

Allusion has also been made, by one of your honored Speakers, to some remarks recently made by myself at Pittsburg, in regard to what is supposed to be the especial interest of this great Commonwealth of Pennsylvania. I now wish only to say, in regard to that matter, that the few remarks which I uttered on that occasion were rather carefully worded. I took pains that they should be so. I have seen no occasion since to add to them or subtract from them. I leave them precisely as they stand, (applause) adding only now that I am pleased to have an expression from you, gentlemen of Pennsylvania, significant that they are satisfactory to you.

25 *New York Herald*, February 16, 1861.
26 *Philadelphia Inquirer*, February 20, 1861.
27 *Buffalo Morning Express*, February 18, 1861.
28 *New York Herald* and *Times*, February 19, 1861.
29 *New York Herald*, February 20, 1861.
30 Ibid.
31 Ibid.
32 *New York Herald*, February 21, 1861.
33 Ibid.
34 *New York Herald*, February 20, 1861.
35 *New York Tribune*, February 22, 1861.

36 Ibid.
37 For Lincoln's attitude toward the Declaration, see Harry V. Jaffa, "Abraham Lincoln," in *American Political Thought*, ed. Morton Frisch and Richard G. Stevens (Itaska, Ill.: F. E. Peacock, 1983), 195–213.
38 *Philadelphia Inquirer*, February 22, 1861.
39 Ibid., February 23, 1861.
40 Immediately following the speech in Independence Hall, Lincoln was accompanied to a platform outside, where he was introduced to the assembled crowd by Stephen Benton, chairman of the Committee on City Property, in charge of the ceremonies. The new flag contained thirty-four stars, the thirty-fourth representing Kansas, admitted to the Union on January 29, 1861.
41 *Philadelphia Inquirer*, February 23, 1861.
42 The Quakers' formal name is the Society of Friends.
43 *Pennsylvania Daily Telegraph* (Harrisburg), February 22, 1861.
44 Written in Nicolay's handwriting, copied from a rough draft by Lincoln.
45 *New York Herald*, February 28, 1861.

11 Coping with Constitutional Crises

1 On the conflicting theories of empire, see Carl L. Becker, *The Declaration of Independence* (New York: Vintage Books, 1958).
2 On the American revolutionary theory of popular sovereignty, see Oscar and Mary F. Handlin, eds., *The Popular Sources of Political Authority* (Cambridge: Belknap Press, 1966), and Donald Lutz, *Popular Consent and Popular Control* (Baton Rouge: Louisiana State University Press, 1980).
3 On the application of that theory, see Handlin and Handlin, *Popular Sources of Political Authority*.
4 On the legalities or illegalities of the Annapolis Convention recommendations and the Philadelphia Convention that followed, see Jack Rakove, *This Constitution*, no. 12 (Fall 1986).
5 On the use of popular sovereignty in the 1850s and the response to that doctrine, see Harry V. Jaffa, *The Crisis of the House Divided* (Seattle: University of Washington Press, 1973); idem, *Equality and Liberty* (New York: Oxford University Press, 1965); and Allan Nevins, *Ordeal of the Union: Fruits of Manifest Destiny*, vol. 1 (New York: Charles Scribner, 1947).
6 On southern doctrines of popular/state sovereignty, see John C. Calhoun's Fort Hill Address, in *Calhoun: Basic Documents*, edited and introduced by John M. Anderson (State College, Pa.: Bald Eagle Press, 1952).
7 On Lincoln's theory, see the Lincoln-Douglas debates in *Collections of the Illinois State Historical Library*, vol. 1, edited with an introduction by Edwin Erle Sparks (Springfield: Illinois State Historical Library, 1908).
8 The timing and manner of Lincoln's death gave his stance mythic status among Americans. See W. Lloyd Warner, *American Life: Dream and Reality* (Chicago: University of Chicago Press, 1962).

9 For the justifications of the civil rights revolution, see Reinhard Bendix and Seymour M. Lipset, eds., *Class, Status and Power: A Reader in Social Stratification* (Glencoe, Ill.: Free Press, 1953).
10 Daniel J. Elazar, "Constitutionalism and Fundamental Political Change in Democracies," unpublished paper prepared for Liberty Fund Conference on Constitutional and Political Change in Democracies, November 30–December 2, 1986.

INDEX

Abolition, 224
Abolitionists, 170, 224
Absolutism, 25
Absolutist: state, 186; tradition, 186
Adams, Abigail, 96
Adams, Henry, 251. *See also History of the Administration of Thomas Jefferson*
Adams, John, 6, 48, 165, 183, 191, 195, 197, 201
Adams, Samuel, 181, 191, 198, 201
Agglomerations, three major urban, 76
Agrarian vision, 58
Agrarianism, 74, 175
Amendment: Civil War, 169; constitutional, 117; Eighteenth, 171; Tenth, 127
Anarchy, stage of, 88
Aristocracy, natural, 247
Aristotle, 101, 152
Army: Continental, 181 197; new model, 187
Articles of Association, 240
Articles of Confederation, 7, 14, 15, 26, 27, 124, 125, 129–31, 136, 142, 188, 246; failures of, 37
Associationalism, 47

Bagehot, Walter, 157
Baptists, 41
Bastille, 187
Bellamy, Edward, 19
Benet, Stephen Vincent, 5
Bible, 93, 149, 152, 168, 218. *See Also Hebrew Bible*
Bicameralism, 172
Bill of Rights, 112, 137, 143, 169, 249; Virginia, 32
Bolsheviks, 186
Boston Tea Party, 191
Bourbons, 186, 196
Britain, 169
British: Empire, 245; North America, 169
Bureaucracies, 174

Calhoun, John C., 127, 247, 248
Calvin, 31
Calvinism, 194; Presbyterian wing of, 59. *See also* Puritan, Congregations
Calvinist, 165
Capitalists, 138
Centralization, 49, 138; government, 26, 29
Chase, Chief Justice Salmon P., 248, 251
Christianity, 210
Civil War, 26, 43, 106, 117, 118, 163, 199, 246, 251; English, 187, 198. *See also* Amendment
Clay, Henry, 228
Collectivism and corporatism, 20, 22; and individualism, 17, 18; origins of, 19–20; pressures of on federalism, 36–37
Commonwealth: biblical version of agrarian, 58; of communities, 58; federal, 138; Pennsylvania, 193; pluralistic, 39–41; Quaker, 237; Virginia, 43, 192
Compacts, 90, 197; governmental, 52; Mayflower, 2, 15, 32; preferred term, 2; social, 31, 121
Compromise: Connecticut, 143; intersectional, 197
Confederacy, 117, 130, 133, 134, 234
Confederal: derivation, 31; standard, 129
Confederalist argument, 151
Confederation, 54, 124, 125, 129, 138, 146–48; American, 125, 126, 130–32, 134; New England, 42; as perpetual league, 198. *See Also* Congress
Congress, 83, 133, 222–24, 241, 250; confederal, 134; Confederation, 54, 181, 246; Continental, 7, 14, 27, 191–95, 197, 199; federation, 198
Consensus, political, 36

Constitution, 2, 3, 33, 107, 108, 110, 124, 128, 141, 142, 145, 150, 166, 168, 173, 188, 197, 200, 213, 214, 216, 219, 220, 226, 229, 231, 235, 239, 240, 248, 249, 251; assumptions of, 121; compactual, 122, 123; federal, 116, 135–38, 191, 192, 198; federalism of, 143; of Fifth Republic, 186; Georgia's ninth, 111; Massachusetts, 33, 91, 107, 108, 111, 121, 191, 197; Mosaic, 144; preamble, 162, 163; ratification of, 188, 193; stretching of, 252; Texas, 118; Virginia, 198
Constitutionalism, 37, 38, 91, 109, 164, 167, 188, 252; American, 110, 197; state, 113
Constitutionalization, 196
Constitutional patterns, 115
Constitutional system, 163
Constitutional traditions, 120; Virginia, 145
Consumerism, 9
Continental Line, 187
Contracts, 90, 91
Convention: Annapolis, 246; constitutional, 27, 107, 117, 134, 144, 146, 167, 193–95, 198–200; Philadelphia, 247
Copperhead, 229
Corporatism, 9, 23, 36; defined, 20; phase of, 20–22
Corporatist: ideas, 22; models, 37
Cortez, 25
Covenant, 100, 115, 128, 136, 144; bonds of, 53; as a compact, 2; concept of, 121; federal theory, 32; idea, 35; making, 33; political, 197; principle, 30, 31; stipulations, 105; tripartite, 106; Workshop, 144. *See also* Declaration of Independence
Covenantal character, 91
Covenantalism, 121

Index

Covenantal principles, 30–33, 136
Covenantal tradition, 90
Crolevan image, 20
Croley, Herbert, 19
Cromwell, Oliver, 181, 187, 189, 201; regime, 185; son Richard, 196
Crosskey, W. W., 140–43
Crow, Jim, 170
Curtin, Governor Andrew J., 236
Cybernetic theory, 141

Darwinian theories, 138
Decentralization, 29, 50, 152; constitutional, 140
Decentralized parties, 49
Declaration of Independence, 3, 6, 94, 101, 136, 163, 188, 191, 195–97, 214, 232, 234–41; as a covenant, 97–98, polemic purpose, 105; Vermont, 32
de Gaulle, Charles, 186, 196
Deists, 194
Democracy, 37, 38; Federal, 7; pure, 28; territorial, 46
Despotism, 185, 186, 242; centralized, 25–27; tendencies toward, 28
Deuteronomy, 144
Diamond, Martin, 49, 139, 140, 142, 145, 149, 165, 182
Dictatorship: constitutional, 27; Jacobin, 27
Douglas, Stephen A., 247
Dred Scott Case, 251
Durante, Jimmy, 149

Egalitarian, 30
Electoral College, 83
Empires: Persian, 25; Ottoman, 25; Russian, 25

Enlightenment, 2, 143, 145, 192; Scottish, 167
Environmental: dimensions, 82; legislation, 79; movement, 81
Epoch: modern, 37, 125; postmodern, 125
Ethnicization, 47
Eulau, Heinz, 141
Executive privilege, 156

Factions, 23
Fascism, 95
Federal: derived, 31; principle, 34; theory, 32
Federalism, 3, 6, 49–53, 126, 127, 140–50, 160, 212; American, 14–16, 24, 33; anti, 150; aspect of, 29; concept, 4; idea of, 31; modern development, 13; orientation, 22; practice of, 144; spirit of, 36, 37; theory of, 198; virtue of, 52
Federalist, 137, 146, 164, 192; American, 14; anti, 23, 35, 146, 164; conception, 109; mainstream, 37; outlook, 138; politics, 250; radical, 135; theory, 168; trackings, 139. *See also* parties
Federalist, The, 35, 107, 108, 125, 140, 143–47, 152, 168, 170, 183, 198, 200
Federalization, 123
Federation, 124, 126, 127, 129, 147, 148; American, 246; modern, 51, 115
Ford, Gerald, 1
Franklin, Benjamin, 191, 193–95, 197
Frontier: American, 70; cybernetic, 79, 80, 83; metropolitan, 62, 84; rural land, 5, 27, 71, 78; urban-industrial, 5, 21, 71, 78

Gallatin, Albert, 108, 138, 198, 250
Gettysburg Address, 208
Gitlow v. New York (1925), 129

Government, 51; centralized, 152; conceptions, 122, 123; confederation, 54; democratic, 28; federal, 168; local, 60; monolithic, 39; plenary, 111; system of, 102
Great Depression, 78, 202
Great Society, 79
Grodzins, Morton, 49, 50

Habeas Corpus, 168
Hamilton, Alexander, 27, 108–10, 142
Hamiltonian policies, 195
Hamiltonian style, 110
Harrington, James, 58, 94
Hebrew Bible, 30, 31; foundations of, 57
Hedonism, 47
Hellenic Leagues, 27
Henry, Alexander, 232
Henry, Patrick, 28, 191, 192, 198
Hessians, 231
History, biblical concept of, 93
Hitler, Adolph, 95
Hobbs, 31, 94, 149
Hobbesian political science, 143
Hoffer, Eric, 202
Huntington, Ellsworth, 44
Hynemann, Charles, 144

Ideologists, 193
Individualism, 9, 17, 18, 22, 109; American, 19, 33; Quaker, 59; radical, 47
Industrialization, Middle States, 60
Institutionalization, 187, 205; initial, 188; political, 203; proper, 189, 190
Ivan the Terrible, 25

Jackson, Andrew, 206

Jacksonian era, 21
Jacobin, 34–35, 195; anti, 197; position, 53. *See also* Revolution
Jacobinism: challenge, 35; premise, 7
James, William, 17
Jefferson, Thomas, 4, 22, 89, 96, 191, 194, 196, 197, 201, 249, 250; legacy, 174; presidency, 198
Jews, 231; first settlement, 40
Johnson, Lyndon, 156

Kennedy, John F., 156

Land: use of, 59; Puritans, 59; policy, 62; division, 64, 66; patterns, 67, 68; and role of government, 72; characteristics of use of, 74, 76; feudal tenure of, 112
Landau, Martin, 141, 159
Laski, Harold, 53
Lee, Robert E., 208
Legislature: national, 223; Ohio, 218
Lenin, V. I., 181, 182, 186, 201
Lerner, Max, 36
Lewis, Sinclair, 20
Liberty, 211; civil, 186; communal, 170; constitutional, 207; federal, 49, 168, 171; government restrictions on, 99; individual, 176; natural, 57, 164, 165, 168
Lincoln, Abraham, 89, 108, 163, 165, 170, 183, 185, 204–30; extra constitutional acts, 250, 251; first arguments, 248; popular government, 241–44; speeches in Pennsylvania, 232, 237
Lipset, Seymour Martin, 37
Locke, John, 25, 31, 94, 145, 149
Lockean view, 31
Louisiana, 119

Index

Louisiana Purchase, 195, 249
Lubbell, Samuel, 63
Lutz, Donald S., 108, 144, 145

Madison, James, 109, 131, 136, 151, 160, 161, 195, 197–99, 201, 213, 249, 250
Majoritarianism, 28
Managerial: view, 110; constitutional pattern, 120
Mason-Dixon Line, 206
Mason, George, 142, 145, 146, 151, 158, 160, 161
Massachusetts, 41, 42; Puritan, 167; Stamp Act, 191
Marxism, 8
Megalopolis, 76
Mesopotamia, 156
Metropolitanization, 63; eastern, 64
Minnesota, politics of, 52
Model: center-periphery, 141, 156, 159; federal, 157
Modernism, 42
Monarchy, 185
Monopolies, 174
Montesquieu, Barou, 25, 94
Morgon, Governor, 226
Morton, Governor Oliver P., 210

Napoleon, 181, 182, 185, 196, 201; regime, 186, 189
Nationalism: idea of, 93
Netherlands, United Province of, 26
New Amsterdam, 40
New Deal, 19, 20, 62, 83, 176; commerce clause, 251
Newman, Franz: "Freedom and Federalism," 53

New York, 4, 40; pluralism of, 41
Nixon, Richard, 1, 156
Noncentralization, 29, 150. *See also* centralization
Northwest Ordinance of 1784, 195

Oligarchies, provincial, 134
Oligopolies, 174
Organization, synergistic, 174
Ostrom, Vincent, 141

Paine, Thomas, 132
Paris Commune of 1870, 196
Parliament, 50, 105, 157, 187
Party: Democrat, 212; Democratic-Republican, 195, 197; Federalist, 196; political, 227; Republican, 212, 229; Revolutionary, 199
Patriotism, 210
Penn, William, 39, 41
Pennsylvania, 40, 42, 59
Plato, 152
Pluralism, 47; American, 17, 44, 49, 127; California, 52, 53, 55; model of associations, 43, 44; model of individuals, 44; religious, 59; six models of, 45, 46; Yankee, 43
Policy, English imperial, 105
Polity, 130; American, 1, 2, 4, 5, 204, 207, 211; federal, 52, 53; Jacobin, 8; North American, 144; three models, 152
Populists, 128
Power: Divine, 219; hierarchical model of, 153, 155, 158; imperialistic, 51; separation of, 122, 135; sovereign, 28
Programs, federal housing, 62
Progressive Era, 21
Progressive movement, 19

Progressives, 128, 138
Protestantism, Reformed, 194
Prussians, 153
Publius, 29, 145
Puritans, 16, 142, 174; and community structure, 58; and English revolution, 185, 187; Massachusetts, 192, 194; tradition of, 108, 144; view of, 165; and yeomanry, 59

Quakers, 39, 41

Reconstruction, 118, 138
Reformation, 142
Reformist perspective, 107
Republic: American federal, 140; democratic, 140, 252
Republicanism, 26, 37, 38, 110, 129, 162; American, 56; democratic, 145, 162, 186, 196; Whig forms of, 109. *See also* Party
Revolution, 101, 193, 200, 203; American, 102, 165, 170, 194, 199, 202, 246; French, 7, 182, 187, 185, 201; Jacobin style, 196, 180, 196, 198; Russian, 182, 185–87
Revolutionaries, 192, 193
Revolutionary War, 43, 230
Rhode Island Assembly, 96
Rights, civil, 127, 129
Riker, William, 141
Robespierre, 181, 182, 185, 186
Roosevelt, Franklin Delano, 250. *See also* New Deal
Rousseau, Jean-Jacques, 31, 164
Rousseauian ideal, 49
Rurban-cybernetic, 6; era of, 21
Russian civil society, 29–30

Secessionists, 212
Sectionalism: new, 77, 83; city-suburban, 79
Segregation, 176
Seivall, Judge Samuel, 96
Slavery, 43
Slavocracy, 170
Socialists, 138
Sovereignty: popular, 188, 253; state, 247
Soviet Union, 186, 196
Stalin, Joseph, 182, 186, 189, 201
Stuarts, 185
Stuyvesant, Governor Peter, 40, 41
Subcultures: political, 114; traditionalist, 61
Suburbanization, 76
Supreme Court: United States, 36, 42, 46–50, 53, 106, 107, 113, 114, 118, 128, 175, 176, 240, 242, 249, 251, 252

Taney, Chief Justice Roger, 251
Texas, 118
Thatcher, Margaret, 157
Theology, federal, 16, 31, 144
Third Republic, 196
Tocqueville, Alexis de, 1, 36
Tories, 188
Totalitarian: democracy, 34; police state, 190; societies, 166; tyranny, 172; USSR, 186
Trotsky, Leonard, 181, 201
Turner, Frederick Jackson, 5, 55, 76

Unionists, 212. *See also* Washington, George
Urbanization, 42, 63, 75, 84

Virginia: House of Burgesses, 199; plan, 198; Resolutions, 213; Resolves, 192, 195
Voting Rights Act, 252

Washington, George, 27, 181, 182, 191, 197, 199, 201, 205, 208; cabinet of, 195
Webster, Daniel, 228
Whig: conception, 110; influence, 134, 137; models, 170; Old, 192; politics, 250; principle, 132; theory, 134, 139; tradition, 109
Whiggism, 174
White, Leonard D., 200
Wilson, Woodrow, 110, 143, 153

Winthrop, John, 22, 36, 128, 166–68
Wolfe, Tom, 165
Wood, Fernando, 229

Yankees, New England, 58
Yeager, Chuck, 165
Yeomanry, principles of, 59
Yorktown, battle of, 200

Zeus, 156